TRIPS WITH CHILDREN
IN NEW ENGLAND

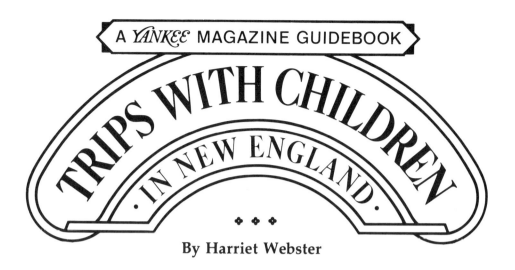

A *YANKEE* MAGAZINE GUIDEBOOK

TRIPS WITH CHILDREN
·IN NEW ENGLAND·

❖ ❖ ❖

By Harriet Webster

Yankee Publishing Incorporated
Dublin, New Hampshire

Yankee thanks John Robaton, Harris G. Smith, and their photo-journalism students at Boston University's School of Public Communication, Department of Journalism, for the substantial efforts they extended to provide illustrations for this book.

The section featuring the Submarine Memorial in Groton, Connecticut, is based on a story by Ellen Fitzpatrick that appeared in the Summer/Fall 1981 issue of *Yankee Magazine's Travel Guide to New England*.

Edited by Lila Walz
Photo Editing and Design by John W. White

Yankee Publishing Incorporated
Dublin, New Hampshire 03444

First Edition

Library of Congress Catalog Card No. 81-71637

ISBN: 0-911658-44-0

For my Ma, who gave me the joy of travel,
And for Jonathan, who helps me pass it on to our kids.

A *YANKEE* MAGAZINE GUIDEBOOK

TRIPS WITH CHILDREN

· IN NEW ENGLAND ·

CONTENTS

Preface
For Parents

TRIPS WITH CHILDREN IN NEW ENGLAND is a book about enjoying a unique region of our country by experiencing it from the perspective of a child. It is a guide to some of the places, activities, and traditions that bring alive the personalities of six unique states: Connecticut, Maine, Massachusetts, New Hampshire, Rhode Island, and Vermont.

As an adult, you know that there are many ways to travel in New England, or in any area. You can focus, for instance, on elegant dining and lodging. Or you can plan your tour to coincide with the special foliage seasons and enjoy unhurried drives on mountain roads, admiring the scenery. Perhaps your interest lies in handcrafts and fine antiques; if so, you might wish to ferret out those intriguing workshops, auction galleries, and antiques shops. If you are a history buff, you can visit dozens of historic landmarks and buildings. And if you are an outdoors enthusiast, you will find ample opportunities for hunting and fishing, technical climbing, or arduous backpacking expeditions. All of these are fine ways to enjoy a region, and there is a wealth of literature available on these topics to help you make your plans.

A DIFFERENT PERSPECTIVE. But there is another way to discover New England, a way that has not received much attention to date. That is to visit the area not by focusing exclusively on *your* particular interests but by focusing instead on your children and some of their tastes and concerns. This book will help you attain that goal. It will show you, for instance, how to involve children in making plans for a trip instead of fitting them into your own plans. This is a book to use before your trip as well as during it. With it your children may sample before they start the treats that await them in New England. Read to them — or have them read to younger children — the bits of history and nostalgia included in these pages. Talk to them about the people who live and earn a living in this region; use the information contained in this book to whet their (and your) appetites, to encourage them to express their own interests.

BE A CHILD AGAIN. As for yourself, before planning a trip through New England with your children, indulge in a little role playing. Put yourself in your child's shoes. Let yourself be five again, or seven, or eleven, or fourteen. Remember how it felt to stare at one Chippendale highboy after another. Remember how itchy you got being patient through cocktails, then dinner, then after-dinner coffee. Determine that this trip will be geared to your children's needs and to their sense of pace, excitement, and exploration. Instead of splurging on that grown-up formal meal at a famous restaurant, plan to indulge in a clambake with all the frills, including lobster steamed over seaweed, with live entertainment afterwards!

Because of the variety and number of attractions that New England offers, both natural and manmade, the area is well suited to family travel. We provide you with a groaning board laden with activities attractive to children.

SELECTIVE COVERAGE. New England has so much to offer that we cannot begin to be exhaustive in our coverage. Our approach, then, is selective. Every entry in this book was chosen for its appeal to children. Every entry also in some way reflects the economic, natural, social, artistic, recreational, and/or historical significance of the region. To this end, we include a turn-of-the-century amusement park similar to those that played an important part in New England summer recreation a hundred years ago, but we do not devote space to some of the newer commercial attractions that one can find in any part of the country. You have chosen to explore New England with your children, so we want you really to experience New England.

It is important to remember that this book represents a personal selection of places to visit and things to do in the New England region. We have chosen to be thorough rather than exhaustive, to give a true sense of each attraction or activity described, keeping in mind the way children will respond. Please understand, then, that many places and even some geographical areas have been omitted — not because they are unworthy, but simply because of time and space considerations. New England has so very much to offer. It is our hope that the trips you and your young traveling companions take here will one day be counted among their special memories of childhood.

WHAT CHILDREN REALLY LIKE. The emphasis here is on participation. We are especially partial to places that invite the senses to come into further play. Besides looking at things, children also like to experience tastes and smells, as well as the sound and feel of things. They like to ride on things, to take things apart, to make things work. They like to pet animals and pick strawberries and hunker down in damp caves. These factors were important considerations in choosing the material in this book.

In addition we include not only places of major interest but also the lesser-known, serendipitous spots that please local children and that will certainly add to your group's enjoyment, too. We tell you, for instance, about a dock where you can rent a canoe for an hour. We are sensitive to the appeal of a particularly well-endowed penny-candy counter. And we know how lovely it is to find a waterfall in which you can dip your toes or a nickelodeon you can operate yourself.

SCOPE AND FOCUS. Although our primary focus is on children from five to fourteen, we have also paid attention to attractions of particular interest to preschoolers and older teenagers, recognizing that many families have children of a variety of ages. The amount of time you allot to visiting a specific place will depend upon the ages of the children involved, but we have tried to provide some general guidelines throughout the book.

Shops, restaurants, and lodgings have been included throughout only where they are especially useful, appropriate, or attractive to families with children. Excellent hotel, motel, and shopping guides abound; it is hoped that parents will use them in conjunction with this book to find suitable accommodations throughout New England. (For further information, consult the latest issue of *Yankee Magazine's Travel Guide to New England.*)

For each attraction in the book, you will find clear driving directions as well as information on what seasons of the year the attraction is open and whether admission is charged; a phone number for each is also included where applicable. Specific information regarding hours or days open and exact admission or ticket prices is not given, since these may change at any time. A word of advice to travelers: always use the phone numbers to check ahead of time on these important specifics; this simple rule of thumb can save many an unhappy arrival after hours or post-season to find the doors closed tight.

In the case of busier locations and attractions where walking tours are feasible, brief directions for how to proceed from one point to another are given in the page margins, beside the text itself. Otherwise, directions appear at the end of each attraction or related group of attractions.

This, then, is a book for parents, grandparents, aunts, uncles, and just plain friends of children. Children and adults can use it together to plan and enjoy their travels. Take it along as a friendly guide that will open your eyes and your children's to the experiences waiting for you in a very special part of the country.

Traveling with Children

C hildren are usually wonderful travelers. Energetic, curious, and eager for adventure, they thrive on the opportunity to visit new places and try out unfamiliar foods and activities. To children on a trip, the world becomes a tremendously interesting place, and they revel in exploring everything and every place they can.

It is this enjoyment of fresh new experiences that makes children such excellent travel companions. Perhaps as an adult you have visited New England many times. Although you love the mountains, the ocean shore, and the sense of history that characterize the region, you may have settled into a pattern of rather sedate expectations. Take a child or two along, however, and you find yourself transported back in time to your own childhood, a time when you too experienced the world with unbounded enthusiasm. You may have seen dozens of covered bridges in your travels, but just wait until you come upon one with a child who has never seen one before.

FAMILY DYNAMICS. Traveling with children, you reap still another reward. Beyond the sheer pleasure that children derive from the trip, beyond the ideas and facts they assimilate from their new experiences, there is the matter of the dynamics of the family unit. It may sound strange, but brothers who fight like wolves at home may suddenly find themselves drawn together in comfortable unity on a trip far from home. Why? Without their friends to amuse them, they have to rely on each other; they may begin to realize that it is a lot more fun to play checkers than to argue constantly. Also, because they are away from home, they discover that it might be *better* to travel with company. A pair of siblings who would never dream of walking to the store to buy ice-cream cones together back home are quite likely to do just that when the trip involves a walk down the block in an unfamiliar town.

Adult-child relationships can also benefit handsomely from the time spent together. Away from the pressures and distractions of home, older travelers have time to listen to younger ones, to pay close attention to them. Because travel involves long hours of close contact, family members do learn to make adjustments, to become more accepting and tolerant of each other. They can take the time to appreciate one another. As an added bonus, they take part in a common experience that they will be able to remember and share in the years ahead.

FAMILY PROBLEMS. Now that we have mentioned the virtues of family travels, such as enriching experiences and increased family solidarity, to be fair we must also point out some of the more controversial aspects of traveling with children. It is most important to understand that traveling with children is a very different situation from traveling without them. For the trip to be successful, you need to form reasonable expectations, and to realize that children have different tastes from adults in almost every area. To have a pleasant trip, you need to squarely face the children's point of view when it comes to eating and sleeping, sightseeing, and even the pace they like to set.

HOW TO PACE YOUR TRIPS. Let's begin with the question of pace. How far and how long you travel in a day can have a strong bearing on the temperaments of your young passengers. If you are traveling by car, plan to get an early start, particularly if you are driving during the hot summer months. Map your route with the idea that you will make a stop every two hours. Perhaps it will be a stop for a meal, or perhaps a visit to a point of interest. Or you will stop simply to let everyone stretch his legs, use the facilities, and buy a cold drink. By letting your young passengers know that you will definitely stop regularly, you will avoid much of the whining that so frequently ruins a family car trip. But once you have told them that you will make scheduled stops, stick to it. Don't push on for another half hour when you promised a break at noon.

If you are one of those people who like to get straight to your destination, you may find it frustrating to abide by our suggestion of frequent breaks. If this is the case, and if you have a long drive ahead of you, try this approach. Take a deep breath and plan to leave about 4 AM! Load the car the night before, including a thermos of coffee, some doughnuts and sandwiches, and a bottle of orange juice. Wake the children and stuff them into the car. With luck you can probably drive about four hours before they awaken and get restless. Dip into the snacks you have brought along to placate the child who is hungry at 5 AM (and the driver, who may be a bit grumpy, too). Then when your carful really begins to come to life, pull in somewhere for breakfast. After a good meal, you'll all be ready to drive another four hours; by early afternoon perhaps you will have covered over four hundred miles. You'll still have time for the children to explore their new surroundings before having supper and settling in for the evening.

TAKE-ALONGS. It's a good idea to supply each child with a small knapsack for personal possessions; you can pack the car so that the child will always have access to the knapsack. In addition to the small toys and books that children are likely to pack for themselves, tuck in a supply of fresh felt-tip markers or crayons and a pad of paper. Also include a small notebook or scrapbook, and encourage your children to keep a journal or pictorial record of the trip. Playing cards are another worthwhile item to take along, particularly if you know some challenging versions of solitaire to teach your group. Stick in each knapsack a copy of the road map you plan to use, so that each child can chart your progress. If you want to supply children with a work surface in the car, cut an arch from the front and back of a topless cardboard carton. Slide the carton bottom-side up over the child's lap; it will fit even if he is strapped into a car seat.

In general, try to anticipate problems before they arise. Instead of arriving in a strange town late at night with tired children, aim to get there in the afternoon. Do the same when it comes to meals. Before you go to bed in the evening, know where you are going to feed your crew breakfast, be it the hotel dining room or a coffee shop in the center of town. If you are out exploring, begin to keep an eye out for lunch spots before the children get ravenous.

EATING OUT TOGETHER. If you relish the thought of a continual round of elegant dinners and leisurely lunches, you won't be happy with your children in tow unless they are old enough to either enjoy such meals or take care of themselves while you dine. Most children just do not take kindly to a constant regime of long dining periods, and although you might be able to force them through the routine, you couldn't make them love it. By the time you paid the bill, you might find yourself so tense that the dinner would seem more like a battle than a pleasure.

This is not to discourage you from trying an occasional elegant meal with your children. The clue to success here is to make it *occasional*. Build them up for it. Make it an event to anticipate. Discuss possible menu items in advance so that they know what to expect — and so you are not treated to long faces the minute they open the menu and find nothing vaguely familiar. Most important of all, don't pay any attention to whether or not they eat their food. This is a splurge, a special treat, and it is important that it be enjoyable for everyone. You are going to have to pay for the ten-dollar steak your seven year old ordered whether or not she eats it, so why make everyone miserable, including yourself, with a lot of nagging and threatening? This is not the time to assert your parental authority; do that at a budget cafeteria!

As for the economics of eating out with children, there are a couple of ways to cut corners. First, you might deliberately choose a restaurant that offers several children's plates. The best way to find out if this is so is to telephone ahead and ask. If you are in the immediate vicinity of the restaurant in question, stop in at an off hour and ask to see a menu.

Second, plan to make your splurges at lunch rather than at dinner. The house specialties are very often the same, but the price drops considerably, sometimes as much as thirty percent. Also, because they are less tired than at dinner time, children tend to be more patient at lunch.

Third, keep in mind that children get stale from too much indoor dining. Picnicking is a pleasant alternative, suitable for all but the coldest months. While picnics most commonly take the form of a midday meal, they are also an excellent way to end the day. After a hard day of sightseeing, children and parents alike might well appreciate a full-fledged picnic in the hotel room instead of having to clean up to go out to dinner. Picnics also provide you with a good excuse to prowl local markets and purchase regional goodies such as homemade blueberry turnovers, apple butter, or fresh-baked bread.

Another technique of reducing restaurant exposure and expense is to have an occasional day when everyone in the family lives on snacks. This means that you are patient when one child wants to buy a hot dog at a country fair, and ten minutes later another child wants to wait in line for a slice of pizza. (Of course, it also means that the children are patient when you decide you need some oysters on the half shell.) Don't worry about nutrition or about starting bad habits. After all, this is a vacation; your children will not expect to be constantly entertained and in your company when you return home, nor will they expect continued liberal access to ice-cream cones, such as they may get on a snack day.

WHERE WILL WE SLEEP TONIGHT, MOM? Most children find hotels and motels exciting places. They like to explore the hallways and grounds, discover the vending machines, and take a look at the swimming pools or playground. If you plan to stay in a conventional hotel or motel, be sure to inquire about budget or family plans, which usually offer a big reduction for children who share a room with their parents. Once you know the room rates, think carefully about the number of rooms you require. Your family may be able to fit into one room — but is it worth it? You may decide that a budget squeeze is worthwhile on an occasional one-night stopover, but that it is not a suitable arrangement when you plan a longer stay. It might even be wise, should money be tight, to cut your trip down a couple of days in order to afford that extra room. This will depend largely upon the number of children you travel with, and their ages.

Don't take anything for granted when booking rooms. If you want two rooms that connect with each other, be sure to specify. Adjoining rooms have a door directly between them but adjacent rooms usually do not. Also, if you require a crib or other special equipment, request it in advance. If you don't know where you will be staying and don't want to be hampered with heavy equipment, consider taking along a small inflatable wading pool. Such a pool packs flat, but when it is inflated it can serve nicely as a makeshift crib. Small babies will be snug and secure, and toddlers won't have to worry about falling out of a big bed.

The type of lodging arrangement you choose depends largely on your personal style as well as budget considerations. If your children are strictly urban creatures, you may want to open their eyes to the rural side of life by checking in to a working farm for a week. Depending upon the specific farm you choose, your children may be able to lend a hand at simple chores: collecting still-warm eggs from the chickens, picking strawberries, helping to feed the pigs. They might also have the opportunity to ride on a tractor or to see cows milked with modern machinery.

If you lean toward an experience steeped in history, you may opt for an old country inn — but choose carefully. Some inns are so preciously appointed that small children are definitely out of place. Also, look for inns that offer activities such as hiking, swimming, and square-dancing, instead of those that focus on the availability of fine restaurants and choice antiques shops. But if you cannot find a first hand source, take the direct approach: write to the innkeeper, describe the number and ages of children in your group, and ask whether he thinks his accommodations are suitable.

SIGHTSEEING: HOW MUCH AND WHAT KIND? Just as you choose your restaurants and lodgings with the specific needs and tastes of your children in mind, plan your sightseeing with a similar approach. Try to integrate active experiences with more passive or sedentary ones. If you plan to visit historic houses, alternate these stops with a sidetrip to a park or zoo, a hands-on museum, or even a beach. Involve the children in planning the day's events so that they know what to expect. Be certain to include at least one activity that really appeals to them. If possible, schedule it for the afternoon, so that they will have it to look forward to if the plans made for the morning turn out to be dull or disappointing.

Keep in mind that parents have rights, too. If a family trip is to be successful, everyone needs to practice some give and take. If you are willing to go off to an amusement park for the afternoon because you know it gives your children pleasure, you may expect them to be willing to go along to a special art gallery that you really want to visit.

MUSEUM-ING. If you do want to visit a fine-arts museum or gallery, do some advance work. Read up on the collections. Try to unearth some interesting stories relating to the art works you will be viewing. From a child's point of view, it is a lot more interesting to visit a room rich with van Goghs when you are privy to the information that this famous painter really did cut off his own ear. The more young children know about the work of art they will be seeing, the more tolerant they will be. Plan your visit so that you know what museum or gallery you want to see first. Be sure to visit that first, so that if your young company becomes too restless, you will be able to leave without feeling cheated.

Convince yourself that it doesn't really matter if your children look at the paintings. If your daughter is happier reading a comic book, leave her alone. Children have an uncanny but dependable way of sensing when an experience is meaningful to them and when it is not. If you've survived for forty years without seeing this marvelous collection, chances are your child will get by, too. So don't make her look at everything. Instead, concentrate on your own pleasure, and then leave before pushing the children beyond their limit.

FAMILY TOGETHERNESS. It is important to note here that two or more adults traveling with their children need not spend every moment together. You don't all spend every minute together at home; part of the reason for that is that you all have different interests. If Dad and one of the older children want to go fishing but the rest of the group has no interest in that, plan to split up for the afternoon. Similarly, if one of the adults wants to pay a return visit to the art museum, the other family members should be able to do something more interesting to them. And those who are bored by shopping trips should never be dragged along. You are all going to have plenty of togetherness on this trip; a little apartness now and then may seem like a breath of fresh air. It makes for better tempers, which in turn make for a happier trip.

TRAVELING WITH OTHERS. Single parents don't have the option of going off by themselves unless they engage in some creative planning. How about teaming up with another adult and his or her children? In addition to being able to get away by yourself occasionally, this arrangement is advantageous in that shy children are often more willing to join in activities designed for their age group if they have a pal along. Of course, you should weigh carefully the other side of the arrangement before entering into a joint trip. You may lose some degree of flexibility when there are more people whose tastes must be accounted for, when you are deciding where to go and what to do. And you may simply want this trip to be a time spent exclusively with your own offspring.

Whether or not you choose to travel with another family, the best way to assure a successful trip with children is to plan carefully and discuss openly. Build realistic expectations in your children. Let them know the scope of activities available, and listen to their opinions. Do some solid advance work; for instance, if you plan to visit Nook Farm, where Mark Twain lived and worked, encourage your children to read one of his books before you go. These and other kinds of activities together will help everyone enjoy himself — and others — more.

*   *   *   *   *

Like anything else worth learning, traveling with children takes some time and effort. It becomes easier and more fulfilling with a little experience. If you are patient and flexible, if you determine to try to experience the places you visit from a child's point of view, you may well find that traveling with children is far more rewarding and far more fun than you ever imagined. In fact, after visiting New England with children along, the idea of visiting the area without them may strike you as just plain dull. See for yourself. Use the information and suggestions in the chapters that follow to bring the history, natural beauty, and recreational attributes of this special part of the country alive for your children and, through them, for yourself.

Getting to know the flowers at Mystic's Denison Pequotsepos Nature Center.

CHAPTER I

Connecticut

E nvision a graceful village green neatly bordered by sparkling seventeenth- and eighteenth-century homes. Add a simple white church with soaring steeple. Fill in the background with rolling hills forested with birch, beech, maple, and hemlock. Now you have the Connecticut hallmark, a portrait of one of the many typical villages that abound throughout the gentle valleys of the country's third smallest state.

Despite its geographical limits, Connecticut is one of the most densely populated states in America; she also has one of the highest per capita incomes in the country. She entered the industrial age with a vengeance in the early 1800s; by 1850 more of her citizens were employed in manufacturing than in farming. She owes much of her success in making the transition to modern urban life to innovators such as her famous resident Eli Whitney, who invented not only the cotton gin but the principle of inter-changeable parts.

The fabric of modern urban-industrial life is enriched in this state by a contrasting thread, that of a colorful and strong allegiance to the past. People in Connecticut appreciate the approaches and accounterments of a slower-paced age. To this end they have developed over a hundred historical societies, whose roles are to oversee the preservation and operation of hundreds of homes, forts, and landmarks important to the state's history. As you visit the museums and historic sites (and many of them are lively places with opportunities for active participation), you begin to appreciate the fact that in Connecticut elements of the past are truly integrated into the present. You will become poignantly aware of this melding of tradition with contemporary concerns when you visit one of the state's many country fairs, where the best blueberry pie still receives every bit as much attention as the most up-to-date tractor, and the newest calf can be just as popular as the shiniest ride on the midway.

Compact and accessible, with many indoor and outdoor activities, Connecticut is perfect for year-round visiting. Just keep in mind that while the climate is moderate, the weather is noted mainly for its changeability — hot waves and cold waves, stormy skies and bright ones alternating at a confusing rate. As has been said, "If you don't like the weather in Connecticut, wait a minute."

Mom can be the frightened patient and daughter the doctor, tucking her into her hospital bed and deftly hooking up her IV.

This is no place for children to be shy. It's the Children's Museum, where they're encouraged to step up front and take part.

New Haven

THE CHILDREN'S MUSEUM. For a real family experience, visit this museum where the staff encourages grownups to actively join their children's play. Mom can be the frightened patient and daughter can be the doctor, tucking her into her hospital bed and deftly hooking up her IV. Dad can play the role of waiter, taking his son's order in the restaurant. There is lots to do here, with dozens of role-playing opportunities designed to stimulate good conversation as well as a healthy exchange of feelings and ideas between the generations.

The main room, called The Village, is where children can participate in all the activities they see around them each day. They can find a job in the employment agency, shop for supper at the grocery store, or fill cavities in the dentist's office. They can become bank president, fireman, policeman, teacher, letter carrier, chef, nurse, or cashier. There are lots of dress-up clothes, everything from heavy work boots to a purple tutu, to help them fill their roles.

On a typical day, one child hobbles across the hospital on crutches while another tries to navigate the wheelchair. A young man stamps letters in the post office while three middle-aged folks sit attentively at their desks, listening to their eight-year-old instructor point out exotic spots on the globe. Cash registers ring, the typewriter clacks away, and a human siren sounds as a "fire engine" speeds to the scene of impending disaster. This is no place to be shy! Just jump right in and find yourself a job in the village.

Cash registers ring, the typewriter clacks away, and a human siren sounds as a "fire engine" speeds to the scene of impending disaster.

A second room contains shelves full of paper punches, paste, paints, scissors, yarn, fabric scraps, markers, paper, and much more. Here in the workshop area, young museum visitors create projects that range from paper flowers to bird feeders, puppets to musical instruments. The projects are designed so that even preschoolers can succeed. The room also contains a minitheater, the perfect place for homemade plays.

Here, children really learn about the world around them and about themselves and their families — imagining and manipulating, touching, seeing, hearing, comparing and creating, and talking it all over with their older friends, the adults in their lives. Plan to spend at least one hour here; the activities are best suited for the three to eight year old.

PEABODY MUSEUM OF NATURAL HISTORY. This Yale University museum features outstanding exhibits in geology, ecology, natural history, and minerals. Dinosaurs are a favorite subject with most children, and here young ones gasp with wonder as they gape at the standing skeleton of a Sauropod dinosaur, the famous brontosaurus. This herbivorous creature, known as the "thunder lizard," is sixty-seven

Dinosaurs are a favorite subject with most children; this mural is at the Peabody Museum of Natural History.

feet long and sixteen feet high at the hips. He is thought to have weighed about thirty-five tons; that's a lot of flesh on a lot of bones! It is believed that he required nearly a thousand pounds of food each day and that he feasted primarily on soft water plants.

There are many other animal parts on display here, some genuine and some replicas. You meet the Otisville Mastodon, discovered in 1872 by one Mr. Andrew Mitchell, an Otisville, New York, farmer, on his own land. You also see the saber-toothed cat, the ground sloth, and the huge Tyrannosaurus Rex skull.

The Indian exhibits here are particularly worthy of notice. For instance, you can compare the elaborate ceremonial masks of the North Pacific Coast Indians, decorated with wood, fur, hair, and feathers, with simpler ones made by the Northern Athapaskan Indians. Then survey the extensive display of artifacts belonging to the Plains Indians. They are divided into categories according to function: transportation, smoking, music, tools, shelter, and art, to name a few. Notice the sun-dance stick and the spirit wand in the section called Religion, Magic, and Medicine; in another area, called Clothing, watch for the man's shirt decorated with 230 locks of hair, and the floor-length war bonnet

Dinosaurs are a favorite subject with most children, and here young ones gasp with wonder as they gape at the standing skeleton of a brontosaurus.

that belonged to Dakota Chief Iron Bull. Children who enjoy making Indian costumes and trinkets find this collection a great source of ideas.

In the Upper Amazon collection, the real shrunken head makes quite an impression. Known as a "tsantsa," its purpose was to capture and subjugate the enemy's soul as a lifelong servant. Here you also see a vivid display of body ornaments made from the bright blue, green, orange, red, and yellow feathers of tropical birds. In addition to the feathers, many pieces incorporate entire animal pelts.

Other exhibits include A Meteorite Lands in Connecticut and a hall devoted to dioramas, showing stuffed North American animals such as the musk ox (from the high arctic tundra of Ellesmore Island, in the Canadian Archipelago), the mule deer (Kaibab Plateau of northern Arizona), and the bison (foothills of the Rockies). This museum is the perfect destination for a rainy day; allow at least an hour to sample its offerings, which are appropriate for all ages but are of special interest to those eight years old and older.

ACCESS

TO GET TO NEW HAVEN. Heading east or west, follow I-95 to I-91. From Hartford, head south about forty miles on I-91 to its New Haven terminus.

THE CHILDREN'S MUSEUM. Directions: Take I-91 exit 3 (Trumbull Street), and turn left onto State Street. The museum is at 567 State Street. **Season:** Year round. **Admission** charged. (203) 777-8002.

PEABODY MUSEUM OF NATURAL HISTORY. Directions: Take I-91 exit 3 (Trumbull Street), continue to Whitney Avenue, and turn right. The museum is on your right, on Whitney Avenue at Number 170. Parking is available along the street. **Season:** Year round. **Admission** charged, but there are some "free" days. Inquire ahead. (203) 436-0850.

Essex

THE VALLEY RAILROAD. From the moment you arrive at the Essex Depot and march up to the ticket office, you find yourself caught up in the hustle and bustle of this busy train station. You learn that the venerable Valley Railroad began operation in 1871. It was later purchased by the New Haven Railroad, which ran it until 1968, when the New Haven Railroad closed down. Several years later, it was revived as a tourist attraction. Today you can travel back in time to the early 1900s — an era when steam-powered locomotives ruled the railroad tracks — and give your children a taste of their grandparents' heritage.

Plumes of smoke and steam swirl about the engine as the firemen shovel coal and the conductor shouts,

"All aboard!" The whistle blows and you are off and chugging, destination Chester, Connecticut. You ride in a vintage coach that has been fully restored. Some coaches have lacquered-straw seats, others sport wooden benches, and still others have comfy, red fabric-covered seats. There is also an open car out back in which you might like to travel on a bright day.

If you are feeling flush, do pay the extra charge required for admission to the parlor car. Here you find yourself comfortably ensconced in a high-ceilinged Victorian "room" with fancy light fixtures, elegant overhead racks (perfect for your hatbox, m'dear), and small pull-down tables where you can write postcards or play solitaire. You can sit in a plush red swivel armchair or a cushioned gold-painted wicker chair, watching the world pass by as you listen to ragtime tunes courtesy of the old wooden Spartan radio. A leaded-glass partition decorated in a fruit-basket motif divides the parlor car into intimate sections and provides an additional splash of elegance. You can swivel your chair toward the aisle when you are feeling sociable or turn toward the window when you want to reflect on the passing panorama in privacy.

As you trundle down the tracks, the conductor, who wears a red carnation, answers any questions you might have. A voice comes over the loudspeaker occasionally, identifying local landmarks or imparting tidbits of historical interest. Your route winds along the edge of the Connecticut River, past fields of sumac, loosestrife, and milkweed, past brooks and back roads, meadows and marshes, until you arrive at Chester. Here you flip your seat around for the return trip.

Although it is possible to take the railroad trip only, you will probably want to take advantage of the riverboat connection. A combination ticket entitles you to leave the train at Deep River, and board the *Viking* or the *Silver Star* for an hour-long cruise on the state's longest river, the mighty Connecticut, which originates near the Canadian border and terminates in Long Island Sound. Both boats have enclosed lower decks and open upper decks that are protected by canopies. As you travel along, your crew discusses cogent matters such as water depth, dredging operations, and the navigational markers that appear. When you pass the *Selden III*, one of the last operating river ferries in the country, you will probably hear about the history of ferryboats, harking back to the time when such boats were pulled along the river banks by mules.

Cruising by Gillette Castle towering high on the rocks, you learn that the great stone edifice was built by the famous and eccentric actor William Gillette. You are also shown the Goodspeed Opera House at East Haddam, where Broadway shows like *Annie* got their start. (Indeed, the dog who starred as Sandy in the original version of this famous musical was rescued

JUDITH DINOBILE

He'll take your ticket and tell stories of the days of steam-powered locomotives while you enjoy a ride on the Valley Railroad in Essex.

Plumes of smoke and steam swirl about the engine as the firemen shovel coal and the conductor shouts, "All aboard!"

Here you can have your picture taken in fancy clothing — how about a derby hat and vested three-piece suit, or a satin dress complete with bustle?

from the East Haddam Dog Pound!) As you approach a drawbridge, you discover that in times of power shortage, it takes twelve strong men a good hour to manually open the bridge. Making your way back down river to the Deep River landing, you see children fishing and families canoeing near the banks of the river. When you leave the boat, board the train for the last leg of your journey, the return to the Essex Depot.

There are several old railroad cars here at the depot to climb aboard and investigate. You might wish to stop for a hot dog or hamburger in the 1915 grill car that serves as a lunch wagon, or purchase popcorn from the popcorn cart. For a really special souvenir, stop in at Photographs & Memories, which is also housed in an old railroad car. Here you can have your picture taken in fancy clothing — how about a derby hat and vested three-piece suit, or a satin dress complete with bustle? There is also a flapper's outfit, an engineer's clothing, a sailor's suit, and a dozen other outfits to choose from as well, not to mention a fine collection of hats: a conductor's cap, a few boaters, and some ladies' hats trimmed with flowers, feathers, and lace. The photographer will outfit you, and spruce you up with an appropriate prop — perhaps a parasol or a rifle — then pose you individually or in a family group.

Your photograph is treated with special sprays to give it a sepia tone, just like old-time photos. You can choose from a number of mattes, including a couple of "Wanted" posters, a marriage announcement, and a Valley Railroad poster. (Frames are available at additional cost.) Try this! You will have a unique remembrance of your journey into the past.

The train and boat ride takes about one and a half hours; allow an extra half hour for browsing about the depot to round out your visit.

ACCESS

THE VALLEY RAILROAD. Directions: From Route 9, take exit 3 directly to Essex, then follow signs to the Valley Railroad. Season: May through the end of October; December (depot only). Admission charged. (203) 767-0103.

Hadlyme/East Haddam

GILLETTE CASTLE STATE PARK. All set for a ferry ride? The short trip from Chester to Hadlyme is one of the last great bargains. The crossing takes only five minutes, no reservation is required, and the ferrymen know that they are providing more than basic transportation. They are happy to talk about the boat as you approach the towering castle on the opposite bank.

The park is located just a short drive from the ferry landing. Indeed, when William Gillette began

Looking at it, you can well understand that the castle was built at a cost in excess of a million dollars.

construction of his home in 1914, he first erected a tramway to carry workmen and materials from the ferry landing below to the work site above. He chose to build his castle on a high peak, the southernmost in a series of hills known as the Seven Sisters. Naturally enough, he called his property "Seventh Sister."

Working from Gillette's own architectural plans, which called for southern white oak and native stone, it took workmen five years to complete the castle, a three-quarter-size reproduction of a castle Gillette had fallen in love with while visiting the Rhine River area in Germany. Looking at it, you can well understand that the house was built at a cost in excess of a million dollars.

Truly a castle, the home has walls four feet thick at the base, tapering to two feet at the tower. From 1919, when he moved in, until his death in 1937, Gillette had a delightful time outfitting his home. Throughout the twenty-four rooms, he had many pieces of furniture built in; you can marvel at the massive oak bureaus and the curious circular, rectangular, and wedge-shaped upholstered banquettes. For the interior doors, Gillette devised intricate wooden locks. While the light switches are also rendered in wood, the light fixtures themselves are decorated with bits of colored glass that he collected from his friends. The walls are coated with raffia mats custom-made and imported from Java.

Since William Gillette was a famous turn-of-the-century actor, you find throughout the castle many displays of theater memorabilia such as programs, props, and newspaper reviews. One of his most famous roles was Sherlock Holmes, which explains why one room is authentically furnished to represent "221B Baker Street," Sherlock Holmes's digs. Can you find the famous detective's knife? (It is, quite characteristically, stuck in the mantelpiece.) His dressing gown hangs on one wall. Over there is his violin, and over here his magnifying glass and microscope. Newspapers are scattered everywhere; you can almost feel the detective's presence in the room.

Gillette was a man of many hobbies. He loved cats, and you will find evidence of this affection throughout his home. Look for them — there are cats in the shape of saltshakers, a soap dish, doorstops, and candlesticks. It is said that he kept as many as fifteen cats as pets. In addition, he had two pet frogs and an assortment of goldfish in his conservatory. Indeed, his overlapping of interests is revealed anew when you peruse his scrapbook collection (he made over a hundred such books). Several, as you might expect, are devoted exclusively to cats!

Gillette's interests extended to the out-of-doors as well. A confirmed walker, he built a network of hiking trails throughout his 122-acre property. He was also a railroad enthusiast; to this end he built a miniature railroad just big enough so that he could frighten the

One of his most famous acting roles was Sherlock Holmes, which explains why one room is authentically furnished to represent "221B Baker Street."

Children delight in exploring the pathways, terraces, and stony arches that surround Gillette Castle in Hadlyme.

wits out of his visitors as he whipped them about the three-mile loop. Although the railroad has long since been dismantled, you will still see portions of the old trestle and roadbed as you wander the grounds. There is also a well-maintained set of trails to explore.

William Gillette was so concerned about the disposal of Seventh Sister after his death that in his will he instructed his executors "to see to it that the property did not fall into the hands of some blithering saphead who had no conception of where he is or with what surrounded." His executors honored his wishes; in 1943 the property was acquired by the Connecticut State Park and Forest Commission. Today, over one hundred thousand visitors enjoy the park each year, hiking, picnicking, and touring the castle. Plan to spend about half an hour inside the castle.

Even if you decide not to visit the interior, children enjoy exploring the pathways, terraces, and stony arches that surround the castle, and can spend a pleasant thirty minutes or so at that pursuit. There is even a huge stone gazebo with tables where you can picnic comfortably no matter what the weather. Munching on a sandwich or an apple here, you feel as though you are dining in a medieval castle all your own.

ACCESS _____

GILLETTE CASTLE STATE PARK. Directions: From Essex, return to Route 9, then head north on Route 9 to 9A. Follow Route 9A toward Chester, then pick up Route 148 and follow that to the car ferry. Take the car ferry across the river to Hadlyme, and follow Route 148 to the entrance of the park, on the left. **Season:** Memorial Day through Columbus Day. **Admission** charged to the castle. (203) 526-2336.

Groton/New London

GROTON SUBMARINE MEMORIAL. Berthed in the Thames River near the site of the Electric Boat Company where she was built, the submarine USS *Croaker* welcomes guests to tour her innards. This impressive gray tunnel of steel, on permanent loan from the Navy and the Federal government, offers a sharp contrast to the whaling boats you will see at Mystic Seaport. Climb aboard this 312-foot hunk of metal and find out what life was like in a submarine. While you tour the *Croaker*, keep in mind that during World War II this very vessel sank more than its share of tankers and enemy ammunition ships, as well as numerous smaller vessels. A ship to be reckoned with, the *Croaker*.

Your tour begins in the Forward Torpedo Room, which is stocked with four two-thousand-pound torpedoes, each mounted for quick loading and firing. A "guppy-class" sub (one that travels at high speed), the

There are two showers aboard, one for the eight officers and another for the sixty enlisted men.

Croaker carried a crew of sixty-eight men within her light-green walls until she was decommissioned in 1971. There are two showers aboard, one for the eight officers and another for the sixty enlisted men. To conserve precious fresh water, showers were off limits to the crew for the first three weeks at sea.

In the Ward Room, you see shelves full of navigational manuals; on a conference table there is a plan book lying open; it reads as follows: "Description of Dead Reckoning Tracer MK 7 Mod 2 Modified for Time Bearing Plotter Operation." Today, you learn, subs are nuclear powered, but in the *Croaker's* day they relied on diesel power. And, to add a human dimension to all the other factors, crew members could not be any more than five feet ten inches tall because the engines and associated equipment took up so much room.

In the Control Room you see the "Christmas Tree," a board equipped with red lights that indicate when diving or ascending maneuvers are imminent or in progress. There are lots of other switches and instruments to consider, too, including the diving alarm, which your guide will sound for you. In the After Battery, examine the dining tables with their built-in checker and backgammon boards, where the crew ate and whiled away the hours at sea. A trip through the Maneuvering Room and the After Torpedo Room winds up your tour. About forty-five minutes here provides a worthwhile experience; your attitude toward old war movies will never be quite the same.

OCEAN BEACH PARK. This New London amusement area has something to offer all members of the family. There are rides, bumper cars, and mechanical things that tilt and swirl located in their own area, to one side of the parking lot. Here you also find a high spiral water slide, appropriate only for the truly daring; teenagers seem to love it.

The broad boardwalk here has many viewers and lots of benches suitable for comfortable people watching; it runs between the wide sandy beach and the arcades, the eateries, and a miniature golf course. You can try your luck at shooting galleries, the latest in video games, or good old-fashioned skee ball. If you want to practice your swan dives, a small fee admits you to the Olympic-sized swimming pool located near the boardwalk; it has both high and low diving boards. A little farther along, there is a pleasant beachside playground where younger children can swing, slide, and climb above the sand. If you want to enjoy luxury while lounging on the beach, you can rent a beach umbrella or a lounge chair from the concession here.

ACCESS

GROTON SUBMARINE MEMORIAL. Directions: Take I-95 north exit 85 onto Bridge Street, then take the

Crew members could not be more than five feet ten inches tall because the engines and associated equipment took up so much room.

Here you find a high spiral water slide, appropriate only for the truly daring; teenagers seem to love it.

first left off Bridge Street onto Thames Street. The submarine memorial is at 359 Thames Street. **Season:** Mid-April through mid-October. **Admission** charged. (203) 448-1616.

OCEAN BEACH PARK. Directions: Take I-95 north exit 83 or south exit 84 (the New London exits), and proceed to downtown New London; then follow Ocean Avenue and signs to Ocean Beach Park. **Season:** Memorial Day through Labor Day. **Admission** charged (parking fee).

The masts of Mystic. This is the **Charles W. Morgan,** *the last of America's wooden whalers, where children can hop on board as whale hunters did 140 years ago.*

Mystic

MYSTIC SEAPORT MUSEUM. Here you can imagine yourself transported back in time to the mid nineteenth century, a time when life moved more slowly than it does today. Pretend that you and your family are residents of this busy seaport set on the banks of the Connecticut River. You've come to shop at the Grocery & Hardware Store, perhaps selecting a curling iron or razor strop. Or you might stop in at the Drug Store to buy some live leeches for an ailing relative or to have a tooth extracted. If you are quite young, perhaps you would be doing arithmetic problems on your slate in the old Schoolhouse, and if you are a sailor ashore, you might drain a mug or two at the Schaefer Tavern.

There are more than forty boats and buildings to visit here. Many of the businesses relate to the whaling trade, such as the Ship Chandlery with its rich odor of

You might stop in at the Drug Store to buy some live leeches for an ailing relative or to have a tooth extracted.

oakum (there is some to pick up and examine) and paint, and the Shipsmith Shop, where you can have your favorite harpoon mended. Don't ignore the Cooperage (where barrels are made), the Ropewalk, and the Sail Loft; and there are many more. Then there are some community institutions to patronize; try the Fishtown Chapel, the Meeting House, and the Mystic Bank, where valuables were stored in granite vaults, more for protection against fire than against thievery.

If you fancy ships, you will have a field day here; you can clamber about the decks of the fishing schooner *L.A. Dunton*, the world-famous wooden whaleship *Charles W. Morgan*, and the square-rigged ship *Joseph Conrad*. And if you visit between May and October, you can chug up the river aboard the coal-fired steamboat *Sabino*. There is also a complete working shipyard to explore, as well as the Shipcarver Shop, where figureheads are made, and the Small Boat Shop, where classic shapes are reproduced.

However exciting the ship activities may seem, you haven't even begun to exhaust the seaport's offerings! Be sure to look at the fabulous scrimshaw and the finely crafted ship models in the formal exhibit buildings, where you find many handsome marine paintings and lots of nautical memorabilia. If you are a craftsperson, stop in at the Mystic Bridge Weavers, where you can watch trained weavers demonstrate the use of nineteenth-century hand-operated looms. You discover that in many early communities it was the men who worked as itinerant weavers. They would go into homes to work by the day, either carrying their own looms or using the spinning and weaving equipment already in each home.

Throughout the seaport, there are generally many special activities and demonstrations under way. For example, you might watch a crew set the sails on one of the square-riggers. There are knot-tying demonstrations, of course, and if you want to learn to shoot the sun with a sextant, this is the place to do it. In the fisheries exhibits, you can see fish split, dried, and salted down. A half-hour-long whaling program, including footage of an actual whaling voyage, is held several times each day. Does your nose detect the scent of hot chipped beef? You can follow the smell to a nineteenth-century hearth, and watch a demonstration of fireplace cookery. If that's not enough, you can observe a whaleboat in action, or see a nineteenth-century lifesaving drill.

At the Seaport Planetarium, you discover how important the stars and planets are to the navigator. The show changes with the season, but you learn how to locate stars in the sky and become acquainted with the ways in which mariners used astronomy to find their way across the world's great oceans. On clear summer evenings, the seaport sometimes sponsors

You learn how to locate stars in the sky and how mariners used astronomy to find their way across the world's great oceans.

Do you know how to roll a hoop or walk on stilts?

Children can curl up in the child's bunk bed, which has its own curtains and a porthole to peek out of.

outdoor observation programs where visitors can do some stargazing using the planetarium's telescopes.

Although almost all aspects of the seaport intrigue children of all ages, there are several activities of special interest to very young visitors. Take them straight to the Children's Museum on your arrival so they can plan their day around the events scheduled just for them. The offerings include such activities as craft sessions focusing on the traditional sailors' arts of scrimshaw or knot-tying, films about the sea, and old-fashioned games (do you know how to roll a hoop? or walk on stilts?). It's really fun for children to visit the parts of the seaport where adults are not permitted. For instance, in the playyard, children can climb the rigging or settle down in an old boat to listen as the Village Storyteller, dressed in nineteenth-century garb, astounds them with tales of the *Flying Dutchman,* a ship destined to sail the seven seas forever, never coming to port.

Another ubiquitous character, the Village Chantyman, often stops in at the Children's Museum to lead a lively sing-along, aided by his trusty banjo and his concertina. He makes up songs with the assistance of his young audience: "Those New York ma's don't bake no pies — they feed their kids on codfish eyes; those Gloucester boys don't use no sleds — they slide down hills on codfish heads; those Trenton grandmas don't make no jellies — they cover their toast with ..." — you guess!

Even when there is no special activity in progress, there is still lots for small visitors to do in this building. The interior is a replica of the captain's family cabin. Did you know that many sea captains took their families to sea with them during the nineteenth century? Remember that while merchant ships might be gone for only several months, whaling vessels often left home for three to five years at a time. It is in this cabin that the children spent most of their time, tended by their mother.

Children eight years old and younger are invited to enter the cabin and pretend they are the children of a sea captain. They can curl up in the child's bunk bed, which has its own curtains and a porthole to peek out of. They can settle down on the oriental rug to play with toys of the period, reproductions of actual items described in the writings of children who went to sea. It's lots of fun to line up the wooden animals that live in Noah's Ark, or to fit the alphabet blocks into the wooden wagon. There is a toy train to play with, a rocking horse to climb upon, wooden dominos to set up and knock down, dolls to hug and play tea party with, and much more. To help the children get in the right mood, Victorian dress-up clothes are on hand.

Older children need not be disappointed either; there is also plenty for them to do here. They are invited to visit the gallery, an area outside the railing that defines the family cabin. Here they can read the correspondence and journal entries posted on the walls, most of which were written by children who went to sea. Young Alice Rowe Snow tells us: "My father being very fond of pets, bought twenty-two monkeys, five parrots, one ant-eater. We already had our dog Jess and two cats." ("Log of a Sea Captain's Daughter") Imagine — all this on a ship?

There is also a table full of Victorian toys for older children to investigate. Try your hand at making the jointed wooden lumberjack dance on a board set upon your knee. Manipulate a fascinating Jacob's ladder. Put a penny in the hand of a cast-iron clown, and watch him swallow it. Or you can drive yourself crazy tossing the wooden ball in the air and trying to catch it in the cup on a handle. You can also draw on an old slate or admire scenic vistas with the aid of a stereopticon. If you are a movie lover, you can tune in for an early version of this medium via the phenakistoscope. And if all this activity tires you out, settle down for a good read with one of the reproductions of nineteenth-century children's books provided.

With all the goodies to be found and enjoyed at Mystic Seaport, plan to spend a full day so that as many interests as there are children (and adults) may be served and satisfied.

MEMORY LANE DOLL AND TOY MUSEUM. This privately owned one-room museum began as the offshoot of one woman's personal passion for doll collecting. Today it contains some fifteen hundred dolls dating from the early 1700s to the present. When you enter the museum, you are immediately fascinated by the sensation that thousands of tiny eyes are staring your way! Here you find dolls from the United States, Japan, France, Germany, Italy, and China. There are dolls made from wood, wax, cloth and bisque, china, papier mâché, metal, and composition.

Some of the outstanding treasures include a 125-year-old papier mâché doll that stands forty inches high; his kid body is stuffed with sawdust and his hair is painted onto his head. And there's an elegant young damsel whose bisque socket head has a human-hair wig and pierced ears. She was made by the Société Française de Fabrication de Bébés et Jouets.

It's fun to find all the famous personalities here — they are in residence by the dozen at the doll museum. Look for Howdy Doody, the Beatles, Charlie McCarthy, W. C. Fields, Jackie Robinson, and Hopalong Cassidy. Even Batman is represented. Children will be intrigued by the many different versions of the Dionne quintuplets (accompanied by magazine articles and advertisements featuring their photographs) and of Shirley Temple. One Shirley Temple doll sits at her pipe organ and plays show tunes for your listening pleasure. You will also meet Buster Brown here: "I'm Buster Brown, I live in a shoe. Here's my dog Tige, he

Everywhere you go, you are greeted by dolls, some dressed as soldiers and sailors and others in gorgeous gowns, the tiny and the tall.

lives there too." — along with old friend Tige, who is just as likely to growl at you as to wag his tail.

While you're on the premises, take time to examine the Pennsylvania Dutch Barn, with its full allotment of hand-carved animals, as well as a well-equipped Humpty Dumpty circus. There is also a turn-of-the-century doll house decorated for the Christmas season. Both boys and girls are fascinated by the profusion of tiny tea sets, doll-sized strollers and carriages, cast-iron trucks, old trains, and riding toys — look for the hobby horse on the tricycle chassis, and the miniature Packard. Everywhere you go, you are greeted by dolls, some dressed as soldiers and sailors and others in gorgeous gowns, the tiny and the tall. Although there are no information panels, proprietor Violet Meier can tell you interesting stories about many members of her collection during a profitable half-hour visit.

The doll museum is located in the Olde Mistick Village Shopping Center. You might wish to browse a bit in this imaginative network of shops and restaurants, which was designed to represent an early-American village in about 1720. You find that the stores are tucked together along winding lanes and paths, lined by generous plantings of flowers. There is a small gazebo, a pond with ducks to feed, and many benches for taking a rest while you examine your purchases or study brochures from the Tourist Information Center, which is also located in the complex.

Just try to pick out a fish that looks like a weed-covered rock in a tank full of real weed-covered rocks!

MYSTIC MARINELIFE AQUARIUM. A division of the Sea Research Foundation, the aquarium sets out to teach visitors some interesting things about how the many animals that live in the sea look, live, and behave. After you are greeted by the well-whiskered sea lions in the outdoor pool by the main entrance, you disappear into a dark world of fish tanks, great and small. Here you find an exhibit centering on adaptation techniques; one of them is camouflage. Just try to pick out a fish that looks like a weed-covered rock in a tank full of real weed-covered rocks!

Want to find out what fish feel like? You can discover this by running your hands over a variety of materials. What does a fish see through its fish eyes? There are some special lenses to look through to find out. Another exhibit shows you that the age of a fish can be determined in a manner similar to that used to estimate the age of a tree. You'll learn that, like other living things, fish continue to grow throughout their lives; they have growth rings on their scales, each ring equaling one year of life. The oldest known fish is a Canada Sturgeon who displayed 152 such rings at the time of his capture! A little farther away, over at the large Open Sea tank, a recorded voice tells visitors about the habits of the sharks, bluefish, bass, and other sea creatures that live here in New England together.

Step outside after a while, and visit another major exhibit, the two-and-a-half-acre outdoor complex known as Seal Island. Do you know what a pinniped is? You will when you leave here. (To give you a head start, the word is derived from two Latin words — "pinna," meaning wing, and "pedis," for foot.)

On Seal Island, there are five species of seals and sea lions; they live in three areas that simulate their native habitats: the New England coast, the Pribilof Islands of Alaska, and the California coast. By the time you leave the area, you will be able to answer such questions as: Which pinniped is tropical? Which one eats shellfish? Which is a circus performer? There is a push-button board where you can try your luck matching pictures of the various pinnipeds with a set of characteristics listed below.

As you walk back to the main aquarium, be sure to take a walk through the marsh area; take a look at the extensive waterfowl collection, which includes many types of dabbling and diving ducks (the former feed on land and just beneath the surface of the water, while the latter reach down deeper for vegetation).

Don't leave the aquarium area without attending one of the daily animal-training sessions; it is sure to be a highlight of your visit. Here you will meet the resident whales, dolphins, and sea lions, who learn their tricks through a special behavior-conditioning technique. The main principle used in training here is that when an animal is rewarded for a certain kind of behavior, he will probably repeat that behavior. Thus you might see Skipper, a four-hundred-pound California sea lion, who will balance a ball on his nose with the aid of his very sensitive whiskers while doing an elegant bellyslide across the stage! Try that yourself in your living room sometime.

If you sit in the front row of the bleachers overlooking the oval pool in the Marine Theatre, prepare to be splashed! The three Atlantic bottlenose dolphins specialize in the high jump, and they displace a lot of water as they return to the pool after a leap some twenty feet into the air. These animals look just like synchronized swimmers as they strut across the pool on their tails with most of their bodies out of the water (you are told that this stunt requires the same amount of energy that a person needs to walk fifteen miles). These gregarious chaps cackle and whistle and slap the water loudly with their powerful tails when displeased. If you get hooked on their antics (which is very easy to do), you can always come back for another session later in the day. Allow at least a full morning or afternoon for your aquarium visit.

BEN FRANKLIN KITE SHOP. On your way out of the Mystic Seaport Museum, you might wish to drive through downtown Mystic for a touch of the more modern world. Besides stopping for gas or a soda, you'll find a shop there to gladden the heart of any

If you sit in the front row overlooking the oval pool in the Marine Theatre, prepare to be splashed!

Whether you favor a dragon kite, a replica of the Wright Brothers' famous plane, or a hang glider with its own pilot, you can find what you want right here.

visitor, young or old — a kite shop called The Ben Franklin Kite Shop. At One-Half Pearl Street in downtown Mystic, your eye will be attracted to the window of this cheerful shop by the profusion of color and the shiny pinwheels and mylar balloons. For this store is devoted to toys that fly. There are kites from all over the world: fisher kites, box kites, sleds, and much more. They are made of nylon, mylar, silk, and paper and they come in the brightest yellows, reds, greens, purples, and oranges that you can imagine. Whether you favor a dragon kite, a replica of the Wright Brothers' famous plane, or a hang glider with its own pilot, you can find what you want right here. The shop also provides reels, line, fancy gliders, and books about kites and paper airplanes.

THE DENISON PEQUOTSEPOS NATURE CENTER. When you need a break from the frenetic pace that seems to accompany the major Mystic attractions, take a short drive out to this small natural history museum located in a 125-acre nature sanctuary. At this outdoor education area, you can take a peaceful walk along one of the self-guiding trails. Here you stroll past ponds and through woods, meadows, and bogs thick with ferns. It is ideal territory for family walks because there are more than six trails to choose from, each less than a mile long.

There is even a twelve-hundred-foot-long trail designed for the blind, which sighted children, closing their eyes, also enjoy while gaining a beginning understanding of what it is like to be blind. Using a rope handrail and braille information panels, the trail encourages visitors to use their senses of touch, smell, and hearing to discover the natural world. One panel, located near a huge bird feeder, announces that some thirty-five species of birds have been identified right here. If you listen hard (closed eyes make it easier to listen hard) you might hear the chickadee saying its own name. Or perhaps you will hear the nasal "yank-yank" of the white-breasted nuthatch, or the whistled "peter-peter" of the tufted titmouse. You are also encouraged to hug a two-hundred-year-old swamp white oak to get a sense of its size.

In addition to the trails, the preserve includes several large enclosures, which are used to house injured or orphaned animals who will eventually be returned to the wild; a visit here is most instructive and rewarding. There are more animals inside the small museum, including a boa constrictor, and lots of fish and turtles in their own aquariums. Here you will also find stuffed examples of many types of birds and small mammals. Then there is a fossil display, a mounted collection of butterflies, and an exhibit that challenges you to match real bird eggs with pictures of their parents. Look, also, for a discovery box where you stick your hand in one of the holes and try to identify a skunk's skull, a turtle shell, and a snakeskin by

What's that splashing in the bog? Youngsters can find out visiting the Denison Pequotsepos Nature Center.

If you listen hard, you might hear the black-capped chickadee saying its own name.

touch. Altogether, this nature center offers a welcome respite from the more popular tourist attractions since it provides a pleasant opportunity to get into the country and experience firsthand some of Mystic's loveliest natural features. Plan to spend at least forty-five minutes here; this center is especially rewarding for five-to-ten-year-olds.

ACCESS

TO GET TO MYSTIC. Take I-95 about seven miles east of Groton to exit 90, then head south on Route 27 a short distance.

MYSTIC SEAPORT MUSEUM. Directions: From I-95 exit 90, head south on Route 27 about one mile; there are two entrances, one north and one south of the museum, and parking is available at both. **Season:** Year round. **Admission** charged. (203) 536-2631.

MEMORY LANE DOLL AND TOY MUSEUM. Directions: Take I-95 exit 90 (Route 27) to Olde Mistick Village complex. **Season:** Year round. Small **admission** charged. (203) 536-3450.

MYSTIC MARINELIFE AQUARIUM. Directions: Take I-95 exit 90 (Route 27) to Olde Mistick Village, on Coogan Boulevard. The aquarium is next to the village. **Season:** Year round. **Admission** charged. (203) 536-3323.

BEN FRANKLIN KITE SHOP. Directions: Follow signs to downtown Mystic. The kite shop is at the corner of Main and Pearl streets, at One-Half Pearl Street. (203) 536-0220.

DENISON PEQUOTSEPOS NATURE CENTER. Directions: From the aquarium, continue down Coogan Boulevard, in front of the aquarium; turn right onto Jerry Browne Road, and right again onto Pequotsepos Road. The nature center is on your left. **Season:** Year round. **Admission** charged. (203) 536-1216.

Hartford

NOOK FARM. Connecticut's capital city is a bustling metropolis best known for the thriving insurance industry. It may not be a city that immediately comes to mind when one thinks about vacationing in Connecticut, but it does have several points of interest to please young visitors. If you have some Tom Sawyer or Huckleberry Finn fans among your number, a visit to Nook Farm, the famous Victorian literary colony, should be part of your plans. Eighteen interrelated families and friends settled here during the second half of the nineteenth century, to share their cultural interests and accomplishments on the 130-acre spread. Today much of the farm land has been turned over to other purposes, but the homes of its two most famous

From the Nook Farm parking lot on Farmington Avenue, walk up the stairs to the visitors' center, where you can purchase tickets for the Mark Twain and Stowe houses.

Children might like to peek behind the screen in the corner of the dining room, where George the butler hid in order to enjoy Twain's hilarious dinner-table stories.

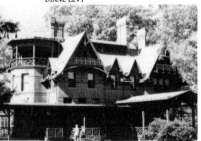

Tom Sawyer and Huck Finn were born in this house, Mark Twain's Hartford home.

residents, Mark Twain and Harriet Beecher Stowe, as well as the attractive grounds and carriage houses preserve the importance of this once remarkable neighborhood.

Mark Twain, named Samuel Clemens at birth, was born in 1811 and was raised in Hannibal, Missouri. He left school at age twelve to try his hand at a series of jobs: printer's devil (an errand boy in a printer's office), newspaper reporter, gold miner, and riverboat captain on the mighty Mississippi. When he settled down as a writer, he chose a pen name that evoked memories of his time on the river: to measure the depth of the river, a rope was lowered from the deck. When the first mark on it disappeared beneath the water's surface, the call was "Mark One!," indicating one fathom (six feet) in depth. When the second mark disappeared, the call was "Mark Twain!" or two fathoms. It was from this experience then that he derived the name that would become synonymous with his written wit and humor.

MARK TWAIN HOUSE. Before your visit to the Mark Twain House, plan to spend a couple of evenings after dinner reading parts of *The Adventures of Tom Sawyer* aloud. This will spark the enthusiasm of those who are new to the story, and perhaps older children who have read the book can relate some more incidents they remember, in preparation for the visit.

Your visit to Mr. Clemens' home takes the form of a fifty-minute guided tour. The guide sprinkles her description of the architecture and furnishings with amusing anecdotes about life in the Clemens family and with its famous father, for this is where the writer raised his family and spent the happiest years of his life. The house is a Victorian marvel that has turrets and bay windows galore; indeed, the whole place is decorated not only with fancy woodwork but also with painted brickwork.

The interior positively drips with tassels, beads, prisms, and fringes, in classic Victorian style. You learn that birthday parties were held in the spacious entrance hall, with its velvet circular mushroom settee. You discover that Mark Twain was enchanted with gadgets and had to have the latest inventions, including the early telephone. The guide reveals the "butter-stamp model," a "phone" wherein one speaks and listens through the same device, quickly transferring it back and forth from mouth to ear. As the guide presses a button in the wall, you can hear actor Hal Holbrook, imitating Mark Twain, complaining about the blasted invention.

Upon your visit to the living room and dining room, you hear a recording of tinkling music from the Clemenses' music box, which the family played in the evening as they sat down for dinner. Yes, the table is still set for dinner, and you learn that Mark Twain sat at the head of it, facing the leaded window over the fireplace, because he loved the sight of snowflakes dancing over flames in the wintertime. Children might like to peek behind the screen in the corner of the dining room, where George the butler hid in order to enjoy Mark Twain's hilarious dinner-table stories.

The bedrooms are interesting to most children because of the lovely oversized pillows. Victorians thought it healthy to sleep in a nearly sitting-up position, and the big fat pillows helped them accomplish the desired posture. In the master bedroom, however, sharp-eyed children will note the fact that the lacy pillows are situated at the foot of the bed! It seems that Mark Twain had purchased the elaborately carved bedstead in Venice at great expense, and he claimed that he and his wife slept in it backwards because they wanted to fully enjoy the intricate headboard. Note also the delightful bedposts with their removable angels, which his daughters liked to play with.

Your guide also takes you through the children's rooms and the conservatory, which boasts a fountain and some Japanese lanterns. In the billiard room, where Twain wrote as well as played, you learn that he smoked about twenty cigars a day, but as he explained, "That's not too bad ... I only smoke them one at a time." The drawing room, library, nursery, and guest room are also shown, each one plumb full of Victoriana and one boasting a Currier & Ives print of two people in an archway; they are suddenly transformed into the image of a skull as you walk by! Now, how does that happen?

Throughout the house, your guide points out pieces actually owned and used by members of the Clemens family, Samuel (or Mark), wife Livy, and their three daughters, Clara, Jean, and Susy. The rest of the furnishings are period pieces similar to those that were probably used by the family.

HARRIET BEECHER STOWE HOUSE. If your young ones are still game for another short house tour, you can also visit the place where the author of *Uncle Tom's Cabin* lived with her husband and her grown twin daughters. With her sister, Catharine Beecher, Mrs. Stowe also wrote *The American Woman's Home*, a popular late-nineteenth-century handbook propounding the most modern ideas on home decoration and domestic economies. Indeed, Mrs. Stowe so enjoyed making household objects pretty that throughout her home you will find furniture, china, and other accessories decorated with her hand-painted flowers.

Less spectacular than the Mark Twain House, the Stowe House nonetheless has a charm of its own and it is certainly worth a visit. If you must make a choice, however, choose the Mark Twain House. The tours at both houses are best suited for children nine years old and older.

Twain smoked twenty cigars a day, but as he explained, "That's not too bad ... I only smoke them one at a time."

The Stowe House is on the same circular drive as the Twain House.

Riding a gray horse with a purple saddle and grabbing for the brass ring, children can enjoy Hartford's Bushnell Carousel much the same way their parents did.

From Nook Farm, proceed east along Farmington Avenue about a half mile to Bushnell Park.

BUSHNELL CAROUSEL. Less than a mile away, in downtown Hartford, the big draw for kids is the fine old carousel in Bushnell Park. This vintage 1914 merry-go-round is housed in a windowed pavilion with stained-glass insets, which makes it attractive even in rainy weather. There are benches where parents can sit if they don't want to take a spin, although that is hard to imagine. Some of the forty-eight carved horses are stationary and others go up and down. Look for the "U" joint at the top of the post securing the horse if you want to ride on a "mover." You can choose from gray horses with purple saddles, cream ones with orange gear, or black stallions with red tack. Some of the animals are covered with fancy flowers painted in vibrant colors; all of them sport golden horseshoes. For the more sedate or the very, very young, there are two fancy upholstered coaches to ride in in elegant style. Nearby you'll find a playground; refreshment carts around the edges of the park offer everything from hot dogs to soul food, ice cream to tacos.

Cross the street to the State Capitol building, which is located at 210 Capitol Avenue, across from the carousel.

STATE CAPITOL. If you look across Capitol Avenue from the carousel, you can see the imposing gold-domed structure that has served as Connecticut's State Capitol building since 1878. Made of marble and granite, the neo-Gothic building looks like an oversized sand castle done drip-style. The ornate interior includes three sky-lit wells that are enclosed on three levels by connecting balconies. Hand-painted columns, stenciled beams, and patterned marble flooring add to the effect.

Free tours of the Capitol are offered on weekdays. You and your children learn here how a bill becomes a law; you also see many historical artifacts — such as bullet-ridden flags and Lafayette's camp bed — relating to Connecticut and to early New England history. The most interesting part of a visit to the capitol, however, is the constant buzz of activity when the legislature is in session. All year, except for the summer months when the legislature is not there, most legislative sessions, hearings, and committee meetings are open to the public; children do seem to enjoy dropping in for an intimate look at government in action. You can come and go as interest dictates. If you are lucky, you might get a glimpse of the governor. Allow about half an hour for a complete visit, unless you stay longer to watch the government sessions.

MUSEUM OF CONNECTICUT HISTORY. Much of the collection in this building deals with antique firearms and clocks, and there is also a gallery featuring portraits of the state's governors. While this is all rather dry, there is one corner that might be of interest to children who are partial to TV drama dealing with crime. In a room to your left as you enter the museum, you find a collection of pamphlets documenting famous Connecticut murder cases. They have titles like "A Sketch of the Life of Albert L. Starkweather, the Murderer of his Mother and Sister." Important issues such as the question of whether or not drunkenness constitutes insanity are raised, along with the matter of false imprisonment. This exhibit is best saved for children ten and older. Allow about fifteen minutes.

Children do seem to enjoy dropping in for an intimate look at government in action. If you are lucky, you might get a glimpse of the governor!

Cross Capitol Avenue to the State Library and Supreme Court building, which houses the Museum of Connecticut History; it is directly opposite the front entrance to the State Capitol.

ACCESS

TO GET TO HARTFORD. Heading east, take I-84 to exit 46. Heading west, take I-86 to its Hartford terminus and the junction with I-84, and continue west on I-84. From New Haven, head north on I-91 about forty miles, then head west on I-84.

NOOK FARM. Directions: From I-84 exit 46, head north on Sisson Avenue; turn right onto Farmington Avenue and follow to Nook Farm parking lot. (A second parking lot is located on Forest Avenue, the next street over on your right.) **Season:** Year round. **Admission** charged. (203) 525-9317.

BUSHNELL CAROUSEL. Season: April through October (weekends only in April and October). **Admission** charged. (203) 525-1618.

STATE CAPITOL. Season: Year round. **Admission** free. (203) 566-3662.

MUSEUM OF CONNECTICUT HISTORY. Season: Year round. **Admission** free. (203) 566-3056.

West Hartford

CHILDREN'S MUSEUM OF HARTFORD. This, the nation's fifth oldest children's museum, specializes in the sciences. Here you find Connecticut's largest planetarium, where shows focusing on celestial

Your child can walk right into the belly of a whale: this life-sized model sits in front of the Children's Museum of Hartford.

phenomena are presented daily. The program changes frequently, but you might learn about anything from seasonal stargazing opportunities to planets bearing both sleeping and active volcanoes.

Frequent live-animal demonstrations are also very much a part of a visit to this museum, with its well-populated Live Animal Center. Reptile enthusiasts are rewarded with a fine selection of their favorites, including three boa constrictors, a red rat snake, an Eastern Indigo snake, and an armadillo lizard. You probably know about hibernation, but have you ever heard of estivation? The Gila monster (he's the only poisonous lizard in the United States, but he doesn't live anywhere near New England) manages to survive the extreme heat of his desert habitat by moving about only at dusk and dawn and living as near to a water source as possible. He also stores surplus fat in his tail on which to live during his long summer fast (or sleep period), when the temperature soars to almost unlivable heights. This is known as a time of estivation.

The museum contains a spacious aquarium, housing both exotic and familiar sea life. You may be familiar with the lethal electric eel, but have you ever made the acquaintance of a catfish capable of rendering a person unconscious with its electrical charge, which it normally uses to catch its prey? Be calm; this frightening animal resides in the swamps and reed beds of tropical Africa.

After admiring the hawksbill turtle, with its speckled flippers and a beak that looks as if it should belong to a parrot, you can pick up an earphone and tune in to "Voices of the Deep." These recordings prove that the sea is really a very noisy place to live. Here you can listen to the whistles and clicks made by whales and dolphins as they communicate with each other, as well as to the sounds produced by the puffer, the pistol shrimp, the sea robin, and the toadfish.

In the Hands-On room, there is a tidepool full of spider crabs, green crabs, rock crabs, starfish, and whelks to pick up and examine. A great sea turtle paddles placidly in a tank in the middle of the room; if you want to know what it feels like to be he, there is a large tortoise shell that you can strap onto your back. Future scuba divers can suit up in rubber vests, fins, and face masks here, as they imagine themselves exploring the ocean depths. Be sure to activate the Fish Shape and Movement display, which illustrates that the fish's body offers the least resistance to water when the fish heads into it. When you reverse the direction of the current, the fish appears to be swimming in place — treading water, so to speak.

When you have had your fill of sea life, there are many other animals to meet here too, such as the burrowing owl, the black-tailed prairie dog, the chinchilla, and "Armand." The last is an attractive nine-banded armadillo, often referred to as a small "pig in armor." For all his armor, Armand is virtually toothless, having only a few molars to his name. He compensates for this with his long and very sticky tongue, which he uses to lap up insects, giving him an excellent reputation for pest control. Armand doesn't see or hear very well, but he has a well-developed sense of smell; he uses his nose to find food and to detect enemies. Once you have seen Armand, you discover that you may as well have seen any armadillo anywhere, for almost without exception the female armadillo gives birth to four babies at a time, all of the same sex, and they are almost always identical quadruplets, down to the number of hairs on their bellies!

The museum contains lots of other exhibits, including some surprising isolated items that appear in odd places. For instance, you may turn a corner and be greeted by a suit of armor. Or take a walk up the stairs and find a Focault pendulum installed in the stairwell to illustrate that the earth does indeed rotate. And there is one room full of artifacts and photographs from the Savanna of East Africa. You see swords, war clubs, even a whisker tweezer; the benches in this gallery are covered with real zebra and lion skins.

As you leave the museum, be certain to pay a visit to the life-sized model of the sperm whale on the lawn. You can walk right into this hollow form made of reinforced concrete. You may be surprised to learn that the male whales grow to fifty feet in length, the females to thirty-six feet, and that some of these beasts weigh about sixty tons. The sperm whale has the largest teeth of any animal on earth, and it inhabits all the world's oceans. You and the children may find it comforting to know that the sperm whale survives mostly on squid.

Have you ever made the acquaintance of a catfish capable of rendering a person unconscious with its electrical charge, which it normally uses to catch its prey?

ACCESS

CHILDREN'S MUSEUM OF HARTFORD. Directions: Take I-84 exit 43, follow signs to Trout Brook Drive, and turn left. The museum is at 950 Trout Brook Drive; the way is well marked. **Season:** Year round. **Admission** charged. (203) 236-2961.

"There was once a fight on board a trolley," our guide said, "when the conductor punched a ticket." Hear other tales at the Connecticut Electric Railway.

Warehouse Point

After years of trusty service, this trolley was shipped back north on a coffee boat; during restoration, volunteers found that coffee beans continually spewed from her innards.

THE CONNECTICUT ELECTRIC RAILWAY. As you enter the premises here, you see a busy sight. More than thirty trolley cars, dating from 1892 to 1947, are scattered about the grounds. Volunteers are hard at work repairing and restoring cars, some soon to be added to the eight already in working condition and traveling on the one-and-a-half mile track. Indeed, ninety-nine percent of the work done on the railway — from restoration to track construction, from general maintenance to trolley operation — is handled by volunteers, who are dedicated to the preservation of a bygone mode of transportation.

One ticket entitles you to ride the trolleys to your heart's content. Perhaps you will travel on Old #840, which began service in New Haven in 1905. An open-sided car, she was used mostly for excursions to the Yale Bowl in the '40s, carrying over two hundred exuberant football fans. Unfortunately, such cars were taken out of service soon afterward, labeled unsafe.

Car #836 hails from New Orleans. Her moment of glory came when she was cast to play the title role in the movie version of *A Streetcar Named Desire*. Madame #850 was built in Saint Louis in 1912, shipped down the Mississippi River by barge, and loaded on a ship bound for Rio de Janeiro. After years of trusty service in Brazil, she was purchased by the Connecticut Electric Railway and shipped back north on a coffee boat. During restoration, volunteers found that coffee beans continually spewed from her innards. Naturally, all her advertising signs were printed in Portuguese.

Riding the trolleys here is a trip back in time; note the bare light bulbs that swing from the wooden ceilings. Be sure to check out the advertising signs promoting such sentiments as "Food Will Win the War — we observe meatless days, wheatless days, porkless days" and such products as "Arrow Shirts — with starched cuffs, are proper and distinctly refined. $1.50 up . . ."

In the old days, the whole family used to ride the trolleys on summer nights, just to get out of their stuffy apartments and cool off. Recognizing a potential market, the trolley companies built small amusement parks, placing them at the ends of the lines so that people would have to get to them by trolley. Piney Ridge, a small park with a spring-loaded dance floor (easy on the feet), was located at the end of this particular stretch of track, the Rockville Branch of the Hartford and Springfield Railway. But the Hartford & Springfield went into bankruptcy in 1926; the cars and tracks were torn up and sold as scrap metal in order to pay eager creditors. Today, loyal volunteers continue to replace the track on this particular stretch, hopeful that one day it will extend to the site of Piney Ridge.

As your ride begins, you hear the air compressor pump up air pressure for the brakes and whistle. Bells ring, whistles sound, and off you rumble. The conductor punches tickets and the motorman drives the car. As you pass an unmarked road crossing, the conductor disembarks to hold up traffic so that the trolley can cross the road. You also travel by the "passing siding," where one car can pull aside to permit another, traveling on the same track in the opposite direction, to pass by safely. At the end of the line, the conductor talks briefly about the history of the trolleys before flipping your seats around for the return trip. Each ride takes about ten minutes. (You can bring your dog along, too, so long as he is on a leash.)

THE CONNECTICUT FIRE MUSEUM. Some folks are just plain hooked on fire trucks, and if one of these lives in your family, walk to the back of the Electric Railway parking lot and pay a visit to a "fire truck heaven," which houses about twenty vehicles used in fire-fighting operations. There is one truck out front to climb on; otherwise the apparatus is strictly for viewing. But search for the black fire truck, and for the hand-drawn hose reel that was used in Stonington, Connecticut, in 1850. Check out the fire sleigh, the one that was used to fight a blaze on Saint Valentine's Day in 1942. All around you, you can see trucks with brass bells, wooden ladders, and wooden-spoked artillery wheels, many of them outfitted with boots and slickers or other items of fire-fighting paraphernalia. Children begin to sense that fighting fires is very hard work.

ACCESS

TO GET TO WAREHOUSE POINT. Follow I-91 north or south to exit 45.

THE CONNECTICUT ELECTRIC RAILWAY. Directions: From I-91 exit 45 (Bridge Street) take Route 140, following signs to the railway, about one-half mile away. **Season:** Memorial Day through Labor Day, weekends only rest of year. **Admission** charged. (203) 623-7417. **Note:** Tracks are strung with colored lights from mid-December through New Year's Day and extra cars are run in the evening.

THE CONNECTICUT FIRE MUSEUM. Directions: Located at the end of the Connecticut Electric Railway trolley tracks, behind the railway parking lot. **Season:** June through August; weekends only in the fall. **Admission** charged. (203) 623-4732.

Manchester

THE LUTZ CHILDREN'S MUSEUM. This small but growing children's museum bills itself as "the Doing Place"; it is easy to see why. At the Lutz, participation means much more than pushing buttons. Take the Communications Center, for example. There is a switchboard for connecting plugs and crisscrossing wires, making imaginary transatlantic calls to your heart's content. Then there is the printing section, where children can spread the written word by composing messages and printing them out, letter by letter, using large rubber stamps and inked sponges. If they should want to experiment with sign language, there are manuals to teach them how to begin. There is also an excellent section on the braille system.

Children are impressed to hear that Louis Braille was only fifteen years old when in 1824 he developed his system of raised dots, which was to revolutionize the world of the blind. You will learn that braille is based on a group of six dots called a cell; the display shows how letters, dipthongs, and punctuation marks are formed. You can try your hand at deciphering a simple message, or run your fingers over the surface of the braille rendition of a picture of a leopard frog, to get an idea of the way in which blind people "see" images. There is even a page from the braille edition of *My Weekly Reader.*

If science is your field of interest, you can build a food chain, using color-coded wooden pieces. The sun provides the plant with energy; the plant uses the sunlight to manufacture food; herbivores eat plants, carnivores eat herbivores, and on and on . . . . It all sounds very complicated until you translate it into a series of tiles showing sun, grass, mouse, snake, etc. There are

There is a switchboard for connecting plugs and crisscrossing wires, making imaginary transatlantic calls to your heart's content.

lots of live animals to investigate here, too, among them some Connecticut residents — an opossum, a woodchuck, a rabbit, a striped skunk, and a corn snake.

If you favor the theater, you can admire the collection of antique puppets on display, and then — go ahead and put on your own production in the handsome puppet theater! Stick puppets and hand puppets wait for you to bring them to life, with a story of your own invention or with one of the scripts provided. There is even a wall screen and projector arrangement, so that shadow puppetry can be displayed too.

With declining enrollments and public spending constraints, many of New England's small neighborhood schools have closed their doors in recent years, surrendering to the more efficient trend of centralization. Housed in the South School building, the Lutz Children's Museum is a fine example of one way in which a former neighborhood school can be recycled as a valuable part of the community. Allow about an hour for your visit at this interesting attraction.

Go ahead and put on your own production in the handsome puppet theater!

ACCESS

THE LUTZ CHILDREN'S MUSEUM. Directions: Take I-86 exit 92 onto Route 44A (Center Street) and continue one-half mile to Manchester. From Center Street, turn right onto Main Street; the museum is at 247 South Main Street. **Season:** Year round. **Admission** free (donations welcome). (203) 643-0949.

East Granby

OLD NEW-GATE PRISON AND COPPER MINE. The magnificent panorama of the Litchfield Hills that greets you as you enter the twelve-foot-high sandstone wall of this former prison seems almost incongruous. It is hard to imagine that such beauty existed so near to this place where men worked and slept in dank underground passageways, first at extracting rich mineral deposits and later at atoning for misdeeds.

Copper was discovered here in 1705 and the celebrated Simsbury Mine was first worked in 1707, financed by capitalists in Boston, New York, London, and Holland. The ore removed from the hill averaged twelve percent copper but sometimes ran as high as fifty percent. Mining activity ceased in 1773. Later efforts to revive the mine were made by the Phoenix Mining Company and the Connecticut Copper Company, but they did not succeed.

In December of 1773, the Colony of Connecticut put the mine to work as a prison, naming the complex after the notorious New-Gate prison in London. Burglars, counterfeiters, and horse thieves were confined here; Tories and British prisoners of war joined them eventually. In 1776, New-Gate became the first state prison in what was to become the United States; during the next forty-two years, more than eight hundred prisoners were incarcerated here.

After listening to a tape-recorded introductory speech, make your way to the mine entrance for a self-guided tour of this subterranean world. You shiver as you leave the warmth of a sunny afternoon behind and descend into an eighteenth-century prison, where the temperature hovers in the mid '40s even in the summer. Young children should be careful here. The going is a bit rough, the damp, packed-dirt floors sometimes slippery. In the Lodging Area, you'll have time to think about the forty prisoners who slept here in wooden "cabinets" designed to afford some protection from the dampness and continual dripping of water. It's hard to believe that when you reach the well where the prisoners got their water, you are forty-five feet under the ground. Continue on, ducking your head to avoid hitting ceilings that are sometimes not even five feet high, to the Solitary Confinement area, where difficult prisoners were shackled to the wall.

You also see the ore shaft, which was used to hoist copper ore to the surface during the early years of the mining operation. Your pathway is lit by strategically placed lamps, but when you peer down the abandoned tunnels, off limits for safety reasons, it is not difficult to imagine the darkness that pervaded the inmates' lives. You can also loop up through the old mine shaft, twenty feet from the earth's surface, which was the only access to the mine until the current tunnel stairway was constructed in 1972. Even though prisoners spent many hours at New-Gate in darkness, many preferred their underground quarters to the above-ground cells because here they could move about and communicate more freely with other prisoners. Indeed, escape attempts were not unusual.

The first prisoner confined at New-Gate escaped by climbing the sixty-five-foot ore shaft after only eighteen days of imprisonment. He was never seen again. The most successful attempt was a mass exit of twenty-one prisoners in May of 1781. They left by way of the old entrance after an accomplice unlocked the above-ground covering to the shaft. In 1806, thirty prisoners forged keys (in the blacksmith shop) from the pewter buttons on their uniforms, unlocked their chains, and attempted a mass escape. Their scuffle ended when one of their ringleaders was killed. But despite continued uprisings and escapes, New-Gate earned a reputation for strength and security. As you wander the dank passageways, you may well hear children plotting their own escape: "I'll hide in solitary until the guard's back is turned, then you . . . ."

In the early years the prisoners were put to work mining copper. (Ask the guide stationed in the tunnels to show you the copper vein.) In later years, as mining proved unprofitable, the inmates were turned to the

The first prisoner confined at New-Gate escaped by climbing the sixty-five-foot ore shaft after only eighteen days of imprisonment. He was never seen again.

production of hand-wrought nails and eventually to shoemaking, New-Gate's major industry in the 1820s.

When you leave the mine and begin to explore the brick and sandstone ruins above ground, you soon find the remains of the treadmill building, which housed offices, a hospital, cells for women, and a grain treadmill during the last years of the prison's operation. The mill was operated by teams of thirty prisoners walking side by side on horizontal flanges on a schedule of ten minutes for work, five minutes for rest.

Much of the pleasure of visiting New-Gate comes in the form of anecdotes, theories, and bits of historical information passed on by the resident guides. They are knowledgeable about both the mining industry and the operation of the prison, and they encourage questions. In talking to a guide, you might discover that in 1810 the Connecticut General Assembly sent a study committee to New-Gate; the committee reported back that conditions were so unsanitary that changes needed to be instituted. Yet, considering the state of medical arts at the time, it is impressive that only 9 of the 255 inmates imprisoned here from 1773 to 1810 died, not counting those who perished from armed insurrection or foiled escape attempts.

And when you look at the daily ration permitted each prisoner, you know that no one starved: "1 lb. beef, 2 lbs. potatoes, 3½ pts. cider, alternated with ¾ lb. pork, 1 lb. flour, 3 gills peas or beans, and 3½ pts. cider." Some even contend that New-Gate represented a new era in prison reform. Previously it was common for prisoners in most jails to have their ears cropped, a practice which was planned to forever mark them as outcasts. This form of punishment was never practiced at New-Gate, although whipping was permitted. Allow about forty-five minutes for your visit.

In 1806, thirty prisoners forged keys (in the blacksmith shop) from the pewter buttons on their uniforms, unlocked their chains, and attempted a mass escape.

ACCESS

OLD NEW-GATE PRISON AND COPPER MINE. Directions: Take I-91 exit 40 (Route 20/Bradley Field), and follow Route 20 west about six miles to East Granby. Turn right onto New-Gate Road and follow signs. **Season:** Mid-May through October. **Admission** charged. (203) 653-3563 or (203) 566-3005.

A Connecticut Country Fair

The air smells of machine oil, horses, and cotton candy. Where else but at a country fair could you stumble on such a combination? Connecticut hosts many such fairs each year and a visit to one can be an exhilarating, memorable event. Here you can watch chickens hatch or see a blacksmith shoe a horse, sip fresh-pressed cider or watch a horse-pulling contest, win a teddy bear by throwing baseballs into a peach basket or take a spin on the ferris wheel . . .

If you have a son who loves to cook, tell him about the baked-goods competition, not to mention the pie-eating contest.

The country fair is a place where folks come together to show off their best efforts — a prize blueberry pie, a perfect heifer, or a handmade quilt. They join together to share and enjoy each other's ideas, talents, and accomplishments and to have a good time. Fairs are family oriented, with many activities for children of all ages. While they are the perfect place to take your brood, fairs also require some planning if they are to reward you with pleasure rather than frustration. Here, then, are several suggestions for making the most of your day at the country fair.

Let your children know in advance that you will be taking them to a country fair. Read up on the fair so that you can tell them about the types of exhibits, contests, and activities they will enjoy. Consider the interests of each child and try to point out exhibits that are particularly appropriate. If your daughter is an aspiring horsewoman, she may be interested in the pony judging. If she prides herself on her ability to sew, pique her interest in the fair by describing contests in quilting, knitting, and dressmaking. If you have a son who loves to cook, tell him about the baked-goods competition, not to mention the pie-eating contest. If he favors machinery, let him know that there will be the newest tractors and related farm machinery to investigate.

Country fairs are exceedingly popular events, and as such they tend to attract huge crowds. Crowds can be confusing when small children are present; it's wise to try to avoid the biggest crush by scheduling your visit for a weekday. If that isn't possible, plan to arrive first thing in the morning. And do your very best to avoid the first and last Saturday of the fair.

Almost every country fair today has a midway chock full of games of chance and skill, as well as loads of mechanical rides. It doesn't seem quite just to take the children along to the fair and designate the midway "off limits," but on the other hand, the midway is almost always the most expensive aspect of attending such a fair. Therefore, it's a good idea to decide in advance how much money or how many rides each child can have. Let the children know of your decision and then make certain you all stick to the limits you have set. Let them take part in the process by deciding when in the day they want to visit the midway — beginning, middle, or end.

As soon as you have paid the general fair admission (usually a blanket charge to cover all events except the midway), sit down on the lawn and read the program and schedule of events aloud. Check off any that the children express interest in. Together, decide whether it is more important to see the ox-pulling contest or the goat showmanship exhibit, the corn-husking bee or the lumberjack competition. Figure out what will be happening, and also *when* and *where* it will take place. Then you can work your fair wandering in among the scheduled events you have chosen.

Before going to any exhibits, choose a meeting place where family members should go in case they become lost or separated from other members of the group. Decide on a conspicuous spot, such as the base of the giant slide or the entrance to the petting zoo. Don't choose a refreshment stand or game booth, because all too late you may discover that there are several of these that look almost exactly the same. The meeting place can also be used for reunions if you should decide to break into smaller groups for a time.

Which brings us to a related point; there is so much to do and see at a country fair that at times it may make sense to split up the family so that different members can visit the exhibits of particular interest to them. Also, particularly when crowds are thick, two people might have an easier time finding seats at the sheep-shearing demonstration or the sausage sandwich stand than would a group of four.

Be certain to vary your activities at the fair in order to keep up the interest level. Try to mix sedentary activities (watching a quilting demonstration) with active ones (taking a hayride). Mix content too, perhaps alternating a banjo concert with a visit to the beekeeper's demonstration hive. If a child is genuinely bored (after watching thirty-three goats pass by for judging, the thirty-fourth goat can get a little dull), don't insist that he remain for the entire event. A child may benefit more from questioning a young 4-H goat specialist caring for his animal in the barn than from watching the formal judging.

Encourage your children to collect leaflets and any other free material that is distributed. Such items will serve as memory spurs when they return home, offering just enough of a reminder to prompt happy reminiscences about their day at the fair.

Here follows a list of major Connecticut country fairs. Although not all the events mentioned above are featured at every fair, most do have animals, home arts, music, crafts, and, of course, rides. Tractor pulls and sulky races are the big news at the Brooklyn Fair, while old-time fiddling contests are important at the North Stonington Fair. Bridgewater has a children's pet show, while gardening, crafts, and cooking are featured at the Durham Fair; and frog-jumping contests are not unheard of at the Four Town Fair. Whichever you choose, you are certain to have a memorable day that will provide pleasure whenever you think of it, a day your children will not soon forget.

For specific dates, write to the Connecticut State Travel Office, 210 Washington Street, Hartford, CT 06106.

Frog-jumping contests are not unheard of at the Four Town Fair.

York's Old Gaol Museum, where you can get locked in stocks.

CHAPTER II

Maine

D eer, moose, black bear, fox. Lynx, porcupine, raccoon, skunk. Dozens of seabirds, song birds, and lake birds. All these make their homes in Maine, the most sparsely populated state east of the Mississippi. Maine, which in land area accounts for nearly half of the entire New England region, remains in many ways very much a frontier society. The climate is generally harsh, the soil rocky and not overly fertile, the distances great. Here is an environment that makes serious demands upon its inhabitants.

Both France and England once claimed the territory that is now Maine, and battles between the French, the English, and the Indians were frequent from 1615 until finally the British prevailed, conquering the French in eastern Canada in 1763. Along with the persistent English, Scottish, and Irish Protestant immigrants (the original "down East Yankees" with their dry, tight-lipped sense of humor), the early settlers came also from Brittany and Normandy, continuing the French influence. And in the latter half of the nineteenth century, French-Canadians migrated to Maine in search of employment in the lumber and textile industries. Today French is still spoken in many parts of the state, particularly in the vicinity of the industrial cities.

Maine is the place to feast on world-famous lobster, to admire whitewashed lighthouses perched on rocky promontories. Explore the colorful harbors, too; take a dip in the icy Atlantic, or go to sea on an excursion boat. And when you have satisfied your appetite for the coast, head inland. Climb the mountains, explore the forests, and look at how life is lived in the small towns of Maine.

On a summer drive from Bangor to Bethel, for example, you pass through town after town marked by no more than a crossroad with a few houses, perhaps a store, a gas station, or a post office. As you drive by the numerous small farms, imagine how it is to live here in the winter, when the deep snow blankets the rocky fields and covers the stands of pine, spruce, and fir. Consider well the isolation, the on-going need to provide your own entertainment. Think about what it really means to count on only yourselves and your neighbors.

Now, as in the past, Maine challenges its people; it also rewards them with a vital way of life. A visit to Maine is an opportunity to enjoy great physical beauty and to discover a truly rural lifestyle, where people pride themselves on their self-sufficiency and their enduring ability to survive and flourish despite an uncompromising environment.

Classic coastal Maine: a clamdigger, spade and bucket in hand, strolls along the York Harbor shoreline.

York

Located less than one and a half hours' drive from Boston, York is an ideal destination for visitors to New England with little time to spare. In York you can both explore Maine's colonial heritage and enjoy the lively tempo of a flourishing seaside resort, all in the space of a single day. Of course, if you travel along the Maine coast in a leisurely fashion, York will simply be the first of the many fine towns, and certainly worth a stop.

Follow signs to York Village, the historic district.

THE OLD GAOL MUSEUM. Begin your visit at the Old Gaol in the historic district of York Village. The Old Gaol Museum is composed of the gaol itself and the neighboring Emerson-Wilcox House. Guides dressed in period costume (circa 1800) conduct thirty-minute tours of the two buildings, explaining the functions and origins of the furnishings and artifacts; they also provide gossipy background about the folks who lived and worked here. In the gaol you see the cells used for women, debtors, and criminals. You learn that the party responsible for sending a debtor to prison was also required to pay the offender's keep.

As you wander from cell to cell, keep your eyes alert for leg irons chained to the floor, and for the straw mattresses where the prisoners slept. From gloomy stone dungeons to the airier upper-story cells, the jail housed many sorts of prisoners . . . including numerous counterfeiters.

The gaol served as the prison for the entire Province of Maine until 1760. For many years it was operated by one William Emerson. When he died in 1790 (and there is no record of his death, not even a headstone), his wife took over the duties, even after running off with the local schoolmaster shortly after her husband's demise. During her tenure as a gaoler, there were nearly a dozen escapes in quick succession, quite a feat when you consider the walls are three feet thick.

Children are intrigued by their guide's explanations of expressions such as "turnkey" and "snug as a bug in a rug." They are interested in the "pass-throughs," where firewood and food could be shoved in to the cells to the prisoners without requiring a door to be opened. This arrangement was devised to prevent the gaoler's wife from being overpowered by the prisoners as she saw to their needs. Notice also that the window shutters are located on the inside of the building, not the outside as we would expect. Makes it a lot easier to close them on a frosty Maine morning!

Before leaving the gaol, pay a visit to the museum area where eighteenth- and nineteenth-century toys, clothing, and household items are attractively displayed. Off to one side is a weaving room where the resident weaver spins yarn and operates the huge loom. Cooking demonstrations are held too, illustrating eighteenth-century skills such as baking in an original old gaol oven. On the lawn in front of the building is a cannon to clamber up on and a set of stocks to try out.

When you finish the gaol tour, cross to the Old Burying Ground and let the children stretch their legs before moving on to the second part of the Old Gaol Museum.

OLD BURYING GROUND. Suggest that the children search for unusual spellings in the verses engraved on the headstones here, some of which date from the seventeenth century. Perhaps they can find Edward Emerson's marker; they will soon be hearing more about this gentleman. His epitaph reads:

> Capricious was his mind
> Benevolent was his heart
> Spotlefs was his character
> Generous, humane, and juft
> But alas! how frail is man. (d. 1803)

Look too for the grave with the large stone block on top of it. According to legend, the block was put there to keep the witch buried beneath securely in her place. But in truth, this was Mary Nason's grave, and her husband Samuel placed the stone there to prevent her remains from being disturbed by roaming cattle.

Here you see the cells used for women, debtors, and criminals.

Cross the side street to the Old Burying Ground, next to the Emerson-Wilcox House.

Walk to the far side of the grave-yard and the Old School House.

OLD SCHOOL HOUSE. On the far side of the graveyard is the Old School House, built in 1745. Look in the door; there is a lifelike tableau composed of mannequins dressed in period costumes. The schoolmaster and several of his pupils, one of them an Indian, are in residence. Note the quill pens and the dreaded whipping post.

Cross back through the grave-yard to the Emerson-Wilcox House.

EMERSON-WILCOX HOUSE. Built in 1742 and occupied until 1953, this house saw early service as a general store, a tavern, a tailor shop, and a post office, often with several functions active at the same time. Your guide shows you some early musical instruments, elegant candle-snuffing devices, and the like in the parlor. In the taproom, you find out what types of food and drink the transients favored (heavy on the rum and ale, they were) and look at the clay pipes and playing cards they used to amuse themselves. In the small post office, your guide points out that in those days the person who received the mail had to pay the postage, not the sender. In the upstairs bedrooms, you see the curtained canopy beds, and discover that they were more than just pretty; they helped reduce drafts and provided privacy, too.

It seems that Edward Emerson, along with his wife and eleven children, lived here from 1757 to 1820. An important figure in the town, Emerson entertained handsomely on Court Days, the quarterly occasions when the traveling judge arrived in York to mete out justice. The table in the dining room is elegantly set for dinner, and on it sits the Court Day Menu. If you were a guest, you could choose from the likes of mackerel, herb soup, veal, chicken, mutton chops, and rabbit before moving on to fruit, custard, and apricot tart. In all, this was a prosperous household. The tour lasts a little less than half an hour, as does the gaol tour. (If your children will be happier with a single dose, opt for the gaol.)

From the parking lot, take Lindsay Road east, staying to the left of Route 1A at the inter-section in the center of York Village; follow signs.

YORK BEACH. For a look at the other side of life in York, follow Lindsay Road to nearby York Beach. Here you find an amusement area, arcades, an old-time photo parlor, and shops and restaurants galore. At the Goldenrod Luncheonette and Soda Fountain, children can watch the production of candy kisses and other mouth-watering confections. The machinery is placed in the large windows for easy sidewalk viewing. Here you can purchase breakfast, lunch, and snacks, including homemade ice cream.

Return to Lindsay Road and follow it to the George Marshall Store.

GEORGE MARSHALL STORE. Are you in the mood for shopping after your sightseeing expedition? You can choose souvenirs reminiscent of the colonial period at the George Marshall Store on Lindsay Road; here you'll find a century-old general store that currently serves as a museum shop. Select from hand-crafted pottery, iron, tin, pewter, brass, and wooden-ware, most of it made by New England artisans. There are old-fashioned books and toys here, too.

BEACHES. There are several beaches to choose from. Short Sands, with its playground and pavilion, is located near the Goldenrod Luncheonette. Long Sands, most popular of the beaches, extends all the way from York Harbor to the "Nubble" (Cape Neddick Light). The boulevard that runs along this beach is crammed with hotels and motels, trailer parks, restaurants, stores, and private homes. York Harbor Beach boasts lovely homes overlooking the water, a yacht club, and two wharves where you can watch fish being unloaded or drop a line and try your own luck. If you wish to explore the harbor or the York River, you can rent a sailboat, a motorboat, or even a canoe here. This is an attractive section, with elegant shops and accommodations. Cape Neddick Beach, the smallest of the York beaches, offers swimming, picnicking, camping, boating, and fishing.

BILL FOSTER'S DOWN-EAST LOBSTER AND CLAM BAKES. While in the York area, you (absolutely) must treat yourselves to a down East clambake and lobster feed. You can't do better than to attend one of Bill Foster's events in York Harbor, where he has been preparing bakes for over thirty years. Five evenings a week in the summer (and Saturdays in the late spring and early fall), he prepares freshly dug clams, succulent lobsters, Maine potatoes, fresh corn, and onions, cooking them slowly over steaming seaweed. Hot rolls and ice-cold watermelon round out the menu. (If some folks don't like lobster, they may choose steak or chicken, or even hot dogs.)

You don't need to dress up to enjoy one of these feeds. As a matter of fact, you should come prepared to do some serious finger licking. It's strictly serve-yourself as you move down the line loading your tray. You sit down to eat your scrumptious dinner at a picnic table, in a large screened pavilion that can accommodate more than three hundred diners in a single sitting. Do plan to arrive early, so that you can watch food preparation, play horseshoes or volleyball, and give the younger children a chance to enjoy the swings in the garden. After dinner, the Foster family and an accordionist lead an old-fashioned sing-along, making this a perfect "down Maine" family evening.

ACCESS

TO GET TO YORK. From the Portsmouth, NH, traffic circle, take Route 1 north (toward Kittery) to York Corner; exit onto Route 1A, and head to the center of York Village.

THE OLD GAOL MUSEUM. Directions: Located on Route 1A in York Village, on your right going north. Follow signs. **Season:** June 15 through September. **Admission** charged; combination ticket to Old Gaol and the Emerson-Wilcox House available at slight dis-

At the Goldenrod Luncheonette and Soda Fountain, children can watch the production of candy kisses and other mouth-watering confections.

Five evenings a week he prepares freshly dug clams, succulent lobsters, Maine potatoes, fresh corn, and onions, cooking them slowly over steaming seaweed.

count. (207) 363-3872.

BILL FOSTER'S DOWN-EAST LOBSTER & CLAM BAKES. Directions: Bill Foster's is on Route 1A in York Harbor, just beyond York Village. **Season:** July through Labor Day, and Saturdays in June and September. **Admission** is the price of dinner. (207) 363-3255. **Note:** A reservation is required, but may be made early on the day you wish to come.

Here's the scoop, or what's left of it, at Barnacle Billy's in Ogunquit.

Ogunquit

This picturesque village, whose name means "beautiful place by the sea," combines a cheerful, prosperous resort ambiance with striking natural features such as a spacious white-sand beach and dramatic cliff and rock formations. Three areas here are of particular interest to children, and Perkins Cove should top the list. This tiny fishing area is filled with lobster shacks and shops, but it is mostly a good place to examine lobster pots, wharves, and boats of all descriptions.

PERKINS COVE. At the entrance to the cove, you pass Barnacle Billy's. It's strictly serve-yourself on the patio at this restaurant where you can eat your lunch or dinner at a table under an umbrella beside the water's edge. Choose from lobsters, chowders, hamburgers, and ice cream and pie. If your wallet is feeling thin, walk a little farther until you come to the Poor Fishermen's Take-Out, where you can purchase hot dogs, hamburgers, and sandwiches to eat on the hoof. A few steps away is Perkins Cove Candies; here your young ones can select licorice whips, spearmint leaves, button candy, Mary Janes, fudges, and chocolates. It's fun to fill a tiny white bag with the confections of one's choice and fifty cents' worth can satisfy even the most demanding sweet tooth. The goodies are attractively displayed on white paper-covered trays and in apothecary jars.

FINESTKIND SCENIC CRUISES. Now that you have eaten, and spent some time near the shore — watching the drawbridge pull up to let a schooner pass, or loafing on the pier — it is time to go to sea. Take a Finestkind Scenic Cruise (the ticket booth is adjacent to Barnacle Billy's). There are several trips to choose from, but the best bet for children is one of the lobstering trips. These fifty-minute jaunts provide a close-up of one of the industries that makes Maine famous. You will travel on a real lobster boat (granted, a generous one) outfitted with benches and comfortable yellow cushions, and capable of holding over forty passengers.

While the lobsterman steers the boat, your hostess discusses the history and geology of the area, peppering her talk with lobster legend and lore. She shows you Lobster Point, where in colonial days these succu-

Here your young ones can select licorice whips, spearmint leaves, button candy, Mary Janes, fudges, and chocolates.

lent arthropods were so abundant that they could be scooped off the rocks. (They were then known as "poor man's food," because only those who could afford nothing else would bother to collect and cook them.) Your hostess then points out The Cliff House atop Bald Head Cliff, where a room with three meals a day went for six dollars a week in the 1890s.

By this time, you've arrived in lobster territory; your hostess turns her attention to lobster-licensing procedures and the color coding of buoys. She explains which lobsters are "keepers" (those over three and three-sixteenths inches from the back of the eye socket to the point where the body meets the tail), and which lobsters must be thrown back ("shorts" and "berried" lobsters, female breeders carrying eggs). Meanwhile her partner slips into a pair of yellow-rubber coveralls and prepares to pull his traps. He uses a gaff to retrieve the buoy and then wraps the line around a hydraulic lift or hauler. The trap is drawn to the surface and its contents revealed — a short, a dead pollock, and several starfish. The pollock is chopped for bait, the short is measured and thrown back into the ocean — and all of the starfish are distributed to eager young passengers.

A second trap reaps greater reward; two of the lobsters are big enough to keep. The third trap contains a couple of sea urchins and a cull (a single-clawed lobster), as well as two shorts. By the time a few more traps have been hauled with only slight reward, you begin to understand why lobster is so expensive.

The hostess explains that lobsters are cannibals and that they will destroy one another in a tank. That, combined with the fact that their human handlers don't like being pinched, is the reason their claws are banded, a procedure you are able to witness. You learn that a lobster can "throw a claw" if it becomes lodged in a tight place or if it needs to flee a predator; a new one will eventually grow in its place. She brings lobsters around so that you can handle them. She also talks about lobstering techniques; for instance, the construction of the basic trap hasn't changed much in the last hundred years. Words like "head," "kitchen," "shark's mouth," and "parlor" are used to describe parts of the traps. (By the time you finish the cruise, you will probably never again be able to sit down to a lobster dinner without having your offspring offer to determine the sex of your dinner for you.)

Be sure to take along a sweater for your lobster-boat trip since it can be cool on the water, even on a hot day. Children like to sit right up front, on the same side of the boat as the steering wheel, if possible. Here they have an excellent view of the traps as they are hauled aboard, but they should expect to get a bit damp from (and enjoy) the salt spray. Trips depart every half hour; if you are early risers, you might

In colonial days lobsters were so abundant they could be scooped off the rocks. They were known as "poor man's food," because only those who could afford nothing else would bother to collect and cook them.

The pollock in the trap is chopped up for bait, the short is thrown back into the ocean — and the starfish are distributed to eager young passengers.

A lobster can "throw a claw" if it becomes lodged in a tight place; a new one will eventually grow in its place.

DON RICHESON

enjoy the 9 AM breakfast cruise, which includes orange juice, coffee, and a doughnut.

OGUNQUIT TROLLEY. Once ashore, head back to town by hitching a ride on the nearby trolley. The bright red and yellow vehicle has open sides, wooden bench seats, and high ceilings. If the seats are full there are brass bars to clutch, and yellow curtains can be unrolled in case of inclement weather. Music plays gaily while you travel. The trolley plies a regular route that takes you past the popular spots, which are marked by a blue-and-white logo. Local businesses foot most of the bill, so the charge for riding the trolley is minimal.

DOWNTOWN OGUNQUIT. The downtown area is filled with shops and restaurants, some of them catering primarily to tourists; others meet the day-to-day needs of local residents. For instance, Einstein's Deli Restaurant offers moderately priced breakfasts, lunches, and dinners in a sprawling arrangement of rooms that includes both booths and counter space. Sandwiches and homemade ice cream, along with an ice-cream smorgasbord, are available until midnight at The Viking. When you have finished exploring the shops, take one of the clearly marked paths leading from Main Street to Marginal Way.

Even children will appreciate art when they see paintings created right before their eyes in Ogunquit.

MARGINAL WAY. This delightful "way" is a path of more than a mile, extending over cliffs and past startling rock formations. There are many benches where you can pause to enjoy the wide-open ocean vistas; there are also lots of places where you can climb down to the water's edge. Children can clamber over rocks and explore tide pools to their hearts' content. There are even two small beaches where swimming is permitted. Beach roses, juniper, and bayberry line the path, which twists and turns along the shore. Be sure to allow plenty of time for your walk, letting children find favorite nooks and crannies. Make sure they wear sneakers, and keep a firm hand on the youngest ones, as there are a number of hazardous spots along the way. If you look hard enough, you will find a cove geared to every ability. In the evening, Marginal Way takes on a romantic aura, as well-dressed ladies and gentlemen promenade en route to dinner. The trail ends at Perkins Cove, very convenient if you have left your car here. Otherwise, hop the trolley for the ride back downtown. (Of course, you can reverse the itinerary too, beginning your visit downtown, taking the trolley to Perkins Cove, and then walking Marginal Way in the opposite direction.)

Children can clamber over rocks and explore tide pools to their hearts' content.

ACCESS

TO GET TO OGUNQUIT. From the Portsmouth, NH, traffic circle, take I-95 exit 1 onto Route 1, just before the York toll plaza. Follow Route 1 north to the center of Ogunquit.

PERKINS COVE. Directions: From Route 1 just beyond the Josias River, turn right and go about a half mile on Bourne's Lane (before you come to the downtown area); bear right again after about a half mile, onto Shore Road, which becomes Oarweed Road, to Perkins Cove.

FINESTKIND SCENIC CRUISES. Directions: Departures from Barnacle Billy's pier, at Perkins Cove. **Season:** July through Labor Day. **Admission** charged. (207) 646-5227.

OGUNQUIT TROLLEY. Directions: Climb aboard at any of the specially marked stops from Route 1 north, to the Ogunquit Playhouse, Perkins Cove, Shore Road, Beach Street, the Main Beach, and back to Route 1 north. **Season:** Late June through Labor Day. Modest **admission** charge.

Wells

Often called the factory-outlet capital of Maine, Wells has much more to offer than just bargains on shoes and clothing (by manufacturers such as Dunham, Hathaway, and Carter). The pace is quick, the summer population dense, the atmosphere cheerful — if a bit frantic. A beach community with a multitude of motels, camping areas, and casual restaurants, Wells is a cheerful vacation spot for families who don't mind crowds with their sun and sand. When you visit Wells, there are two points of interest worth special consideration.

Cars Grandfather once drove can be seen at the Wells Auto Museum.

THE WELLS AUTO MUSEUM. This well-stocked museum contains New England's largest collection of antique, classic, and special-interest cars. For example, there is a 1904 Curved-Dash Olds Runabout (originally priced at $650), a 1904 Stanley Steamer with a raised rear seat for the driver ($725), and a 1907 Rambler Roadster with an oak glove box and deeply padded bucket-like seats ($1350). Other interesting models include a 1908 Baker Electric, originally owned by John D. Rockefeller, with a custom-made rear section containing facing double seats for his children ($2500). Then there is the 1904 Northern, which got thirty miles per gallon, and a 1901 Orient Buckboard, which had no reverse gear and weighed in at five hundred pounds. (It had to be lifted to be turned around.) The most modern vehicle on display is a 1963 Studebaker Lark. After you look the cars over, you and the young ones can all go for a ride in the 1911 Model T Ford awaiting passengers in the parking lot.

While the cars are just for looking at, the museum boasts a different facet as well, one that calls for participation. If your children are hooked on pinball and video machines, they will be amused by the old-time models in operation here. One thin dime lets you try your luck on a Fleet pinball machine dating from the 1930s (a generous ten balls for your money, too). Here you can bet on the "Moving Horses" or try your skill at an old-fashioned hockey/soccer game. There are also "mutoscopes" to operate; put a dime in one of these old-fashioned moving-picture machines and crank yourself out some vintage entertainment. The choices include "A Ticklish Situation," "The Exotic Mirror Dance," and "Revealing Rhonda's Balloon Dance." (Believe us, they are nowhere near as risqué as they sound!) Just a nickel will let you in on a set of pictures such as "The Unattainable," "The Lure of Youth," and

The 1908 Baker Electric, originally owned by John D. Rockefeller, has a custom-made rear section with facing double seats for his children.

"The Form Divine," all approved by the New York censors. Or, you can always nudge the children in the direction of the Charlie Chaplin number, or Rin Tin Tin in "The Night Cry."

The museum also contains a fine collection of nickelodeons such as the Seeburg Orchestrion, the Mills Virtuoso, and the Regina Changer. The orchestrion (which operates for twenty-five cents) melds the tinny tones of mandolin, triangle, piano, trap and snare drums, cymbal, flute, violin, castanets, organ, and bass drum. And ragtime rhythms fill the exhibit area, intensifying the sense of nostalgia.

RACHEL CARSON WILDLIFE REFUGE. The second don't-miss point of interest in Wells is this wooded sanctuary, where you feel as if you are a hundred miles away from the hustle and bustle of the rest of Wells's frenetic vacation community. The aroma of pine combines with the scent of the salty air as you wander along the pathway carpeted with pine needles. It takes about half an hour to walk the trail in the leisurely fashion it deserves. The going is easy and the trail cool and shady on the most blistering day. Even toddlers can undertake this hike and enjoy it.

The route is clearly marked with bright yellow arrows. As you follow the trail, you soon see the barrier beach and the ocean beyond. A fragile, narrow strip of sand and dunes separated from the mainland by marshes and estuaries, the barrier beach offers the mainland protection from powerful ocean storms. Such a beach is always evolving, always changing in form and size according to wind and wave patterns.

As you stroll the trail, look for squirrels and chipmunks. Use your ears to pick up the sound of the ocean lapping gently in the distance, or the cry of the redwing. At one point the trail becomes a boardwalk suspended over a section of salt marsh. Explain to the children that the marsh is an important feeding ground for larval clams and lobsters, crabs, and fish as they grow to maturity. Redwings and other songbirds can be spotted in the cattails and cord grass, so important to the waterfowl and shorebirds that migrate along the Atlantic coastline.

The sanctuary is not usually crowded; you may well be fortunate enough to find yourselves alone as you experience the special qualities of this delicate environment. Author and environmentalist Rachel Carson spent many years in Maine, and worked diligently and passionately to raise public consciousness to the plight of the seabirds and their fast-disappearing habitat, the marshes and wetlands. Along with the wading birds, gulls, and terns who live here, the Canada geese, black ducks, and green-winged teal that rest here on their spring and fall migrations are a graceful testimony to her life and work. "All the life of the planet is interrelated," wrote Carson, ".... each

The wading birds, gulls, and terns here are a graceful testimony to Carson's life and work.

As you and your young ones stroll through the Rachel Carson National Wildlife Refuge, watch for squirrels, chipmunks, and songbirds.

species has its own ties to others . . . and all are related to the earth.''

ACCESS

TO GET TO WELLS. Take I-95 exit 2 onto Route 9, and follow Route 9 east to Wells.

THE WELLS AUTO MUSEUM. Directions: At the junction of Route 9 and Route 1, turn right onto Route 1 and follow signs. The museum is almost immediately on your right. **Season:** Daily mid-June to mid-September, and weekends in the spring. **Admission** charged. (207) 646-9064.

RACHEL CARSON WILDLIFE REFUGE. Directions: From the junction of Route 9 and Route 1, follow Route 9 just under a mile toward Kennebunkport. The sanctuary is on the right; be alert for the sign. **Season:** Year round. **Admission** free. **Note:** There is no parking area; you must park along the road. (207) 646-9226.

Old Orchard Beach

OLD ORCHARD BEACH AMUSEMENT PARK. For a real old-time beachside amusement park in the kind of town your grandparents might have vacationed near, you can't do better than Old Orchard Beach. Orchard Street, leading down to the beach and the pier, is lined with stores hawking bathing suits, beach towels, suntan oils, plastic backscratchers, buckets and shovels, sun hats, ashtrays, T-shirts, and just about any other souvenir you can think of. Wares are displayed on the sidewalks and the doors stand open, rock music and disco seeping out into the street.

Refreshment stands punctuate the stores. Surely this is a junk-food fan's paradise. Run-of-the-mill snacks include buttered corn-on-the-cob served on a stick, chocolate-coated bananas on a stick, clam cakes, saltwater taffy, fudge, fried chicken, cotton candy, and fried shrimp. If you look a little harder, you can also enjoy a veggie-burger, chili and cheese on pita bread, tacos, Belgian waffles, spaghetti-to-go, or Chinese food. Everywhere you look, folks are chomping down the goodies.

As you approach the water, you come to the amusements. There is the Haunted Village (largest walk-through spook house in New England), a scary place with a torture chamber and witches' coven, staffed by live actors who specialize in scaring the daylights out of willing customers. You will also find a couple of studios where you can pose behind a full-sized color drawing of a Victorian costume. If you want your palm read, you can have that done, too.

Children are drawn to the rides, and there are plenty to choose from. There are roller coasters and things that swirl and twist. Choose from the likes of

This is a junk-food fan's paradise, with chocolate-covered bananas, clam cakes, saltwater taffy, fudge, cotton candy, and fried shrimp.

Space Island and Flight to Mars, or tamer fare like Fort Apache (a big trampoline), the carousel, or tiny cars to navigate. Bumper cars are here, too, along with many other favorites.

OLD ORCHARD PIER. If you want to try your skill at throwing games, stroll out onto the old pier, at the foot of Orchard Street. Built in 1898, the pier was destroyed by a severe winter storm not long ago. It has been completely rebuilt now, and extends out over the water just as it did at the turn of the century. Here you can get a good view of the beach itself as it stretches out on either side, part of a seven-mile strip of sand. Souvenir shops and eating places are also in evidence on the pier.

Part of the fun for children at Old Orchard Beach is derived from the fact that this is a popular vacation destination for French Canadian tourists as well as for Americans. You will see signs in both French and English in the shop windows ("Ici nous parlons français.") and hear French spoken frequently on the streets.

Put a child with a shovel on a beach and watch what happens. On a mid-autumn day at Old Orchard Beach, these two brothers had a grand time in the sand.

ACCESS

OLD ORCHARD BEACH AMUSEMENT PARK. Directions: Take I-95 exit 5 (Saco Interchange), then Route 1 north to Route 98. Follow Route 98 to Old Orchard Beach (well marked); signs will bring you to Orchard Street. **Season:** Memorial Day through early fall. **Admission** free.

Saco

AQUABOGGAN WATER SLIDE. North along Route 1 about one mile from the amusement park, you find the Aquaboggan Water Slide, in nearby Saco. A relatively new form of entertainment, the water slide is a fiber-glass chute with a stream of water running down it. You sit on a foam mat and slide down the twisting passageway for splashdown in the small pool below. Here there are three water slides that travel over ramps and through tunnels, and two "Suislides," which are steeper straightaways for the courageous. Although the water in the pool is shallow enough so even a six-year-old can easily stand, children should expect to get good dunkings when they land. In case you haven't guessed, bathing suits are appropriate dress. The slides are recommended only for children who are really comfortable in the water.

Other attractions here include a forty-by-eighty-foot swimming pool, with lots of deck chairs to relax on, an eighteen-hole miniature golf course, a shuffle-board court, and a little tots' play area. The slides are heated, and they are open rain or shine. (Other water slides are located at Mount Attitash in Bartlett, New

You sit on a foam mat and slide down the twisting passageway for splashdown in the small pool below.

Hampshire and at Alpine Ridge in Gilford, New Hampshire.)

ACCESS

AQUABOGGAN WATER SLIDE. Directions: From Old Orchard Beach, take Route 5 west to Route 1, and head north one mile to the water slide. **Season:** Late June through Labor Day. **Admission** charged. (207) 282-3112.

Quick snacks to suit both juvenile and adult tastes are available in plenitude throughout the Old Port Exchange.

Portland

Located on a peninsula bordered by Casco Bay, Back Cove, and the Fore River, Portland is Maine's largest city. Yet this active metropolis, with its several colleges and museums and a bustling waterfront, is only a short drive away from some splendid stretches of unspoiled coastline. Thus in one area you can experience both the pleasures of a lively city and the beauty of wide-open spaces as you combine sight-seeing with hiking, swimming, and picnicking.

OLD PORT EXCHANGE. Begin your visit to Portland with a leisurely walk through the historic Old

Port Exchange district, a lively area of shops and restaurants graced by nineteenth-century buildings that have been lovingly restored. Leveled by the British in 1775, financially devastated by the Embargo Act and the ensuing War of 1812, and once again demolished by the Great Fire of 1866, the Old Port has been resuscitated within the past decade and today provides a sense of the lively ambiance of a flourishing nineteenth-century New England seaport community.

Start your walking tour from Commercial Street, in the Old Port Exchange district.

Nestled among the dozens of fashionable shops and businesses are several attractions of particular interest to children. It's fun to watch the printing presses roll and the typesetters at work in the large windows of The Anthoensen Press (37 Exchange Street). The Old Port Emporium (384 Fore Street) features oriental items such as a huge cloth goldfish to stuff with newspaper and hang from the ceiling, and intricate offerings such as bamboo canary cages, paper lanterns, mobiles, fans, and parasols. It also carries bags of penny candy, candy sticks in dozens of flavors, and tiny tins of imported confections. Necessities, Etc. (4 Moulton Street) has lots of toys, both small and large, inexpensive and costly. If you fancy a handsome wooden sailboat for the beach, you can get one here.

Be certain to stop in at A Likely Story (10 Exchange Street; located inside The Exchange mall); it's a bookshop devoted exclusively to the reading needs of preschoolers through young teens. Fully stocked with fairy tales, science fiction, mysteries, picture books, contemporary young adult fiction, and a special section of Maine books, the store also carries records and some fine stuffed animals representing famous figures in children's literature — such as Peter Rabbit and Winnie the Pooh. There is a plump blue couch where you can settle down to discuss possible reading choices with the helpful proprietor. Be sure also to climb the carpeted stairs up to the second-story loft, which contains an ample selection of activity books. Here are drawing manuals, games to play in the car, magic trick books, puzzles, and more. There is a comfortable rocking chair to rest in while making your decision. Altogether, it's a perfect place to restock on vacation reading matter.

Here are bags of penny candy, candy sticks in dozens of flavors, and tiny tins of imported confections.

The historic district is laced with eateries, both the elegant and the simple. If your brood prefers to dine alfresco, eat lunch at one of the picnic tables in tiny Tommy's Park (at the corner of Exchange and Middle streets); feel free to park yourselves on the grass if the tables are all taken. The park is backed on one side by the Jose Building, built in 1886, which now houses The Coffee and Sandwich Shop on the street level floor. The facade of the building facing the park has been painted in the trompe d'oeil style, a lifelike mural recreating two turn-of-the-century businesses, Gould's Drugstore with its apothecary counter and soda foun-

Consult the outdoor directory at Tommy's Park, at the corner of Exchange and Middle streets, to locate shops and eateries.

The big excitement on this tour is the opportunity to see seals basking in the sun, not in a zoo but in their natural habitat.

From Tommy's Park, follow Exchange Street across Fore Street to Moulton Street. Walk one block to the intersection of Moulton and Commercial streets, crossing Commercial Street to Long Wharf.

MICHAEL QUAN

A fine midday alternative is the luncheon cruise aboard the M/V Longfellow.

tain, and J. Lipson & Co. — Fine Goods. Ask the children to scrutinize the upper floors of the building, pointing out which windows are real and which are just pictures of windows. (It's not as easy as it sounds.) If you come for lunch on a warm summer day, you may well be treated to live music performed by a bluegrass group or a jazz ensemble.

If you want to choose from a menu broader than the simple fare offered at The Coffee and Sandwich Shop or if the weather turns gray, go to the nearby Market Street Market complex (on Middle Street, one block beyond Tommy's Park). Here you can purchase salads, and fresh-fruit-and-yogurt concoctions at Salad Days; subs, pizza, and cheesecake at The Cheesecake and Pizza Place, or sandwiches and ice cream treats at The Soda Fountain. There is a common area of tables and chairs serving the three restaurants; The Soda Fountain also has its own small counter where you should sit if you want to read the magazines and newspapers supplied for the use of patrons. For home-made soups and more substantial fare, you might try the downstairs Ratskeller Restaurant. It has a bar and several video games, so parents can relax with cold beers or frosty daiquiris while the children do combat with aliens from outer space. Allow about an hour for shopping and browsing in the Old Port Exchange.

M/V *LONGFELLOW.* Another lunch-time alternative is to buy some take-out fare at one of the restaurants mentioned and sign on for the 12:05 luncheon cruise aboard the ninety-one-passenger sightseeing boat the M/V *Longfellow.* (Trips originate at Long Wharf, at the foot of Moulton Street.) There are also many other cruises to choose from. You might decide on the Fort and Island Tour or the Lighthouse and Shipwreck Tour if you are interested in local history or in how people, events, and natural phenomena have affected the way residents of the island fishing villages live and work. Children might prefer the afternoon Naturalist Tour, during which they can feed the sea gulls while the captain discusses the nesting habits of those familiar seabirds. The big excitement on this tour is the opportunity to see seals basking in the sun, not in a zoo but in their natural habitat. There are also harborlight cruises and sunset cocktail cruises. Most tours operate seven days a week in the summer.

GULF OF MAINE AQUARIUM. Also located at Long Wharf, this interesting attraction makes its home aboard a barge where you will find tanks filled with examples of local sea life organized according to habitat. Watch for the giant scallop, the queen crab, and the northern red anemone, residents of the pelagic habitat (offshore or deep water); and the Jonah crab, longhorn sculpin, and simple cunner, inhabitants of the harbor waters. There are also tanks devoted to sandy and rocky habitats, as well as one set aside for "special visitors." As you make your way past the tanks, a museum staff member stands ready to explain the animals on view and to answer your questions. He might point out that the nasty wolf fish grows to six feet in length and eats crabs and lobsters with its very sharp teeth. Or he might mention that the shaggy stuff on the homely sea raven is the same shaggy stuff that clings to underwater pilings.

Other features here include a small theater where films and slides relating to sealife are shown regularly, and the Touch Me—Feel Me tide pool where a youngster can roll up his sleeves and dip into the water for a close encounter with a hermit crab or a sea urchin, a starfish or a sea anemone. There is also a small shop where you can purchase both authentic and artificial samples of sea life. About a half hour should prove sufficient for all ages here; if you see a film or other presentation, allow an extra thirty minutes or so.

DEERING OAKS. Need a break in the sightseeing and shopping routine? Head for Deering Oaks, a downtown expanse of green where you can shoot a few baskets or enjoy a picnic. Here you can also feed the eager ducks that live in the pond, which comes complete with a handsome Victorian nesting house and a fountain.

CHILDREN'S MUSEUM OF MAINE. After your picnic break, jump in your car and head out to this outstanding museum, where there are lots of opportunities to actively participate in exhibits. Here children can proudly operate a full-sized traffic light, or pound out a tune on a piano with Plexiglas front that allows them to see how the instrument works. There are also their favorites, the "feely boxes," which encourage them to stick in their hands and guess the identity of hidden objects. An active art room is available; the smocks and paints stand ready at all times. Children are encouraged to paint on a large clear Plexiglas board, which can be moved a little away from the wall. It's fun to stand behind it and let your child "paint" your face. Crayons and clay are available, too, as are magnifiers and kaleidoscopes to further stimulate young imaginations.

One perennially favorite exhibit is Tom and Bill's Market. Here you find a post office with its own sales window, typewriter, rubber stamps, stool, and mailbox. There is also a well-stocked grocery store, with a check-out counter and two working cash registers. Line up your purchases and tally the total! If your young one favors a career in medicine rather than commerce, she will enjoy a trip to Dr. P.D. Atricks Clinic, a complete hospital-room setting that includes an examining table, a wheelchair, a hospital bed, surgical masks and gowns, stethoscopes, and associated paraphernalia. All these items have been assembled to take some of the fear out of the hospital experience.

A youngster can roll up his sleeves and dip into the water for a close encounter with a hermit crab or a sea urchin, a starfish or a sea anemone.

Children can proudly operate a full-sized traffic light, or pound out a tune on a piano with Plexiglas front.

There is a well-stocked grocery store, with a check-out counter and two working cash registers. Just line up all your purchases and tally the total!

Station KITE is another popular exhibit. What child can resist becoming an instant TV star or radio celebrity? Here's where he can put himself on the tube using three video monitors or enter the sound booth, don a headset, and broadcast the news or play some taped music. In another area, the POWER! exhibit demonstrates the basics of muscle, wind, and solar energy. There is a specially monitored bike to pedal that indicates how much energy you are generating. In Snug Harbor, there is foul-weather gear to try on, a ship's wheel to steer, and a pirate's den with a treasure chest to explore. Over at Animal Acres, you meet some nice mice, turtles, fish, a canary, and a couple of rabbits. Julius, a New Zealand White Rabbit, enjoys coming out of his cage to "ham it up" with his visitors. Other areas include The Firehouse, The Quiet Room (books, games, and puppets), and The Wood Room.

Before leaving the museum, check out The Alligator's Bag, in the rear of the building. This is a small consignment shop that carries children's clothing, furniture, and toys, all in good-to-excellent condition, as well as handmade items. Here you can pick up an extra sunsuit for your toddler or a back-to-school outfit for a fashion-conscious preteen, at very reasonable prices. This is a small but attractive and well-organized shop; the profits help support the museum.

In the museum lobby there is also a small shop where children enjoy browsing through the collection of educational toys, books, games, and science items. It takes less than one dollar to buy a top or a tiny lock and key, a spaceman eraser or a ring with a shiny stone, or any of a half dozen other amusing things. The three-to-ten-year-old set will find this museum most interesting. Allow about an hour for your visit.

CHILDREN'S RESOURCE CENTER. Across the street from the museum, the center is an independent entity that also offers good browsing. Actually, this is a fabulous place for children to shop, perhaps more so because of the process of buying taught than for what they actually purchase. The center recycles industrial-waste products ranging from wood, leather, and fabric scraps to zippers, bottle caps, and pieces of foam rubber. Upon entering the center, each child is supplied with a clipboard and a shopping bag. As he makes the rounds surveying the wares displayed in boxes and barrels, he notes each item he puts in his bag. By the time he finishes inspecting the heaps of buttons, bracelets, shoelaces, dowels, plastic game pieces, pieces of colored wax, and much more, he has a complete shopping list of purchases. Since the center operates strictly on a self-service basis, there are scissors and rulers available (for measuring and cutting lengths of fabric and paper), and scales for weighing items that are sold by the pound.

The center is divided into four rooms — two all-purpose rooms, the Paper Room (with rolls of com-

What child can resist becoming an instant TV star or radio celebrity?

Kids do the shopping at the Children's Resource Center.

As a child makes the rounds, he notes each item he puts in his bag. By the time he finishes, he has a complete shopping list of purchases.

puter paper, glossy paper for finger painting, envelopes, all manner of cardboard, scraps of colored paper, and more), and the Fabric Room (with ribbons, canvas, carpet scraps, velour, vinyl, fabric sample books, and other accessories). Throughout the rooms you see on display many projects that suggest ways of putting the materials to use. Materials include games, art equipment (weaving materials, homemade rubber stamps), toys, and pieces of jewelry; all can be duplicated or expanded upon, depending upon your and your child's inclination. There is also a children's book exchange where young ones can swap a book they have already read for a fresh title, no money involved. Again, the three-to-ten-year-olds will enjoy the Resource Center — allow about half an hour for your visit here.

ACCESS

TO GET TO PORTLAND. Take exit 6A from I-95, and follow Route 295 northeast to Route 1A. Follow Route 1A (which becomes Commercial Street) to the Old Port Exchange district.

M/V LONGFELLOW (ATLANTIC NAVIGATION COMPANY). Directions: Continue east on Commercial Street to Moulton Street. The Atlantic Navigation Company is located at Long Wharf, across from the intersection of Moulton and Commercial streets. **Season:** Late April through early fall. **Admission** charged (varies according to length of cruise). (207) 774-3578.

GULF OF MAINE AQUARIUM. Directions: The aquarium is located on Long Wharf, across from the intersection of Moulton and Commercial streets. **Season:** Mid-April through fall. **Admission** charged. (207) 772-2321.

DEERING OAKS. Directions: Located downtown, across from the Federal Building. **Season:** Year round. **Admission** free.

CHILDREN'S MUSEUM OF MAINE. Directions: Take I-95 exit 8 (Route 25/Brighton Avenue) and head east for two miles; then turn left onto Stevens Avenue. The museum is at 746 Stevens Avenue. From I-295, take the Forest Avenue North exit. Follow Forest Avenue one and a half miles, then turn left onto Route 9 (Walton Street). Turn right on Stevens Avenue, and go to Number 746. **Season:** Year round. **Admission** charged; there is a maximum charge per family. (207) 797-3353. **Note:** Parking is available along Stevens Avenue and in any of the Westbrook College parking lots. After visiting the museum, you are entitled to visit three other Maine museums at half price (Seashore Trolley Museum, in Kennebunkport; Maine Maritime Museum, in Bath; Owls Head Transportation Museum, in Owls Head).

CHILDREN'S RESOURCE CENTER. Directions: Located on Stevens Avenue, across from the Children's Museum of Maine. **Season:** Year round. **Admission** free. (207) 797-0525.

MICHAEL QUAN

All children love a lighthouse; this, the Portland Head Lighthouse, was first lit in 1791, making it the oldest in Maine.

Cape Elizabeth

FORT WILLIAMS PARK AND PORTLAND HEAD LIGHTHOUSE. When you have finished exploring the sights in Portland, why not head out to nearby Cape Elizabeth to visit a state park or two? At Fort Williams Park, you can feast at a picnic table overlooking the Atlantic or dip your toes in the icy ocean at the small rocky beach. Here you can also visit Portland Head Lighthouse, Maine's oldest and also one of the oldest in the country. Authorized by George Washington, the white clapboarded structure with green trim and red roof was first lit with whale oil lamps on January 10, 1791. These lamps were later replaced with kerosene lights, but today the lighthouse is illuminated by a thousand-watt lamp visible from approximately twenty miles away. The lighthouse sits on a rocky promontory; if you visit on an overcast day, you may hear the sound horn bellow its deep-throated

There is plenty of opportunity for a brisk walk along the bluff overlooking the ocean as you ponder the fate of ships at sea.

warning every fifteen seconds.

PORTLAND HEAD MUSEUM. Although you cannot enter the towers at the lighthouse, there is a tiny room in the side of the building proudly called the Portland Head Museum, where visitors are welcome. Here you will see pictures of former lighthouse keepers; look for the bearded Joshua Strout, in bow tie, vest, and cap, who manned the Portland Head Lighthouse from 1869 to 1904. There are also pieces of naval-uniform memorabilia and scraps from shipwrecks. When you leave the museum you notice writing on the rocks: "Annie C. McQuire Shipwrecked here, Christmas Eve, 1886." You also see a plaque devoted to Henry Wadsworth Longfellow, who often walked here from Portland to visit with his friends, the lighthouse keepers. This site is believed to have inspired his poem "The Lighthouse." There is plenty of opportunity for a brisk walk along the bluff overlooking the ocean as you ponder the fate of ships at sea, then and now.

TWO LIGHTS STATE PARK. If your children really do want to climb a lighthouse tower, take them to this inviting state park, a forty-one-acre spread of rocky headlands and uplands that derives its name from the two lighthouses operated here from 1828 to 1924. One is now privately owned, but you are welcome to climb the cement tower of the still-operative eastern light. The park also has a network of footpaths to wander, a picnic area, and a small playground.

CRESCENT BEACH STATE PARK. Down the road a stretch is another park, six times as large as Two Lights State Park and boasting a mile of sandy beach. If you are willing to walk, you can always find a private spot here for sunning. You may, however, wish to spread your blanket fairly near the parking areas in order to be within range of lifeguards, snack bar, and bathhouse. There is also a pleasant playground with swings, Jungle gym, slide, and other equipment. In the mood for a picnic? Why not wander out to one of Crescent Beach's 130 picnic sites situated in lovely groves stretching back from the shore and connected by narrow paths. Grills are located near each picnic table so you can take along a steak or hot dogs and hamburgers to barbecue. Here you see beach roses growing wherever you look; and if you stray from the concentration of visitors you may see raccoons, rabbits, woodchucks, skunks, or even white-tailed deer. Seals are sometimes spotted offshore, so take along the binoculars. Altogether, this is an attractive, low-key park where you can happily pass a warm summer day. There are just enough facilities to satisfy basic needs, but nothing to spoil the pleasant scenery.

If you stray from the concentration of visitors you may see raccoons, rabbits, woodchucks, skunks, or even white-tailed deer.

ACCESS

TO GET TO CAPE ELIZABETH. Take I-95 exit 6A

(following signs to Route 114 and Cape Elizabeth), then take Route 114 east to Route 207. Head east on Route 207 to Route 77, then head north on Route 77.

FORT WILLIAMS PARK. Directions: From Route 77, follow signs to Portland Head Lighthouse; the entrance to the park is on your right. **Season:** Memorial Day through Labor Day. **Admission** free.

TWO LIGHTS STATE PARK AND CRESCENT BEACH STATE PARK. Directions: Both are located off Route 77 in Cape Elizabeth. **Season:** Memorial Day through Labor Day. **Admission** charged per person.

Bath Iron Works: birthplace of the big boats.

Bath

Lodged on the banks of the Kennebec River only a few miles from the Atlantic, Bath was once the fifth busiest seaport in the United States. Her waterfront bustled with activity in the latter half of the nineteenth century as great sloops, schooners, and even mighty men-of-war were produced and launched in the shipyards clustered near the wharves. The air was thick with the scent of pitch and pine chips as the caulkers and joiners went about their tasks.

The advent of steel ship production in the 1890s, however, put many of the shipyards out of business; only a few of them successfully weathered the transition to new production methods. One notable exception was the Bath Iron Works (BIW), which was founded in 1884 and which has operated continuously ever since (with the exception of a two-year hiatus following World War I). Bath fell into disrepair in the early part of this century, but the past decade has witnessed a major revitalization effort. Today Bath is a fascinating town to visit, with a charming downtown area and a wealth of intriguing historical sites that bring to life her seafaring tradition.

MAINE MARITIME MUSEUM AT BATH. The major attraction in Bath is a group of locations bound together and known as the Maine Maritime Museum at Bath. Three of the sites are located in the downtown area, while the fourth is located about two miles out of the center of town.

PERCY & SMALL SHIPYARD. Since there is convenient parking at the Percy & Small Shipyard at 263 Washington Street, you may prefer to start here. After purchasing your all-inclusive admission ticket, take the children trooping through the Paint and Trunnel Shop, where paints and finishes used on wooden ships were manufactured. Here, elegant cabin paneling was varnished, painted, and grained. Look for the piles of treenails (pronounced trunnels), wooden pins used in assembling the hulls of the great vessels. Each schooner built here required two thousand or more locust or white oak treenails. Percy & Small produced forty-one huge masted schooners between 1894 and

1920, including the *Wyoming*, a six-masted beauty measuring 329.9 feet in length. She was built in 1909, at a cost of one hundred ninety thousand dollars.

At the Mill and Joiner Shop, where cabin interiors and other fancywork were produced, keep an eye out for the awning doors. These doors swung upward to permit long timbers to be passed from outside in through the saw and planer stored within the building. Upstairs you find a formal exhibit devoted to the many facets of the building of wooden ships. There are the riggers' tools called "lizards" and "hanks." There is a section on ropemaking, where you learn the meaning of the saying "Worm and Parcel with the lay, turn and serve the other way," an instruction for protecting rope from chafing and hard use by binding it with thin strands of additional rope and long strips of canvas to form a stiff protective covering.

At the Oakum Shop down by the river, you see where the caulkers stored their materials. In bad weather they sat inside and spun oakum, often picking apart old rope and soaking it in pine tar to recycle materials. It's interesting to learn that the caulkers traditionally feuded with the carpenters. If a vessel leaked, the caulkers maintained it was because the carpenters had done a poor job on the planking. If the ship was nice and tight, the caulkers said it was because they themselves had done such an excellent job of sealing the seams.

Do pay a visit to the Small Craft Center where you see a large display of small boats. Here shipbuilding trainees make replicas of traditional crafts similar to those on exhibit, eagerly explaining their work to visitors. Perhaps you'll see the *Seguin*, the oldest United States registered wooden steam tugboat, which may still be undergoing major restoration when you visit. Outdoors nearby, the schooner *Bowdoin* is being given a massive overhaul.

Percy & Small is best enjoyed by children who are eight years old and older. Much of the fun here is due to the fact that visiting Percy & Small is much more like being given license to snoop around an active shipyard than like visiting a museum. Allow about forty-five minutes for your visit, and come and go as you please. If some of the children aren't all that fascinated by the old tools, they will enjoy exploring the river bank, the wharf area, and the flurry of activity taking place wherever an active project is underway. There is a hot-dog cart where you can purchase light refreshments; or, you can take along a picnic and settle down at one of the tables overlooking the Kennebec.

When you are ready to move on, board the M/V *Sasanoa*, a twenty-foot motor launch, for a narrated swing upriver to the rest of the museum sites. Your route takes you past BIW, where you are likely to see a well-seasoned ship hoisted up in drydock for its

Percy & Small produced forty-one huge masted schooners between 1894 and 1920, including the Wyoming, a six-masted beauty.

When you are ready to move on, board the M/V Sasanoa, a twenty-foot motor launch, for a narrated swing upriver to the rest of the museum.

twenty-year overhaul. You will probably also travel alongside several steel frigates (more than four hundred feet long) whose primary function is anti-submarine warfare. There is also a four-hundred-foot-high crane which can pick up loads weighing two hundred twenty tons, swinging them three hundred sixty degrees. Your captain explains what is going on at the moment, as well as relating some of the history of the ironworks. You are close enough to hear the hum of gas turbine engines and the ring of hammers as workers go about their chores on the decks far above. Then you leave the ironworks behind as the launch is maneuvered under the bridge which carries U.S. Route 1 (upper level) and a railroad route (lower level) across the river. As you approach your destination, your captain sounds a horn announcing the boat's arrival; be certain to cover your ears, as he requests, if you are sitting in front of the wheelhouse! As you disembark, he will warn you that the boat leaves hourly for the return trip to Percy & Small; if you miss the last trip back you will have a long walk back to your car.

The round-trip boat ride is included in your admission charge; children consider it one of the highlights of the visit. The boat leaves every hour; the two-mile trip lasts about fifteen minutes in each direction.

SEWALL HOUSE. Begin your visit to the downtown area at this 1844 mansion, which is now the home of extensive maritime collections. There are many impressive paintings here, but children favor the exquisitely detailed dioramas depicting activities in the shipyards and related businesses that flourished here during the height of the wooden-ship era. For example, at The Sewall Shipyard you see tiny vessels in various stages of construction, while miniature men and work animals go about their tasks. The Donnell Ropewalk diorama offers a detailed portrait of Bath as it appeared in the 1880s. If you look very carefully, you are likely to find some of the humorous touches diorama makers frequently add to their work; can you find the tiny mermaid basking on the bank of the Kennebec, or the small figure running frantically toward the outhouse? Since rope making was one of the most important ship-building-related industries, this diorama shows hemp being hackled (combed and cleaned), treated with tar, and spun into yarn, with the yarn then formed into strands. This is important when you learn that the typical thousand-ton vessel required over twelve thousand feet of rope for the standard rigging alone, so there was plenty to keep the rope makers busy. In the Skolfied Shipyard diorama, look for the warehouse, gate house, barn, workmen's boarding house, cookhouse, privy, well, saw pit, blacksmith shop, and lumber schooner offloading.

In the Navigation Room, turn your eyes to the ceiling for a sample panorama of the stars as they

Can you find the tiny mermaid basking on the bank of the Kennebec, or the small figure running frantically toward the outhouse?

would have been used by a navigator off the coast of Maine to find his way at 10 PM on July 4, 1966. Downstairs is a small children's room entered via a ramp with rope railings. Here is a loud ship's bell to ring, several ship-steering mechanisms to try out, and a mock ship's deck with wheel, ropes, and pulleys to handle. There is also a mural of a battleship, with eighteen portholes; if you peek through them, you will see vignettes of life aboard a navy vessel.

WINTER STREET CENTER. Here there is a huge diorama, again depicting the Bath waterfront in the 1880s. This one features a flour and grain mill, a coal-and-ice company, a freight house, a grocery, a junk dealer, a sail loft, a steamboat wharf, and much more. Nearby you find the answers to questions such as, "Why are vessels christened by breaking a bottle of champagne over the bow?" Answer: This is a Christian/pagan ritual that survives from a time when sailors made sacrifices to the sea gods at launching time. Modern ship-christening ceremonies continue to combine prayer or dedication with the symbolic sacrifice of the champagne.

In one of the center's small exhibits, titled Statistics, you will discover facts about the cost of living in Maine in the 1880s. For instance, the average shipworker was 42 years old; he averaged 10 hours of work per day. He earned $1541 per year, and his annual budget allowed $200 for food, $37 for fuel and light, and $100 for clothing. If he owned a home, it was worth about $1508, and the average family size was 3.7 people. Children may enjoy comparing present-day prices with these.

Most children will be intrigued by the second-floor exhibit, Life at Sea. Here you will see the actual contents of a nineteenth-century seaman's chest, including his clothing, shaving kit, bedding, money, and books (to help improve his seamanship skills and make him eligible for advancement). There is a full-sized replica of a ship's forecastle, and you realize here that the sailors were stuffed as tight as sardines into their quarters in the dark, dank space below board. Other sections of the exhibit focus on victuals at sea, leisure activities such as macramé, accordion playing, and checkers; and presents brought home to loved ones from India, Japan, and the South Seas.

Exhibits at the Maine Maritime Museum complex are practical and realistic rather than flashy. This is the sort of place where the success of the visit depends largely on the adults' ability to help their offspring understand the significance of the shipyard and the entire museum complex. This takes patience. One young lady about eight years old moaned pitifully in the Paint and Trunnel Shop ("This stuff doesn't *do* anything!"), became contemplative in the Mill and Joiner Shop, and cracked her first full-strength smile

Here you find a loud ship's bell to ring, several ship-steering mechanisms to try out, and a mock ship's deck with wheel, ropes, and pulleys to handle.

Do you know why a new vessel is christened by breaking a bottle of champagne over its bow?

when the M/V *Sasanoa* came into view. However, when encountered two hours later at the Winter Street Center, she was enthusiastically planning the inventory of her own seaman's chest: "I'd take my Monopoly set for sure!"

Your final stop is the Apprenticeshop up the road, where programs in boat building and seamanship are conducted. If your young companions have already satisfied their appetite for shipbuilding, skip the shop and board the M/V *Sasanoa* for the return trip to Percy & Small and another close-up view of the ship fitters, welders, and machinists working at the BIW.

It's wise to allow a full day for your visit to Bath. Because the museum sites are spread around the city, you can easily alternate your museum visits with some center-city strolling.

DOWNTOWN BATH. Perhaps you'd like to take a lunch break in the downtown area. If you want to picnic, try Waterfront Park on Commercial Street. There are pebble walks, benches, and grassy stretches to relax on; if you come on a summer Saturday, replenish your fixings with fresh produce, lobsters, fish, and baked goods from the weekly farmers' market at the corner of Front and Broad streets, very near the park.

If you prefer a restaurant try Kristina's at the corner of Center and High streets. A bakery at heart, Kristina's features fancy tortes and delectable cheesecake, homemade breads, cookies, muffins, and sticky buns. You can also purchase full breakfasts and lunches; and dinner is served several evenings a week. Start the day with a "smoothie," a combination of fruits, yogurt, peanut butter, and honey, even carob or chocolate if you like. There are pancakes served with bananas, blueberries, or sautéed apples, and you can order French toast in small or large portions. For lunch, choose from a half dozen varieties of grilled-cheese sandwiches, more than a dozen kinds of omelets, or several varieties of hamburgers. There are also salad plates and pocket sandwiches. This is a spacious, unpretentious eatery with comfortable booths and a counter that seats seven. Even if you can't stay for a meal, stop in to purchase a morsel from the bakery case.

You can't explore downtown without rambling along Front Street, the main thoroughfare, attractively punctuated with brick sidewalks, nineteenth-century lighting fixtures, and bright awnings. Unlike many revitalized downtowns, Bath manages to maintain a sense of perspective. You find many functional shops here, as well as trendier stores geared to tourist tastes. Children like Shaw's Book Shop, which has activity books, board games, and small toys. Right next door is Animal Crackers, which carries a good selection of children's clothes. Hallet's Drugstore is a favorite place to stop for an ice-cream cone; while you are there, be certain to check out the notices posted in the window.

Start the day with a "smoothie," a combination of fruits, yogurt, peanut butter, and honey, even carob or chocolate if you like.

It's fun to read the various announcements of local chicken barbecues, baked bean and casserole suppers, and lobster feeds — all entice you. There are lots of benches where you can pause to enjoy your ice cream, and everywhere you roam you are treated to glimpses of the Kennebec River, so important to the city of Bath.

ACCESS

MAINE MARITIME MUSEUM AT BATH. Directions: From Portland, take I-95 north to the exit for Route 1/Brunswick-Bath Coastal Route; continue on Route 1 to the Washington Street exit in Bath, turn right onto Washington Street, and continue about one mile to the Percy & Small Shipyard, on your left. **Season:** All four sites are open mid-May through mid-October; some sites may be open at other times of the year; telephone for information. (M/V *Sasanoa* operates only from May through October.) **Admission** charged; maximum family charge may be opted for in preference to individual admission charges; under six free. (207) 443-6311. **Note:** Free second-day admission is provided with a validated ticket. You can also ask for a discount ticket good for half-price admission to three other Maine museums (Owls Head Transportation Museum, in Owls Head; Seashore Trolley Museum, in Kennebunkport; and the Children's Museum of Maine, in Portland). Or, if you already have such a ticket, you can use it here.

Route 1: Rockland To Ellsworth

If you want to reach northern Maine as quickly as possible, stick to the Maine Turnpike. If, however, you'd rather enjoy the scenery and explore the coastal towns with their busy harbors, do plan to spend some time negotiating the slower traffic along Route 1. (The Rockland-to-Ellsworth stretch is ideal for vacationers who want to visit the Owls Head Transportation Museum on their way to Acadia National Park.)

Much of the pleasure derived from traveling the coastal road comes in the form of discoveries you make on your own. Instead of rushing, poke about in the towns along the way. Stop at small simple restaurants featuring home-cooked foods. If you pass through Rockland on a Friday in the summer, make a sidetrip down to the farmers' market at the public landing where you can purchase fresh produce, pickles, and preserves from the people who grow and prepare them. Route 1 becomes Main Street in Rockland; if you want to spend time here, watch for signs to the Public Landing, where the Chamber of Commerce is also located and information is available.

Try to catch a glimpse of the honorary harbor-master, André the Seal, running through his antics in a pen in the middle of the harbor.

CAROLYN J. CASEY

Buoys will be buoys. They are popular souvenirs for those traveling the central Maine coast.

ROCKPORT. As you continue along Route 1, and if you chance to come through Rockport in the late afternoon, try to catch a glimpse of the honorary harbormaster, André the Seal, running through his antics in a pen in the middle of the harbor with the assistance of his trainer. This orphaned harbor seal has become something of a celebrity. For years now he has wintered in Boston at the New England Aquarium, returning each summer to his own turf in Rockport harbor. He used to make the entire harbor his home but he made such a nuisance of himself in recent years, tipping over dories and the like, that he is now in an enclosure. He stages his show at 4 PM.

CAMDEN. A few miles farther ahead, make a stop at Camden, with its picturesque harbor and streets lined with shops and galleries. On a weekend keep your eye out for two of the tall-masted windjammers, pride of the region, who put in here. You might see the *Adventure*, once featured in a television version of Rudyard Kipling's classic, *Captains Courageous*, or the *Mattie*, a veteran of the West Indies fruit trade.

BELFAST. In Belfast, stop off at Perry's Tropical Nut House. Here you can buy toys, moccasins, fudge, and souvenir novelties, with stuffed ostriches, boxing bear cubs, and turtles looking over your shoulder. Yankee trader Irving S. Perry started this unusual business in 1926. He had invested in some pecan groves in the south when a bumper crop of the nuts and not nearly enough warehouse space to store them prompted Perry to move some of the crop north; here he tried to sell them at a roadside stand. A world traveler, Perry decided to display some of the curios he had collected in his travels along with his pecans. Passersby couldn't resist the combination, and that is how Perry's Tropical Nut House got its start.

The huge man-eating clam (now safely stuffed) Treat brought back from a Navy tour in the Pacific would surely have warmed Perry's heart.

As the business continued to thrive, Perry moved it into an old cigar factory, where he had plenty of room for expansion. He traveled throughout Cuba and South America, adding more nuts and more curios to his collection. A showman at heart, he had huge carved animals erected in the yard and installed trick mirrors inside the store. Stuffed alligators, birds, and mammals continued to be added to the display.

When Perry died in 1940, the business was taken over by Joshua Treat, who continued to add to the collection. The huge man-eating clam (now safely stuffed) he brought back from a Navy tour in the Pacific would have warmed Perry's heart. His other (stuffed) contributions include a full-sized gorilla from Africa, a bull from India, and an albatross from the South Seas.

Although many of the specimens show their age, it is an unusual experience to pick out pine pillows and bumper stickers with animal eyes staring at you wherever you turn. Oh yes, do be sure to take a look at the nut collection while you are here. It contains just about every species known to man, including some real gems like the Hypalene nut, from Egypt, the size of a rubber ball.

Continuing on Route 1 north of Belfast, you can stop for a meal at Duffy's Home Cooking. There are thirteen tables here and a counter with just three stools. The fare is good and inexpensive; you can get hearty meals "like Mom used to make." Top it off with homemade pie; Duffy's has raspberry, lemon meringue, chocolate cream, blueberry, Boston cream — you name it. There are many other restaurants like Duffy's along Route 1 that offer a refreshing alternative to the fast-food joints and other chains you generally have to rely on when traveling on a highway. If you haven't eaten by the time you get to Ellsworth, look for the Rosebud Cafe on Main Street.

ACCESS

ROUTE 1: ROCKLAND TO ELLSWORTH. Directions: From Bath, take Route 1 east through Rockland, Rockport, Camden, and Belfast.

PERRY'S TROPICAL NUT HOUSE. Directions: Heading north on Route 1 in Belfast, you'll find Perry's on the right. **Season:** Spring, summer, and fall. **Admission** free. (207) 338-1630.

Owls Head

THE OWLS HEAD TRANSPORTATION MUSEUM. You must see this fascinating collection of vehicles that travel both in the sky and on the ground. Some of the early airplanes look like insects out of a science-fiction movie, with their bright coloration, delicate wing structure, and antenna-like propellers.

Some of the early airplanes look like insects out of a science-fiction movie, with their bright coloration, delicate wing structure, and antenna-like propellers.

Here you can see a World War I Fokker triplane, a T-6 trainer, and others named Spad, Jenny, and Waco. The ground vehicles include a 1901 Oldsmobile, a 1903 Mercedes Simplex, a sixteen-cylinder Cadillac, and several Packards as well as those old favorites, the Ford Model T's and Model A's. Early tractors and motorcycles are displayed, too.

The museum is situated on an airstrip, with a hangar serving as the main exhibit hall. But what is special about this museum is that much of the machinery actually works. During the week it is on static display, but on weekends the place really comes to life. Model T and Piper Cub rides are available; special events are scheduled for many Saturdays and Sundays from Memorial Day through mid-October. (To request a calendar of special events, write to: Owls Head Transportation Museum, Knox County Airport, Owls Head, ME 04854.) Demonstrations are held each weekend afternoon, weather permitting; but for a really terrific visit, come when an air show is scheduled.

In such a show, you might see the Flying Farmer take to the skies. He begins his act by staggering out on the field in overalls and an old hat, chugging down a bottle of whiskey. The next thing you know, the fellow has stolen a small plane and taken to the skies. An announcer provides commentary on the escapades that follow; it seems the "farmer" hasn't the slightest idea how to operate the plane! As the plane banks and turns, flips over and rights itself, the announcer cries, "Oh no! He's backward in the cockpit now!" (And he *is.*) ". . . he's flying with his feet! . . . he's coming down sideways — that'll never work!"

The plane makes a series of somersaults, goes through some graceful loops wiggling its tail behind, takes a pass at the runway, and soars straight up in the sky. The engine cuts out! The plane tumbles to the earth nose first, only to swoop upward seconds before hitting the runway. This show is a true cliffhanger, an exciting display of skill. (Turns out the flying farmer is a darned fine pilot after all.)

Other special events include Wayne Pierce's Wing-Walking Aerobatic Show, model-aircraft flying demonstrations, car rallies with costumed drivers and passengers, and an auction of mechanical Americana. Be certain to call ahead to find out what will be going on when you plan to visit. Children will probably appreciate it if you arrange your trip to coincide with one of the aerobatic shows.

Back in the hangar, check out the Wright Model Ex "Vin Fitz" replica. Cal Rogers made the first transcontinental flight in a biplane just like this one in 1911. If you think flights are subject to delay today, consider the statistics for Rogers' landmark flight. It took him 54 days to cover the 4,321-mile route, including 70 landings and 15 crashes. Says something for the man's (and

The Flying Farmer begins his act by staggering out on the air field in overalls and an old hat, chugging down a bottle of whiskey.

the aircraft's) durability, doesn't it? The air shows usually last from one to two hours; they are enjoyed by all ages, but particularly by children ten years old and older.

ACCESS

OWLS HEAD TRANSPORTATION MUSEUM. **Directions:** From Bath, take Route 1 north about forty-five miles to Rockland, then Route 73 south two miles to the museum at the Knox County Airport; follow signs. **Season:** Memorial Day through mid-October. **Admission** charged. (207) 594-9219.

Mount Desert Island/ Acadia National Park

NATIONAL PARK SERVICE VISITORS' CENTER. Begin your visit to New England's only national park by stopping at the visitors' center, where you can pick up trail maps and program schedules. You can also watch a brief orientation film introducing you to the many features of the park and get answers to any questions you might have about camping, hiking, and related activities. Acadia consists of thirty-three thousand acres of magnificent landscape highlighted by rounded mountains and rocky seashore.

The Abnaki Indians were among the first people to hunt and fish at Mount Desert, the island that contains most of the national park. While there is no written record, archeological evidence indicates that the Norsemen were probably the first Europeans to discover the area. But it was the French explorer Samuel de Champlain who, in his ship's log, provided the first written descriptions of the island. It was Champlain who coined the name "L'Isle des Monts Déserts," which translates, "island of the deserted, lonely, or barren mountains." You will find that some people pronounce the name Mount *Des*ert and others say Mount Des *sert*. According to a park naturalist, "both are correct, depending upon whether you follow the Sahara (desert) or ice cream & cake (dessert) school of thought."

Champlain made his discovery of the island in 1604, and in 1613 a group of French Jesuits came to settle. Although they were plagued by continual rivalry and conflict with the British, they continued to hold a footing here until the French were defeated at Quebec in 1759. Their influence is still evident today.

After the American Civil War, Mount Desert Island saw increased popularity as a favorite vacation destination, particularly for writers, artists, and others in search of tranquility. Those who came found room and board with local farmers and fishermen. Some of the wealthy, prominent families active in the east coast

Even babies in back-packs appear on many of the walks.

commercial sector purchased large tracts of land here and built elaborate summer "cottages." These families ultimately donated much of their holdings to the national park; notable among these is the eleven-thousand-acre parcel given by John D. Rockefeller, Jr., who also built the many miles of carriage paths that crisscross the park.

As you learn at the visitors' center, there are two campgrounds in the park, Black Woods and Seawall, as well as many private campgrounds located just outside park boundaries. Stays within the national park campgrounds are limited to two weeks. If you wish to swim, the park contains a lovely sandy beach at Echo Lake (very popular and often crowded, however). The only other beach staffed by park lifeguards is Sand Beach, where hearty souls plunge into the icy ocean surf. The park also contains over a hundred miles of trails, from easy walks to strenuous climbs. In order to enjoy both camping and the park to a satisfying degree, plan to stay at least two or three days; a longer stay is even better if the members of your group are enthusiastic (and experienced) campers.

The Park Loop Road, a twenty-mile drive connecting lakes, mountains, and seashore, leads to Cadillac Mountain Summit Road, which winds up the mountain to the highest point on our Atlantic Coast. A trip to the summit is a good beginning to your Acadia visit, providing views of Blue Hill and Penobscot bays as well as Frenchman Bay.

For a thorough tour of Acadia at your own pace, you can rent or purchase a cassette tape at the visitors' center and let it guide you. Prepared by the National Park Service, this tour provides full background on the geology and history of the area, including stories about famous landmarks such as Cadillac Mountain, Thunder Hole, Jordan Pond, and Otter Point. The tour covers a fifty-six-mile route and takes four to six hours to complete. Cassettes and players are rented by the twenty-four hour period, so you can take half of the tour in the afternoon, and half the next morning, if you choose.

ACADIA NATIONAL PARK NATURALIST PROGRAM. During the summer months, and on a restricted schedule in the spring and fall, the National Park Service operates a comprehensive program of nature activities. There are mountain hikes, nature walks, sea cruises, and special-interest events. The program is designed to help visitors "interpret" the natural environment of Acadia, to learn more about the geology, flora, and fauna of the park. Different levels of endurance and ability are required for the various events, but there is something for every member of the family; even babies in backpacks appear on many of the walks.

The mountain hikes (which are not recommended for small children) run from two and a half to five and a half hours, and are rated from "moderate" to "very strenuous." Participants are requested to wear sturdy walking shoes, to bring drinking water, and to pack a lunch if appropriate to the time of day you'll be hiking.

Two of the nature walks include an exploration of the plants and an investigation of the effects of glaciation atop Cadillac Mountain, and a two-hour forest, field, and marsh walk; both are rated "easy." Other walks take participants along carriage roads and across bridges as they study the ways in which man has intervened with the natural topography. A two-hour Night Prowl offers a chance to explore the shadows and sounds of the forest community after dark.

Dress warmly for the naturalist sea cruises, which last two to four and a half hours. Children enjoy the tour of Frenchman Bay, cruising among the islands in search of eagles, ospreys, seals, and porpoises aboard a comfortable sightseeing boat. On the Islesford-Somes Sound cruise, you become acquainted with the history of Acadia. You can look for wildlife with the help of your naturalist/guide as you cruise to Little Cranberry Island, where you have an hour ashore to explore the Islesford Historical Museum. Still another cruise focuses on the lobstering industry; here you have a chance to see sea life brought aboard in a lobster trap.

Special events include bird-watchers' walks, biking tours, and astronomy watches. Children seven to ten years old can sign up for "What's That?" — the one-and-a-half-hour nature walk geared specifically to their interests. Fourteen-year-olds with a serious interest in becoming competent with map and compass are eligible for "Introduction to Orienteering," a four-hour session. Both of the national-park campgrounds have outdoor amphitheaters where evening programs are conducted daily in the summer. The subjects vary, but you are likely to see a narrated slide show on some aspect of the flora and fauna in the park or nearby waters. People of all ages attend these programs, bringing along blankets to wrap up in or stretch out on, as the mood dictates. By the way, you need not be staying at a park campground to attend.

With the exception of the cruises, the naturalist activities are free. Some of the events, however, require a reservation (made at the visitors' center), as only a certain number can be accommodated.

SIEUR DE MONTS SPRING. Here you will visit the Robert Abbe Museum of Stone Age Antiquities and take a self-guided tour of the Wild Gardens of Acadia. There is also a small nature center containing the skeleton of a pilot whale found beached on Prince Edward Island in Canada. There are grassy lawns to run on, and a pond and stream to explore.

The one-room museum is a treasure chest packed full of handsome Indian artifacts. One display traces the evolution of the crooked knife ("biketagenigan," to

A two-hour Night Prowl offers an opportunity to explore the shadows and sounds of the forest community after dark.

the Penobscots), beginning with an animal's curved incisor tooth and working up to a lead blade set into a wooden handle. The knife was used to make basket splints, paddles, and birch-bark canoes.

Look for the Indian woman's kit of tools containing her personal possessions; can you find an awl for punching holes in leather, a beamer to soften skins, and a weaving needle to make rush mats? After spending nine years (1689 to 1698) in Indian captivity, John Gyles wrote in *Curious Adventures:* "If an Indian girl is educated to make 'monoodah' (Indian bags), birch dishes, to lace snowshoes, sew birch to canoes, and boil the kettle, she is esteemed a lady of fine accomplishment."

In the Wild Gardens, you will find plants that you have seen on your walks through the bogs and forests and along the shores of Acadia. They are organized according to habitat. In the Mixed Woods habitat, you will see lady's-slippers, wild oats, wood anemone, Canadian lily, and the bright (but poisonous) red and white baneberries. The Roadside habitat contains edible berries such as the blackberry and the huckleberry, as well as the familiar aster and goldenrod. The Beach habitat features beach pea, sea milkwort, and skullcap. Other habitats are Dry Heath, Meadow, Mountain, Island, For the Birds, Coniferous, Ponds and Marshes, and the Bog. All species are fully identified; a guide is usually present to answer any questions you might have. Using the handy map provided, head for the appropriate habitat and satisfy all those "what's that?" inquiries that have punctuated your nature walks.

SHIP HARBOR NATURE TRAIL. If your schedule makes it impossible for you to take part in one of the naturalist-led walks, or if you prefer to explore on your own instead of in an organized group, purchase the guide to the Ship Harbor Nature Trail at the visitors' center and take the self-guided nature walk. This route focuses on the interrelation of man, nature, and disaster, with the booklet identifying and explaining points of interest related to that theme. For instance, you become acquainted with the dependence of certain animals on specific types of vegetation. You learn how a change in habitat affects the animals who live there, and you find out how trees adjust to lack of light. You walk to the ocean's edge to see the spot where a shipwreck occurred in 1740. Ask yourself what you would do if you were cast ashore here with no weapons and few tools. What would you eat? Where would you sleep? How would you survive? The trail leads through the woods and along the shore, to a place where land and sea overlap, where flowering plants and seaweed share the same soil. Your walk will take one to one and a half hours to complete. When you purchase the booklet, be sure to inquire about other self-guiding options.

ACADIA NATIONAL PARK. Directions: Follow I-95 to Bangor, then take Route 1A south twenty-six miles to Ellsworth. From Ellsworth, take Route 3 south to Mount Desert Island. On Mount Desert Island, follow Route 3 to Hull's Cove, toward Bar Harbor; the park entrance and visitors' center on your right are clearly marked. From the center, take the Park Loop Road to Sieur de Monts Spring entrance. **Season:** Park open all year. Visitors' center maintains limited hours November through April. **Admission** free, except for cruises; donation requested at Abbe Museum. (207) 288-3338, or 288-5262.

COURTESY MOUNT DESERT OCEANARIUM

Children can find out how much they weigh under water at the Mount Desert Oceanarium.

Southwest Harbor

MOUNT DESERT OCEANARIUM. In Southwest Harbor, you can climb aboard a retired lobster boat, "radio" a message, and pretend that you are steering your trusty craft across a cold and salty ocean to pull your lobster traps. Inside the oceanarium, children like to begin the visit by plunging an arm through a slitted piece of rubber secured over an old keg in The Great Barrel Challenge. There are several of these kegs, and the idea is to identify by touch the sea items below. Is it a starfish, a piece of seaweed, perhaps a horseshoe crab or a sponge or even a sea cucumber? When you have checked your answer, move on to the shelves labeled "Beachcombers' Treasures" to handle and identify dozens of items such as a Deadman's Finger Sponge, the lower jaw of a monkfish, or a snail's eggcase.

In the Commercial Fishing Room, you can dress up in foul-weather gear, float wooden boats, and learn about fishing techniques that range from handlining to modern dragging and trawling methods. There is a push-button board where you can check your knowledge of the seafood industry by answering questions like "how many saltwater species of fin fish and shellfish are commercially available for food?" or "how fast can a sardine packer pack?"

Try to identify by touch the sea items below: Is this a starfish, a piece of seaweed, perhaps a horseshoe crab or a sponge or even a sea cucumber?

You can dress up in foul-weather gear, float wooden boats, and learn about fishing techniques from handlining to modern dragging and trawling methods.

Do you know how much you would weigh under water? You can step on a scale to find out. Then, here's another challenge; when you taste two types of salt, can you distinguish the sea salt from the table salt? There is a participatory exhibit that teaches you how to minimize the risk of hypothermia (subnormal body temperature) should your boat capsize. If you put on a set of earphones, you can listen to the sounds of the humpback whale. And you can use a hydrometer to determine which bucket holds sea water and which holds fresh. There are lots of facts to learn about sea gulls and marine algae. And that's just the beginning.

In the Lobster Room, a licensed lobsterman explains how the lobster eats and reproduces and how it is caught. He also shows you how traps are constructed, baited, and set.

Be sure to see the room full of aquariums containing eels, scallops, spider crabs, and other specimens found in local waters. Don't miss the Touch Me tank, where you can hold a starfish, a crab, or a sand dollar — or how about a slimy sea cucumber? One of the oceanarium's friendly, knowledgeable staff members will tell you about the behavioral traits of your new acquaintance (and bolster up your courage, should you need it).

The oceanarium is very crowded on rainy days since it is one of the few indoor places to visit on Mount Desert. That doesn't mean you can't have a good time on a rainy day, just that you should be forewarned. Do be sure to allow plenty of time for your visit. This is a place for people of all ages to get involved with the exhibits, which range from the sophisticated to the simple. You might even get a bit wet in the process! Plan to spend an hour or more here for an experience that will be enjoyed by all ages.

ACCESS

MOUNT DESERT OCEANARIUM. Directions: From Ellsworth, follow Route 3 south to Mount Desert Island and Route 102; follow Route 102 south to Southwest Harbor. Turn left at the flashing light at the intersection; the oceanarium is on your right. **Season:** Mid-May to mid-October. **Admission** charged. (207) 244-7330.

Naples

The Sebago/Long Lakes Region of inland Maine is one of the state's oldest resort areas. Today vacationers arrive by car, but in years past they came by train or by horse and buggy. Earlier still, they traveled here by stagecoach and canal boat. The switch-back Songo River runs from the twenty-two-mile-long giant Sebago Lake to Brandy Pond and then to Long Lake.

The river is the last remaining useable portion of the Cumberland-Oxford Canal.

THE NAPLES HISTORICAL SOCIETY. This large and fascinating barn full of treasures tells you a lot about how people worked and lived in the Naples area in past generations. Here you will find sleighs and carriages, even an early snowplow. The latter was constructed in about 1896; you learn that the huge wooden cylinder was drawn by a team of horses. In the off-season, it was also used to roll newly seeded areas around the farm or town. There are lots of kitchen utensils and tools here, too. Look for the corn knives, which are used in local packing factories to strip the kernels from the cobs.

Many old clothes are displayed here; you see everything from a lacy Victorian wedding dress to a red flannel undershirt, a demure blue middy dress to a gentleman's bathing suit, circa 1890, with its knee-length drawers and long tunic top. Ask also to see the two-celled jail in a nearby outbuilding. You'll find a metal cage that looks just perfect for bears or other fierce beasts. Actually, it never did house many criminals. It did serve, however, as a "tramp house" in the early 1900s. It was furnished with straw mats and the doors were left unlocked so that hobos and other itinerants passing through without a place to stay could bed down for the night.

The society maintains an extensive library of slides and movies focusing on early transportation, including railroads, canals, and steamboats. You might see pictures of the Bay of Naples Hotel, one of the finest of the grand old summer lake hotels in the state. If the young ones get restless, send them over to the adjoining Naples School playground (when school is not in session, of course) to work off their excess energy. Allow about twenty minutes for your visit.

OLD CHURCH TAVERN ANTIQUES. Another cavernous barn, this shop contains hundreds of intriguing bits of nostalgia. The selection is eclectic, with sections devoted to glass, furniture, and china, and dozens of other collectibles. Children can add to their collections here without spending a lot. One dollar can buy a couple of turn-of-the-century photographs, a few special postcards or buttons, old magazines from the '50s, or perhaps an old advertising card or two. With just a bit more cash, you can add to your cache of pocketknives or spectacles. Although this is a very well organized shop, with most items clearly priced, there are plenty of nooks and crannies, boxes and piles to explore to keep it interesting.

When you get hungry, walk through the door to the adjoining Victorian Ice Cream Parlor. This attractive room has a fine soda fountain and lots of little round tables with metal ice-cream-parlor chairs. (There is even a toddler-sized set.) The menu is

You see everything from a lacy Victorian wedding dress to a red flannel undershirt, a blue middy dress to a gentleman's bathing suit, circa 1890.

Take a seat at the center table, which has a checkerboard painted on top, and have yourself a friendly match while you down your hot fudge sundae.

painted on gold framed mirrors that hang above the counter. The bill of fare includes ice cream sundaes, sodas, and cones — and salads and sandwiches too. Table lamps with decorated glass shades, an old wooden radio, and a collection of rag dolls further enhance the atmosphere. But the best touch of all is the profusion of advertising memorabilia that covers the walls. One poster features a beaming young miss boasting, "My Daddy bought me a government bond at the Third Liberty Loan — did yours?" Another one shows a proud mother holding her robust baby in the air. The sponsor is Cummings Milk ("laboratory controlled") which philosophizes, "Yours to love, ours to protect."

If you don't have enough to look at, take a seat at the center table, which has a checkerboard painted on top and game pieces ready at hand, and have yourself a friendly match while you down your hot fudge sundae. Children of all ages can spend a profitable and delicious forty-five minutes in the interesting old shop and at the ice cream parlor.

ACCESS

TO GET TO NAPLES. Take I-95 exit 8, follow signs to Route 302, and head north to Naples.

NAPLES HISTORICAL SOCIETY. Directions: The society is located on your left off Route 302, immediately after you cross the Causeway. **Season:** Summer through mid-October. **Admission** is a voluntary donation.

OLD CHURCH TAVERN ANTIQUES AND VICTORIAN ICE CREAM PARLOR. Directions: The tavern is located on Route 302 just east of the Causeway. **Season:** Year round; ice-cream parlor Memorial Day through Labor Day. **Admission** free. (207) 693-6550.

West Paris

PERHAM'S MAINE MINERAL STORE. Established in 1919, this unusual store is housed in a rambling farmhouse at Trap Corner, where the Indian princess Mollyocket buried gold and hung a trap in a tree to mark the spot. If you are a rock hound, or think you might like to become one, you have come to the right place. Oxford County, where Perham's is located, contains (for its size) the largest selection of minerals in the world.

Perham's carries a large selection of jewelry and mineral specimens, as well as all the necessary tools for finding, sanding, and polishing your rocks. There is an excellent inventory of field guides and other books to help you find and identify minerals. And the store contains a museum area, where you can examine local

At the Harvard Quarry, you might find purple apatite crystals, while fluorescent minerals can be discovered at the Willie Heikkinen Quarry.

If you are a rock hound or would like to become one, Perham's Maine Mineral Store is the right place for you.

minerals so that you have a better chance of recognizing them in the field. There is a very interesting small exhibit that addresses the question, "What is fluorescence?" You discover that it is not a reflection but is instead the conversion of energy from an invisible to a visible form; it is the light given off by certain minerals and organic materials when they are struck by ultraviolet light.

But the best feature at Perham's is the people who work there. To help you to get started at finding your own specimens, they provide a free map locating and describing thirteen area quarries where you can dig and scratch to your heart's content. Five of the quarries are owned by Perham's, and there is no charge for the privilege of collecting at them. At the Harvard Quarry, you might find purple apatite crystals, while fluorescent minerals can often be discovered at the Willie Heikkinen Quarry. Some of the quarries are on private land, such as the Mount Mica feldspar quarry, where some of the world's largest and best tourmalines were found around the turn of the century; to dig here, you must pay a user's fee. Mount Mica, as the name suggests, is full of chunks of multilayered shiny mica.

The quarry site usually consists of a pit or excavation that has since filled with water, and a dump or pile of discarded rocks. As you dig through the heaps, keep your eyes alert for interesting colors and formations. Perham's sells hammers and chisels and all the other equipment that can be useful to the rock hound, but for your maiden trip, all you really need is a pair of gloves to protect your hands from scratches and cuts as you dig through the rock heaps.

Wear sneakers or sturdy walking shoes on your expedition, and be prepared to do some hiking to get to the site. Take along a plastic bag or container to hold the specimens you find. It's fun to strike up conversations with other rock hounds, most of whom enjoy sharing their knowledge and experiences. If you still find specimens you can't identify, cart them on back to Perham's for some assistance. And the store is the place to stock up on inexpensive samples of those Oxford County minerals that somehow you missed. Take along a picnic lunch to enjoy while you take a break from "quarrying," and spend one to two hours, or as long as the interest of your group dictates. Children eight years old and older especially enjoy this activity.

ACCESS

PERHAM'S MAINE MINERAL STORE. Directions: Take Maine Turnpike north to exit 11 (Gray), then take Route 26 north to West Paris. The store is located at the junction of routes 26 and 219. **Season:** Year round. **Admission** free. (207) 674-2341.

This ship replica at the New Bedford Whaling Museum is a treat for inquisitive moppets.

CHAPTER III

Massachusetts

Massachusetts is synonymous with history. The Pilgrims landed here, the American Revolution got its start within these boundaries; the Boston Tea Party, "Old Ironsides," and John F. Kennedy left their historic marks. And Massachusetts respects and honors this heritage, both for its intrinsic worth and for its value to tourism. Here in a very special way the past comes alive; you can experience it in restored homes, museums, cemeteries, churches, factories, and lavish reconstructed villages. Today you can relive the adventures of the New Bedford whaling crews, the Gloucester fishermen, or the Salem merchant seamen who plied those lucrative routes to China and the West Indies. Literary tradition comes alive as you follow in the footsteps of writers such as Louisa May Alcott, Herman Melville, and Nathaniel Hawthorne — just a few of the talents nurtured in Massachusetts.

No visit to the Commonwealth is complete without a stay in Boston, still the Hub of the Universe to many residents. The cultural center of New England, Boston combines the charm and grace of centuries-old architecture with sleek, contemporary expanses of glass and steel. The city is populated not only by Anglo Saxon descendants and healthy numbers of Irish and Italians, but also by impressive numbers of Greeks, Slovaks, Poles, Canadians, Russian Jews, Scandinavians, Syrians, Germans, French, and Chinese. Today the "melting pot" concept is as alive and well in Boston as it is anywhere in New England.

Part of Massachusetts' historical importance lies in her economic development. The state became a major manufacturing center as early as the 1640s, when a saltworks was opened in Beverly, and ironworks were built in Saugus and Quincy. Items produced in the state (some still are today) included guns, hand tools, rocking chairs, motorcycles, leather goods, paper, silverware, razor blades, shoes, and textiles. Currently sixty percent of all the world's cranberry supply is grown in southeastern Massachusetts including Cape Cod. (Take a train ride through the bogs, or stop in at the visitors' center to get the complete lowdown on cranberry culture and lore.)

The state has almost as much variety in its geography as in its ethnic and manufacturing mix. Begin with Cape Cod, for example, with its sand dunes, gnarled jack pines, and scrub oaks, and consider that Massachusetts has a total of fifteen hundred miles of coastline. Although the land in the eastern part of the state is mostly rocky and sandy, central Massachusetts has rolling plains fed by many streams, which give way to the broad and fertile Connecticut River valley. In the west, the land rises again, becoming the Berkshire Hills, and the still higher Taconic and Hoosac ranges. There are nineteen main river systems, and over twelve hundred lakes and ponds, many of them bearing long Indian names. Ponder this rather severe example: "Chargoggagoggmauchuaggagoggchaubuna-gungamaugg," or "You fish on your side; I fish on my side; nobody fish in the middle."

How many gables can you count? There should be seven; this is the house immortalized by Hawthorne.

Salem

Justly proud of her maritime and colonial history as well as her literary heritage, Salem is chock full of museums, historic sites, attractions, and activities that bring her rich past to life. Because most of the highlights cluster together in the Derby Waterfront area and the Essex Street/Salem Common area, this is a city that is best explored on foot. Park your car in the Riley Plaza parking lot and stroll down Derby Street, directly across the plaza from the post office.

From Riley Square in downtown Salem, follow Derby Street east to Pickering Wharf; the entrance is on your right, next to the Salem Chamber of Commerce, where you should stop to purchase a touring map.

VOYAGE OF THE *INDIA STAR*. Pickering Wharf, the new commercial and residential complex overlooking Salem harbor, houses dozens of shops, a smattering of restaurants, a year-round marina — and a multimedia presentation that brings alive Salem's days as a busy seaport. The last, titled The Voyage of the India Star, is perfect for children of all ages. The program is presented in a seatless theater in which the audience moves around to face the action. Here you can relive the loneliness, excitement, and danger of life aboard a nineteenth-century merchant ship out of the busy port of Salem as the story unfolds all about you in the circular auditorium.

Voices pierce the dark, speaking words extracted from the diaries, letters, and ships' logs of the men and women who lived in early Salem. "A fellow's got to hang by his eyelids . . . ," "Bodies floated up from the deep . . . ," "This coast of Sumatra is a vile place . . . ," "The good sailor, Mr. Barnes, is dead, having been stabbed in the back and side . . . ." As the voices grow stronger, they take on a physical presence in the form of mannequins representing a ship owner, a young couple preparing for their first separation, a cabin boy anticipating his first trip at sea. The lilting sounds of nineteenth-century sea chanteys enhance the mood.

As the presentation continues, you see a riotous July Fourth celebration in Salem; a barker can be heard urging customers to risk their money on a wheel of fortune; you see bodies piled high on the deck of the India Star, the ring of swords testifying to the pirate attack that is in full swing. A lively, well-researched production, "The Voyage" lasts about forty-five minutes and whets your appetite for further exploration of Salem. It is excellent for children six years old and older.

SALEM MARITIME NATIONAL HISTORIC SITE. Here you see Derby Wharf, typical of the wharves that dominated the waterfront during the era of the China trade (1789 to 1830). There is the Custom House, where inspectors, clerks, weighers, gaugers, measurers, and the collector processed imported cargo. The tour guide shows you the office once used by Nathaniel Hawthorne, Salem's most famous author. Continuing along Derby Street, you pass Ye Olde Pepper Company, the oldest candy company in America. Don't let its name fool you. This is the place to stock up on licorice whips and horehound drops as well as dozens of other confections.

THE HOUSE OF THE SEVEN GABLES. On the water side of the street a bit beyond the Olde Pepper Company, you come to the home that inspired Hawthorne's famous novel of the same name. Take a twenty-minute guided tour of the home, including a peek at the secret stairway. Three other old buildings have been moved to this spot (Hawthorne's Birthplace, Hathaway House, and the Counting House), and they too are open for inspection. The buildings are grouped around a nineteenth-century garden overlooking Salem harbor. Refreshments are available here in

You can relive the loneliness, excitement, and danger of life aboard a nineteenth-century merchant ship out of the port of Salem.

Return to Derby Street and turn right. Follow signs to the nearby Salem Maritime National Historic Site.

Continue down Derby Street to The House of the Seven Gables. The entrance is well marked, on your right.

"Do you believe in witches? Millions of your ancestors did," states a voice in the dark at the Salem Witch Museum.

Return to the Pickering Wharf entrance, cross Derby Street, and proceed up Hawthorne Boulevard to the Essex Street/ Salem Common area. When you reach Washington Square, you will see the Salem Witch Museum, located in an old church on your left behind the statue of Roger Conant, one of Salem's founders.

warm weather, providing a pleasant break. Allow about forty-five minutes for your visit (although children under eight may become bored).

SALEM WITCH MUSEUM. Here you find another excellent multimedia presentation, this one depicting that infamous period in Salem's history, the time of the Salem witch trials. "Do you believe in witches?" asks a voice from the dark. "Millions of your ancestors did." (Because this show is sometimes scary, it is not recommended for children under six).

Members of the audience gather around the Sabbath Circle, an illuminated red and black witchcraft symbol set into the floor and bearing ominous words like "Lucifer Rex" and "Beelzebub." The bodiless voice explains the terrible hysteria that afflicted some of the young women of seventeenth-century Salem. Soon you meet young Ann Putnam, a girl as accountable as any other for the unsavory events to follow. You learn of the tedium of her life and those of her friends: "They were not encouraged to run and play, to meet boys, to become frivolous." Perhaps understandably, they turned to their imaginations for amusement.

The narrator describes how young Ann and friends Abigail Williams and Betty Paris would while away their long winter afternoons listening to tales of magic and sorcery as told by Tituba, the Parises' maid from the West Indies. As they became more involved with her stories, they began to lose sight of the distinction between superstition and reality. Eventually, they were stricken with fits of hysteria. They accused Tituba and others of witchcraft, of being agents of the Devil. Their tales were believed, arrests made, and the pattern began to spread.

Arrangements of life-sized mannequins are illuminated to illustrate particular incidents in the story. For example, you see the accused women caged like animals in tiny jail cells, atoning for crimes they never committed. The narrator goes on to say that prisoners had to pay not only for their meager food but also for the chains that were used to restrain them. Consider the pathetic tale of Sarah, accused and acquitted, but left to languish in prison because she could not pay the costs required for her release. Finally, you discover that before the hysteria passed, nineteen people lost their lives and hundreds of others were jailed, humiliated, and otherwise ruined.

The prisoners had to pay not only for their meager food but also for the chains that were used to restrain them.

ESSEX INSTITUTE. This museum complex includes collections of early costumes and uniforms, furniture, silver, and pottery as well as documents. Although many of the exhibits do not particularly appeal to most children, they might enjoy visiting the three small buildings in the garden behind the institute. The John Ward House dates from the seventeenth century and boasts a parlor, a kitchen, an apothecary shop, and even a "cent" shop (predecessor of our now nearly obsolete dime store). The Doll House shelters an extensive collection of dolls, doll furniture, and doll accessories, while next door, the tiny Lye-Tapley Shoe Shop depicts the shoe industry from 1750 to 1850.

Leaving the Salem Witch Museum, walk one block back toward Pickering Wharf. Turn right onto Essex Street. The Essex Institute is on your right.

Two buildings located adjacent to the institute and managed by it may interest children. The Crowninshield Bentley House has a fully outfitted eighteenth-century children's room, and the Gardner-Pingree House has a nineteenth-century playroom.

Nearby, a very special shop, Pattee-Anne, carries lots of imported clothing and specializes in classic styles. It is exactly the place to buy a baptismal outfit or a proper suit or dress for your child to wear to a wedding or other festive occasion. But Pattee-Anne also carries durable clothes in basic everyday styles.

Walk across Essex Street from the institute to Pattee-Anne, a children's clothing store.

ESSEX STREET MALL. This lovely pedestrian walkway is paved in brick and cobblestones. Since there are no cars threading up and down the street, your children can play outside while you wander into the shops. They will particularly like the East India Square Fountain, located in the square at the beginning

Continue another block on Essex Street to the Essex Street Mall.

of the mall. Built in 1976, the fountain was designed to symbolize Salem's historical relationship with the Orient. The water pours from a Japanese gate into a pool representing Salem harbor. Two levels of stone reach into the pool, symbolizing Salem's shoreline in the 1700s and as it is today, with large portions of the harbor filled in. The upper level represents the shoreline of the 1700s, while the lower indicates the shoreline of today, pushed farther into the water itself. The fountain was designed to be used. Children can wade and float their boats in it without a moment's hesitation. About ten yards beyond the fountain is the entrance to the East India Mall, a winding maze of restaurants and shops just perfect for rainy-day exploration.

The Peabody Museum is on Essex Street at East India Square.

PEABODY MUSEUM. This imposing modern structure houses important maritime, natural-history, and ethnology collections. Children will particularly enjoy the detailed dioramas depicting early days on the Salem waterfront. Can you find the miniature kegs of rum? bits of cod drying in the sun? a tiny wharf rat?

The museum has toys and armor from Japan, China, East India, Siam, and other exotic locations. There is also a full-sized stuffed ostrich with her own genuine ostrich egg, as well as the preserved body of the largest sea turtle ever harvested off the Eastern United States coast. The museum is suitable for children of all ages and the duration of your visit depends upon their interests and temperaments. Films and workshops for children are held frequently on weekends. Telephone ahead for details.

Leave this area and return to Riley Square and your car.

PARKER BROTHERS FACTORY TOURS. This is the place where you can see Monopoly made before your very eyes, not to mention more recent favorites in the board-game business such as Risk and the Mad Magazine Game. On the hour-long tour, you learn about the history of the famous company as you walk through two floors of the factory. You see board tables attached to hard cardboard squares to form game boards, and you see the bagging machine, packing up tokens and other pieces. Visitors must be at least seven years old.

Because Parker Brothers tours are extremely popular and because there is both a minimum and a maximum tour-group size, you must make plans well in advance. It's wise to telephone the tour coordinator two months ahead to secure space for your family. But, if you just happen to be passing through Salem unexpectedly or if you plan your visit only a few days ahead, call anyway; the tour coordinator notes that she can often squeeze a few more visitors in with a scheduled group.

You see board tables attached to hard cardboard squares to form game boards, and the bagging machine packing up tokens and other pieces.

SALEM WILLOWS AMUSEMENT PARK. Located about two miles from downtown Salem, this turn-of-the-century amusement park has a dark green bandstand (where there are frequent concerts in summer) and sprawling green wooden refreshment concessions dating from the early 1900s. Children like to watch the concessionaires making fresh saltwater taffy right on the spot, the good sticky kind your grandparents chewed on in their courting days. Piped-in music appropriate to that long-gone era adds to the ambiance.

The only adult ride at the Willows is the bumper cars. Children, however, can choose from over a dozen, including a century-old merry-go-round with ornately carved circus animals. There are old-fashioned amusement machines (put a nickel in and make the puppet dance) as well as skee ball.

M/V MISS SALEM. If you plan to be in Salem for just one day, you might want to park your car at Salem Willows and take a narrated tour of Marblehead harbor and the Salem waterfront aboard the M/V *Miss Salem*, which departs from the pier at the amusement park. The boat is equipped with snack bar, rest rooms, heated cabin, and open upper-deck seating. You can disembark at Central Wharf in the Derby Street area, tour downtown Salem on foot, and then return to Salem Willows by boat. Or, you can simply take a loop trip from Salem Willows to Central Wharf and back, listening to your guide point out landmarks that played a role in the Revolutionary War.

Located approximately half way between Boston and Cape Ann, Salem is a convenient place to spend the night should you wish to continue on to Beverly, Gloucester, or Rockport. Since it is also a stop on the commuter rail service line from Boston, the city is accessible to those who wish to leave their cars at home. You will not be able to see all the attractions outlined here in a single day. Should you decide to stay overnight, your best bet is to book a room at the pleasant, comfortable, and informal Hawthorne Inn conveniently located across from the Essex Institute end of Essex Street, next to the Salem common. The hotel atmosphere is in itself a novelty for children more familiar with impersonal motels. The inn is located next door to Russell's Ice Cream Parlor, where you can feast on homemade ice cream and other goodies.

Children like to watch the concessionaires making fresh saltwater taffy right on the spot.

ACCESS

TO GET TO SALEM. From Boston, take I-93 north exit 11E (I-95 and Route 128 north), and follow I-95 and Route 128 to exit 25E (Route 114). From Route 114, follow signs to Salem; proceed downtown to Riley Square.

VOYAGE OF THE INDIA STAR. Season: Year round. **Admission** charged. (617) 745-9540.

SALEM MARITIME NATIONAL HISTORIC SITE. Season: July and August. **Admission** free. (617) 744-4323.

THE HOUSE OF THE SEVEN GABLES. Season: Year round. **Admission** charged. (617) 744-0991.

SALEM WITCH MUSEUM. Season: Year round. **Admission** charged. (617) 744-1692.

ESSEX INSTITUTE. Season: Year round. **Admission** charged. (617) 744-3390.

PEABODY MUSEUM. Season: Year round. **Admission** charged. (617) 745-9500.

PARKER BROTHERS FACTORY TOURS. Directions: From downtown Salem, turn right onto Bridge Street (which is also Route 107 north and Route 1A south). The factory is at 190 Bridge Street. **Season:** Year round. **Admission** free. (617) 927-7600, extension 2249.

SALEM WILLOWS AMUSEMENT PARK. Directions: Follow Essex Street to the Essex Street Extension, then follow signs to Salem Willows about two and a half miles ahead on your right. **Season:** Memorial Day through Labor Day. **Admission** free. (617) 745-0251.

M/V MISS SALEM (PIER TRANSIT COMPANY). Directions: Located at the pier at Salem Willows. **Season:** Late spring through early fall. **Admission** charged. (617) 744-6311.

Beverly

Located adjacent to Salem just off Route 128, Beverly has one super attraction that absolutely should not be missed: treat yourself and your young ones to a performance by Le Grand David and His Spectacular Magic Company, at the Cabot Street Theater on Cabot Street downtown. From the moment the tuxedoed doorman welcomes you, you know that you are in for something very special.

LE GRAND DAVID AND HIS SPECTACULAR MAGIC COMPANY. You pass by the counter where clowns sell candy, entering the inner lobby with its large, hand-painted puppet theater. Here early arrivals (forty-five minutes before show time) are treated to stories, songs, and dances performed by a group of antique and contemporary puppets. When you enter the main part of the theater, be sure to look at the collection of magic-trick paraphernalia on display before finding seats in the beautifully kept hall. Find seats as close to the stage as possible so that your children can keep a sharp eye focused on the magicians' maneuvers. There is also occasional action in the aisles, and it is therefore particularly nice for children to sit at the end of a row. Or, if you prefer, there is also balcony seating.

The inspiration behind the two-and-a-half-hour production that unfolds right before your very eyes is Marco the Magi, Le Grand David's teacher and himself a most prominent member of the cast. Marco grew up in Cuba, where he began performing as a magician at age thirteen. It took him nearly five years to assemble and train the company of more than forty members, which has performed at the Cabot Street Theater since 1975. Marco summarizes his attitude toward magic: "I have no supernatural powers. I want us all to have fun together, to share what is theater magic."

It is difficult to believe that Marco and his associates have no supernatural powers as you watch them pluck silks and feathers from thin air, emerge whole and healthy from boxes pierced with swords, and sometimes even reel in live goldfish from fishing lines they have cast into the audience. When Seth, a very young member of the company, demonstrates the art of levitation, more than one child in the audience has been heard to murmur, "Do you think I can learn to do that, Ma?" The pace is quick, one illusion following another with hardly a break. Oriental music, a barber-shop ensemble, and trombone, accordion, and piano music enhance the atmosphere.

An opulent collection of curtains and backdrops in spectacular colors also adds to the fantasy — one moment there's a turn-of-the-century European lake-and-mountain scene, and another moment a red silk sash with dashing dragon motif. There are constant changes of costume, too. The properties and wardrobe are made by members of the company, and they do not spare the spangles or the color. Marco himself sometimes wears ten different outfits in a single performance, sporting up to five kimonos at one time to make for quick costume changes.

Intermission is a pleasure in itself. You can purchase refreshment from the clowns, who make their way down the aisles with trays of pastries and candy. Or you can climb the stairs to the second-floor lobby and sample the frozen yogurt and pastries, or sip coffee or tea at one of the small café tables. If the children need to stretch their legs, they can wander out to the first-floor lobby to gape at the old-fashioned player piano as it performs all by itself. When you exit through the lobby after the second act, members of the cast are present to shake hands and sign autographs, so have your pens and programs ready. And come prepared to enjoy a long and delightful experience.

Marco and his associates pluck silks and feathers from thin air, and sometimes even reel in live goldfish from fishing lines they have cast into the audience.

ACCESS

LE GRAND DAVID AND HIS SPECTACULAR MAGIC COMPANY. Directions: From Salem, take Route 1A north to Route 22, and follow Route 22 about two miles to the traffic light. Turn right (to avoid going the wrong way up a one-way street), and proceed one block to Cabot Street. The theater is across the street, slightly to your left. **Season:** Year round, afternoons and evenings. **Admission** charged; reservation advised. (For schedule, write to Cabot Street Theater, Cabot Street, Beverly, MA 01915.) (617) 927-3677.

Note: We do not recommend the show for children under six unless they are unusually patient. Children are not permitted to travel randomly up and down the aisles during the performance, and it is a *long*, albeit a wonderful, show.

Cape Ann

An island attached to the mainland by two bridges, one large and stationary, and one a small drawbridge, Cape Ann is a rocky promontory that juts out into the Atlantic. The cape is made up of Gloucester and Rockport, and no matter where you drive you are treated to one splendid ocean vista after another, the harbors and coves speckled with lobster pots. The two communities attract large numbers of visitors in the summer months; daytrippers come from the Boston area to escape the city heat, and longer-distance travelers come to stay for prolonged periods of time. There are many guest houses and motels to choose from in Rockport, as well as several modern facilities in Gloucester. Both towns are home to lots of restaurants, too.

If the weather treats you well, you will want to spend much of your time on Cape Ann out of doors. For a brief, readable guide to the flora and fauna of the area (so that you will be able to identify tide-pool treasures and find good blueberrying patches), pick up a copy of *The Wilds of Cape Ann*, by Eleanor Pope (published by the Audubon Society), at either The Bookstore, on Main Street in downtown Gloucester (there's a couch here where children can read while their parents browse, and toys for prereaders to explore) or Toad Hall Bookstore, on Main Street in Rockport (with a downstairs room, reached via a circular stairway, housing children's books, records, and posters).

Gloucester

If you plan to take your children to Gloucester, head first to the library and check out a copy of Rudyard Kipling's classic tale, *Captains Courageous*, the story of a spoiled wealthy boy who falls from the deck of a luxury steamer and is rescued by a fishing boat out of the port of Gloucester. Selfish, whiny Harvey is eventually transformed into a compassionate, self-sufficient young man during his months aboard the schooner as he learns firsthand about the talent, sweat, and tears that are all part of earning a living at sea. A visit to the Gloucester waterfront is certainly enriched by an acquaintance with Harvey, Manuel, and the rest of the Kipling characters.

GLOUCESTER FISHERMENS MUSEUM. Gloucester proudly claims to be the oldest commercial

There are drawings and models to study, ropes and sinkers to handle, and dried salt cod to sample (very salty!).

fishing port on the east coast; and the city's maritime heritage certainly comes to life within the walls of this quaint institution. The museum houses a variety of exhibits that encourage children to activate all their senses; for instance, there are drawings and models to study, ropes and sinkers to handle, and dried salt cod to sample (*very* salty!). It's fun to operate the 1895 bellows-powered foghorn with its deep, foreboding voice. And everything smells like seaweed!

At a table full of "found" articles contributed by local fishermen and others who live in the Cape Ann area, there are odd bits of both natural and manmade "sea stuff" to handle and examine up close. Although the collection is continually changing, you might find huge lobster claws, a bait bag, a Russian trawl float, or a small disc issued and set afloat by our government in order to test the drift of the ocean. (If you find one of these that has floated ashore, follow the instructions printed on it and Uncle Sam will reward you with fifty cents for your contribution to the advancement of scientific knowledge.)

In another room, children can use some of the hundred-year-old shipwright's tools to try out techniques used in building fishing boats at the turn of the century. Caulking seams by hand doesn't seem too trying until you learn that a typical hundred-foot

Be sure to stick your fingers into the dried specimen of the lowly monkfish to feel how sharp its teeth are.

Children who have read Captains Courageous *will recognize Gloucester as the story's setting. This monument,* Man at the Wheel, *pays tribute to all those brave sea captains.*

schooner would have about three miles of seams to attend to! There is always a mast to shape; it's a very satisfactory feeling to see the shavings you produce with a wooden plane, even if the mast doesn't look much thinner. There is also a huge post and a hand drill that beckon children to drill holes similar to those used to accommodate the treenails (called "trunnels"), hardwood pegs used in fastening the timbers and oak ribs on the old boats. This too is fun, until you notice the sign stating that each ship required ten to fifteen thousand such holes. Imagine the sigh of relief when electric drills came into use, about 1920!

In yet another room, you can sit on comfortable carpet scraps on the floor to watch short films about the fishing industry. Although the schedule changes, you might see "41 North, 67 West," which shows the business end of the industry, including shots of the Boston fish auctions.

In the museum, there is a row of aquariums to explore. But instead of exotic sea life, these tanks present a diver's eye view of the sea life that surrounds you in *local* waters. You'll see tiny mussels and scallops, shrimp in the process of spawning, baby flounder, sea anemones, and many more fascinating specimens. Farther on, there is a real swordfish sword to spar with ("feels like wood and doesn't smell too great," as one small observer commented). Be sure to stick your fingers into the dried specimen of the lowly monkfish (poor man's lobster) to feel how sharp its teeth are.

A visit to this museum should be an unhurried excursion. It's fun any day, but really perfect for a rainy day. Part of the museum's charm lies in the friendly people who staff the place. If you are lucky, you might meet up with one of the retired fishermen who often help out. They have lots of stories to tell and enjoy answering questions, too.

The museum also sponsors special events: walking tours, whale-watching trips, craft workshops (where you can learn to make a fish net), and others. All in all, a perfect place to bring children filled with curiosity about the sea, its history, and its inhabitants.

HAMMOND CASTLE MUSEUM. As you drive along Stacy Boulevard to reach this museum, take a good look at the famous statue *Man at the Wheel*, overlooking Gloucester harbor. He stands as a symbol of the Gloucester fishing tradition, honoring the men who make their livelihood at sea. When you reach the museum, you'll see a reproduction of a twelfth-century castle — and yes, it has its own moat, parapets, and turrets, and lots of winding passages as well. The castle was built from 1926 to 1929 by inventor John Hays Hammond, Jr., to serve as both home and museum.

A prolific inventor, Hammond was responsible

for developing many diverse items such as an automatic pilot, a hair restorer, some radio-directed torpedos, and a magnetic bottle opener. Altogether, he held nearly a thousand patents, many of them in radar and radio electronics. Ultimately, however, his musical inventions contributed the most to his fantasy. As a result, the focal point of his castle is an instrument of his own making, a massive organ containing over eighty-two hundred pipes. Indeed, the castle was actually built around the organ, which spans eight stories in an eighty-five-foot tower.

Your visit to the castle takes the form of a guided tour. Most of the tour leaders are sensitive to the interests of children; they tend to pepper their talks with intriguing anecdotes as well as offering serious discussion of architectural features and the many art objects exhibited. Children are usually quite impressed with the small interior courtyard, which contains a small swimming pool. John Hammond also thoughtfully equipped the courtyard with a glass ceiling that opened up to the sky so that on a warm, clear night he could swim under the stars.

Children also might like to know that even though Hammond had loads of money to spend on his home, even he could not have everything his heart desired. One of the more outrageous ideas (he never quite managed to put it into use) had to do with the many guest rooms in the castle. He'd planned to arrange them like stage sets, with revolving walls and parts of the floors installed on turntables. With such an arrangement, an unsuspecting visitor might fall asleep in a modern room overlooking the ocean only to waken the next morning in a windowless medieval torture chamber!

At the museum, there is also a small café where you can purchase sandwiches, quiche, and salads as well as other light refreshments.

WINGAERSHEEK AND GOOD HARBOR BEACHES. Much of your time on Cape Ann is likely to be spent on the beach, and Gloucester has two that are particularly attractive. Wingaersheek Beach is a calm, sandy stretch perfect for young children. Older ones in search of body-surfing opportunities will prefer the waves at Good Harbor Beach.

Parking is severely limited at the beaches, so if you come up for the day on a weekend, plan to arrive before 11 AM to procure a parking space. If you can't park, the beaches are largely inaccessible. However, if you are staying at an area hotel or guest house, you will probably either be within walking distance of a beach or supplied with a guest parking permit (which allows you to park even when the lots are closed to nonresidents). Inquire when you make your reservation. (The situation with beach parking is similar in Rockport.)

With such an arrangement, a visitor might fall asleep in a modern room overlooking the ocean only to waken the next morning in a windowless medieval torture chamber!

ACCESS

TO GET TO GLOUCESTER. From Boston, take I-93 north exit 11 (Route 128) and follow Route 128 north to its conclusion, the Gloucester rotary. Take the first exit from the rotary, onto Washington Street, and follow to downtown Gloucester.

GLOUCESTER FISHERMENS MUSEUM. Directions: From the Gloucester rotary, follow Washington Street to the Joan of Arc statue. Turn right on Middle Street, and immediately left on Angle Street. Turn left at the arrow (onto Rogers Street), and turn left off Rogers Street to Porter Street. Museum is at the corner of Rogers and Porter streets, near the waterfront. **Season:** Year round. **Admission** charged. (617) 283-1940.

HAMMOND CASTLE MUSEUM. Directions: From the Joan of Arc statue, turn left onto Middle Street and then right onto Stacy Boulevard. Follow Stacy Boulevard, bear left onto Western Avenue, and then turn left onto Hesperus Avenue. Follow signs; museum is at 80 Hesperus Avenue. **Season:** Year round. **Admission** charged. (617) 283-2080. **Note:** There are frequent organ concerts here and other special events including programs for children. Telephone about two weeks ahead for schedule and reservation, since the demand often exceeds the supply.

WINGAERSHEEK BEACH. Directions: Take Route 128 north exit 13 (Wingaersheek) to the beach.

GOOD HARBOR BEACH. Directions: From the Gloucester rotary, take the second right, onto the Route 128 Extension. Turn left onto Eastern Avenue (at traffic light), and then right onto a nameless street after Foster's Gas Station. At the bottom of the street, turn left and go a quarter mile to the beach parking lot.

Rockport

A well-kept small town, Rockport is a lovely place to explore on foot. The on-season traffic is so thick anyhow that you will probably have to park at one of the outlying parking lots (many signs direct you to them) and take a shuttle bus into town. The bus delivers you to Dock Square, the main downtown intersection. From here, wander down Bearskin Neck (which leads directly off Dock Square), where children can climb on the rocks that extend into Rockport harbor. Remember that for rock climbing, leather shoes are treacherous. Wear sneakers; bare feet will also do.

Shops border the neck on both sides. Several of particular interest to children include The Dancing Bear (for stuffed animals), the Happy Whale (for hand-crafted wooden boats), and the Country Store (with its operable nickelodeon, hot dogs, lemonade, penny-candy counter, and souvenirs galore).

Rockport's Bearskin Neck: a great place for strollers or those in strollers.

THE TOOL COMPANY. As you proceed out of Rockport, you pass The Tool Company, on your right. The forges are generally going full-tilt on weekdays, and children are intrigued by the fact that, because of the noise, all the workers are wearing protective coverings that look like earmuffs. The factory produces many kinds of machine tools. Because of the excessive heat involved, the building is equipped with large flaps that open up in warm weather, making it very easy for slow-driving observers to sneak a peek inside.

THE PAPER HOUSE. Near The Tool Company is a sign directing you to The Paper House. As the name implies, everything here is made from paper; even the walls consist of paper — two hundred sheets thick! All the furniture is made from paper, including the piano, and close examination of the writing desk shows that it is made of newspapers, some of which feature stories about Charles Lindbergh's famous solo flights across the Atlantic. You will probably only spend ten to fifteen minutes here, but the novelty level is high.

Everything here is paper; even the walls consist of paper — two hundred sheets thick!

OLD FARM INN. While you're in the area you might wish to stop at this very popular spot for Sunday brunch (children especially like the pancakes and apple pie) as well as for dinner.

HALIBUT POINT. Administered by the Trustees of Reservations, a conservation-oriented agency, Halibut Point is the outermost tip of Cape Ann and is an ideal picnic spot. From the parking lot, you can wander about a half mile down a winding footpath lined with blueberry bushes (the berries are in season from mid-July to early August) and lots of other local foliage. You emerge from the woods to a spectacular ocean view, one often punctuated by sailboats and lobster

At low tide there is plenty of opportunity to find starfish, sea urchins, limpets, and other tiny creatures in the many tide pools.

boats. Great slabs of granite stretch out into the sea, and at low tide there is plenty of opportunity to find starfish, sea urchins, limpets, and other tiny creatures in the many tide pools. It is also rather fun and very challenging to clamber about on the rocks, to hide in nooks and crannies, and to jump from one great rock to another.

A warning or two is in order, however. The rocks become very slippery at low tide. And Halibut Point is *not* a place for swimming. The waves beat hard against the shore and the currents are extremely strong. Several drownings have occurred here because people decided to take a swim, not realizing how difficult it was to come ashore.

LOBSTER POOL. As you leave Halibut Point, you soon come to this special eating spot, on your right. Featuring picnic tables with one of the most wonderful water views we have ever had the pleasure to dine near, this very popular serve-yourself restaurant specializes in seafood plates and casseroles as well as lobsters and lobster rolls. Of course, there are hamburgers and hot dogs, too. It's all very informal; the food is served on paper plates, with plastic cutlery. There are also indoor dining areas, again taking advantage of the view. This is an excellent restaurant for children (highchairs are available), but be certain to avoid the rush hours (noon to 1:30 PM on weekends, and about 5:30 to 7 PM almost every evening). When the crowds get fierce, the wait gets long.

Families visit Cape Ann for periods lasting from a single day to a whole summer. If your brood enjoys the beach, you may wish to stay several days. There is plenty to do on a rainy day, and even a cool autumn weekend can be happily passed hiking in Dogtown (the wooded interior of the Cape where about one hundred families lived in the eighteenth century), browsing in the shops, and visiting the castle and the Fishermens Museum.

ACCESS

TO GET TO ROCKPORT. From the Gloucester rotary, take the second exit (Route 128 Extension), and turn left at the first traffic light; follow signs to Rockport.

THE TOOL COMPANY. Directions: From Rockport, take Route 127 (Granite Street) toward Pigeon Cove; the Tool Company is about a mile and a half out of town, on your right, at Curtis Street.

THE PAPER HOUSE. Directions: From The Tool Company (on Route 127), take Curtis Street about a half mile to The Paper House, following signs. **Season:** Memorial Day through Columbus Day. **Admission** charged.

OLD FARM INN. Directions: From The Paper House, continue one mile farther on Route 127 to Gott Avenue and the inn. **Season:** Spring through fall. (617) 546-3237.

HALIBUT POINT. Directions: From Route 127 heading toward Gloucester, turn right at the Old Farm Inn onto Gott Avenue; visitors' parking lot is immediately ahead.

LOBSTER POOL. Directions: From Route 127 heading toward Gloucester, continue a half mile beyond Halibut Point to the Lobster Pool, on your right. **Season:** May through October. (617) 546-9471.

COURTESY CHILDREN'S MUSEUM/STEVE ROSENTHAL

You remove your shoes (of course) to enter the Japanese House in Boston's Children's Museum.

Boston

Don't bring lazy children to Boston! Youngsters who visit the home of the bean and the cod have a full schedule ahead of them. During their stay they may make a TV appearance or two, match wits with a computer, eat an oyster, and become political activists. A lively city for visitors of all ages, Boston provides an opportunity to explore past, present, and future. Here you can tune in to the Boston Tea Party and space exploration, the Freedom Trail and Fenway Park, and much, much more.

MUSEUM WHARF. This area is the city's newest family attraction. Located in downtown Boston near the financial district, this complex is the home of the Children's Museum and the Museum of Transporta-

Begin with a visit to the Children's Museum, at 300 Congress Street.

tion. Housed in a massive renovated warehouse overlooking a small corner of Boston harbor, the two museums share a lobby and gift shop, but beyond that they operate independently.

CHILDREN'S MUSEUM. A visit to this amazing establishment starts with the Giant's Desktop, where there is an oversized push-button telephone to climb aboard, huge sunglasses (much too big to lift up) to peer through, and a coffee cup to hide in. Toddlers quickly discover the nearby Playspace, a protected area where they can play without fear of attack from the "big kids." There is a castle to explore, with ramps, a slide, a lookout tower, private compartments, and caves underneath. The carpeted "moat" is filled with playthings and partially encircled by a wall of mirrors.

By this point you have probably realized that this is a museum where children are encouraged to touch, to try on or try out, to really get involved with the exhibits. In Grandparents' House, a Victorian home with a full-sized kitchen, a parlor, an attic, and a basement workshop, there is some fine turn-of-the-century clothing to wear. In What If You Couldn't?, an exhibit focusing on what it feels like to be handicapped, there is a wheelchair to manipulate (just try angling it up to the telephone booth), various prostheses to strap on, and a braille typewriter and Monopoly game to try out.

Up at Station WKID, children can turn themselves into instant celebrities via closed-circuit TV cameras. If they are ardent cartoon fans, they might enjoy making drawings and animating them on a zoetrope carousel.

Work is a network of exhibits encouraging the development of children's insights into different areas of the world of work through role-playing. Here a child may be a doctor or dentist in the Health Care Center, interview a prospective employee in the personnel office, or try out his skills as a cashier in the Congress Street Superette. Downstairs, children can learn firsthand about the realities of automation as they put in a shift on the assembly line and turn out spinning tops — to take home, naturally.

On the Giant's Desktop, there is an oversized push-button telephone to climb aboard, huge sunglasses to peer through, and even a coffee cup to hide in.

Another popular exhibit is the Ruth Harmony Green Hall of Toys, which is filled with antique toys and doll houses, the latter exquisitely furnished and protected by Plexiglas so that you don't have to worry about warning the children not to touch. Then there's the computer area, where a child can learn about these incredible machines by competing with them in games such as Tic-Tac-Toe, Hunt the Wumpus, and Inchworm.

The only part of the museum where you may want to keep an eye on young children is in the Japanese Home, a genuine two-story artist's house and shop imported from Kyoto and assembled here by skilled Japanese craftspeople in the traditional manner. You visit the house via a guided tour that takes about twenty minutes. (The staff is used to having babies along.) You take off your shoes before entering the house, of course. In addition to the bathroom, kitchen, and living and working areas, you may also see an exhibit on making noodles, tatami (mats), shoji (paper screens), or kites.

Plan to allow at least half a day for your visit to the Children's Museum. If at all possible, avoid weekend visits, when the museum often becomes unpleasantly crowded. It isn't much fun to wait in line for a quarter hour to spend two minutes at a computer, and it is annoying to have someone hankering after your plastic fruit in the superette when you haven't even had a chance to weigh it. If you must go on a weekend, by all means go early.

Are your teenagers somewhat reluctant to visit a "children's" museum? Then tell them about "Detours," a new museum-based program that provides area trip planning advice specifically geared to the interests of eleven-to-sixteen-year-olds. Membership costs five dollars a year, but is a worthwhile investment even if you only plan to be in town for a few days. "Detours" members receive complimentary MBTA tokens for use in Boston's public transportation system, an illustrated map of the city's major transportation lines, thirty dollars worth of free or discount admissions to Boston's museums and attractions, and a set of ten printed tour guides that cover themes such as sports, food, art, fashion, music, and work — all of particular interest to teenagers. They discover instructions for taking a self-guided roller skating tour as well as directions on finding a suburban shop featuring old baseball cards and other sports memorabilia.

Housed in a red and yellow 1954 city bus, "Detours" gets around. For further information, or to make certain the roving headquarters will be accessible when you plan to visit, call (617) 426-6500.

MUSEUM OF TRANSPORTATION. As a fitting introduction to this fascinating place, travel to its upper story in a glass-enclosed freight elevator that climbs up the exterior wall of the warehouse and provides a fine bird's-eye view of the waterfront. The major exhibit inside is Boston/A City in Transit, which traces the city's history from 1630 to the present by focusing on the development of transportation technologies and showing you how goods, people, and ideas are moved from one place to another. It's fun to start your tour by walking through the re-created hold of the good ship *Arabella*, which carried Boston's original settlers. Then wander through notorious Scollay Square, re-created to be as it was in 1895, before making a stop at a 1930s-style Howard Johnson's. Your head will be spinning and your sense of time challenged by the time you reach the container unit of a contemporary cargo ship.

The feeling of each time period represented is enhanced through the use of multimedia shows,

A child may be a dentist in the Health Care Center, interview a prospective employee in the personnel office, or try out his skills as a cashier in the Congress Street Superette.

Go next door to the Museum of Transportation.

Children always enjoy taking turns at the controls of a full-sized mockup of a Boston elevated railway car.

appropriate building facades, vehicles, and even road-paving materials. There are artifacts, such as the century-old high-wheeler bicycle you can pedal yourself, that invite visitor participation. Children also enjoy taking a turn at the controls of a full-sized mockup of a Boston elevated railway car.

However, the big action for children is on the lower level, in the Crossroads Hands-On Center. Here one young chap slides down a fire pole and rushes toward a nearby fire engine, stumbling along in full-sized fire-fighting regalia. Nearby, his companion sweats from exertion as he activates the hand-operated fire pump.

In another area, children can work as employees on the Model T assembly line, using a system of templates and work stations to create scale drawings of that fine old vehicle. There's also a tugboat bridge and radar-radio room to explore, a sailboat to climb on, and a vintage taxicab to settle into. The do-it-yourself hovercraft has long been a favorite attraction, but the recently installed aerial gondola is providing a formidable rival.

While at Museum Wharf, don't forget to visit the museum gift shop, off the lobby. Stuffed to the gills with toys — some imported, some educational, some hand crafted, and some just plain fun — this is far more than a souvenir shop. The more expensive items are in a room separate from that housing the less costly ones, making it easy to point a child in the appropriate direction. You can visit the fast-food eatery in the same building, or you can purchase salads, fruit cups, yogurt sundaes, and oversized cookies at the refreshment stand housed in the huge wooden milk bottle outside, on the wharf. An old piece of Hood Milk Company memorabilia, this giant bottle now serves as the Museum Wharf logo.

BOSTON TEA PARTY MUSEUM. At this famous home of dramatized Boston history, travel back in time to that famous day in 1773 when angry patriots gathered at the Green Dragon Tavern shouting, "Rally, Mohawks! Bring out your axes! And tell King George we'll pay no more taxes!" At the Old South Meeting House later the same day, Sam Adams told the band of patriots, "This meeting can do nothing more to save the country." But within an hour, a small, very determined band of Bostonians made their way down Milk Street towards Griffin's Wharf. Disguised as Indians, their faces darkened with shoe polish and their bodies wrapped in blankets, they boarded the brig *Beaver II* in Boston harbor. And so began the Boston Tea Party.

At the museum, you and your children learn about the events leading up to this famous act of protest. You find, for instance, that there are many myths about the tea party, such as the common misconception that the patriots hefted chests of tea over their shoulders and into the briny water below. Actually,

Go just a few steps to the right from Museum Wharf to the Boston Tea Party Museum, next to the Congress Street Bridge.

Playing patriot at the Boston Tea Party Museum.

"Rally, Mohawks! Bring out your axes! And tell King George we'll pay no more taxes!"

this would have been rather difficult, since the chests were lined with lead and weighed about four hundred pounds each. It appears likely that the patriots did a lot more chopping than hefting, first smashing the chests open and then dumping the hundred thousand pounds of tea into the brink.

Most children have a good time here, clambering up and down steep steps and ladders and over the deck of the ship to the accompaniment of piped-in fife-and-drum music. There are slide shows, a tea exhibit, a collection of shipbuilding tools, and a push-button map illuminating Boston in 1773. Aboard the *Beaver II*, a guide serves cups of hot tea, while children enjoy tossing the imitation tea chest into the brink. It's fun to wait for the inevitable splash, particularly when you know that since the chest is secured to the deck by a sturdy rope, you can always pull it back up and throw it in again.

Be sure to get a museum brochure. It contains a quiz to help you determine whether your politics fall predominantly with the patriots or with the loyalists. One ten-year-old who took the test emerged as either a liberal loyalist or a conservative patriot, depending upon how you interpret the official designation "middle-of-the-roader." There is a series of statements to agree with ("strongly" or "somewhat"), or disagree with ("strongly" or "somewhat"). Statements such as this, for instance, appear: "Government is more often the enemy than the friend of liberty."

By now you have probably had your fill of sightseeing, yet you have only just begun to uncover the city's treasures. Boston has several lovely hotels to choose from, but they can put a formidable dent in the family budget. If you're watching your pennies, consider renting a room through New England Bed & Breakfast (1045 Centre Street, Newton, MA 02159; 617-244-2112). You will be placed in a private home in the greater-Boston area, within walking distance of public transportation if you so request. The rates vary,

Children enjoy tossing the imitation tea chest into the brink.

but you will probably pay about half what a major hotel charges.

WATERFRONT PARK. The Museum Wharf museums are fun to explore even in the worst weather, but other parts of the waterfront area are best saved for a bright, sunny day. Waterfront Park has a play area featuring a crow's nest and ropes to swing from. This is a good spot from which to watch the boats go by; it's also a perfect spot for a picnic. You can pick up the fixings a few blocks away at Faneuil Hall.

FANEUIL HALL MARKETPLACE. An immense indoor/outdoor spread of shops and pushcarts, Faneuil Hall Marketplace is dominated by the long central building that formerly served as the heart of the city's wholesale food market, and also includes North Market and South Market — each with lots for children to explore. Now made up of dozens of chic shops and restaurants, this market area, many maintain, has the best take-out food in town. You can choose baklava, goose-liver pâté, or fresh oysters while the children select pizza, Chinese food, fresh fruit cups, and fried dough — to name only a few possibilities. Prices are steep, so consider carefully before asking for a half dozen butterscotch brownie bars; you may decide you can make do with four.

You can choose baklava, goose-liver pâté, or fresh oysters while the children select pizza, Chinese food, fresh fruit cups, and fried dough.

A particularly popular place on warm afternoons, this is where the people who work in the nearby government buildings come to eat lunch. On weekends, the market becomes even more crowded. We would suggest that you avoid Saturdays and Sundays altogether, except that street entertainers are out in full force on weekends and are worth battling the crowds for. Most children find the entertainers as big a drawing card as the edibles. On a recent Sunday, we watched a clown magician perform tricks, we put a dime in the organ grinder's monkey's tin cup (if you give him a penny he throws it back in disgust), we listened to a pair of folk singers, and we grimaced as a sword swallower forced a blade down his gaping throat. Remember, the entertainers are paid solely through contributions, so it seems only right to give a little when they pass the hat.

DURGIN-PARK. If you want to sit down for a proper meal, go to Durgin-Park, or the Market Dining Rooms as it is sometimes called. Founded in 1827, Durgin-Park is best known for its gruff waitresses and generous portions. You might be seated at an individual table, but more often you are placed at a long table along with lots of strangers. Everyone starts off with a plate of homemade corn bread, but after that you make your own decisions.

Durgin-Park is best known for its gruff waitresses and generous portions.

Here you can choose from a huge assortment of homecooked goodies; special features are such old New England standbys as Yankee pot roast, frankfurts and beans, oyster stew, and Boston fried cod. Of course, there are fried chicken, chops, and great chunks of roast beef, too. Apple pandowdy and Indian pudding with ice cream are good choices for dessert, but conservative children may wish to opt for hot fudge sundaes.

The menu brags that the restaurant was "Established Before You Were Born," and this is not difficult to believe. The cooking area is in the midst of the dining rooms, and the cooks and waitresses are a high-pitched lot. The pace is quick and you need to be aggressive to get what you want, but that's part of the fun. It doesn't matter a bit if a young one topples over a glass of water or wails on occasion. You don't need to dress up to go to Durgin-Park. Just bring cash (no personal checks, no credit cards, and no reservations) and a hearty appetite. There are highchairs available. Aim for the off-hours to avoid the crowds.

WATER PARK. Now that we have lunch under control, let's get back to the waterfront. Your visit begins with a stroll through Water Park, on the plaza in front of the New England Aquarium. It is a place to relax on a warm day, a place to enjoy the sights and sounds of water. There are cascading pools and, best of all, a series of steps leading down to the deepest pool. What a wonderful place to dangle hot, sticky feet on a steamy day! You can look at a lovely bronze sculpture, *Dolphins of the Sea*, and a pool full of frisky harbor seals who love to perform spontaneously for your entertainment. You'll find a refreshment stand and usually a couple of vendors, too, making this a good place for snacks or a casual lunch if you haven't wished to take on Durgin-Park.

NEW ENGLAND AQUARIUM. The large building for this, the major attraction on the waterfront, was designed so that the only light inside comes from within the exhibits and displays. As you wander along, you soon feel as though you are traveling beneath the surface of the sea. The aquarium features the largest circular glass-enclosed tank in the world. It's exciting to travel up a four-story-high tank, watching the sea turtles, sharks, moray eels, and other creatures pass by.

There are seventy other tanks too, housing a total of more than seven thousand fresh water and saltwater fish. You meet Siamese fighting fish, catfish, seahorses, and shovelnose sturgeons, to name just a few. Did you know that an eel can produce more than six hundred volts of electricity? Or that the color of an octopus varies with its mood? (Honestly now, did you even know that an octopus *had* moods?)

Don't miss the Tidal Pool on the third level; here children can reach into the water to scoop up sea urchins, horseshoe crabs, starfish, and other cooperative creatures. They are likely to get quite wet in the process, but that's all part of the action.

Next, head on over to the floating pavilion *Discov-*

Street entertainers step to a different beat at Faneuil Hall Marketplace.

Did you know that the color of an octopus varies with its mood? (Honestly now, did you even know that an octopus had *moods?)*

There are no bad seats in the house, but if you sit down front, be prepared to get rather completely splashed!

ery to see the forty-five-minute sea-lion and dolphin show. There are three performances a day and no charge other than regular aquarium admission. Orange bleachers stretch up either side of the *Discovery*, separated by a forty-five by thirty-five-foot swimming pool some fifteen feet deep. There are no bad seats in the house, but if you choose to sit down front, be prepared to get rather completely splashed! There is a small stage at one end of the pool, but most of the activity takes place in the water itself, which is filtered in from Boston harbor.

The performance begins with a movie centering on the characteristics and habits of sea lions and dolphins. Then, from a door below the surface of the water, watch for the stars of the show! If Merlin and Deacon don't steal your heart away, Kathy, Apollo, and Dixie are sure to do it.

Merlin and Deacon are sea lions who like to retrieve colored hoops, balance beach balls on their noses, play catch, and show their appreciation of their own antics by clapping enthusiastically. They are followed by Kathy, Apollo, and Dixie, the three Atlantic bottlenose dolphins, considerably larger animals. We learn that the dolphin, like the sea lion, is a mammal, and that it uses the blow hole on top of its head for sound production as well as breathing. To show us how strong and smart they are, these animals travel rapidly across the pool balancing on their powerful tails, three-quarters of their bodies above the water surface. This aquatic trio also specializes in synchronized jumping.

MUSEUM OF SCIENCE. Like the aquarium, this outstanding museum has plenty of interesting exhibits for all ages: even the toddlers, especially the teenagers. There are over three hundred displays, some of them permanent and others just visiting. Sometimes the simpler displays make a real impact; for instance, there's the one on jogging that tells us that a typical child's feet move about a thousand tons of cumulative weight per day! And, if you think the moon is far away, consider this: in a normal life span, each one of us will walk a distance equal to the moon and back. . . .

Very young children are usually quite enchanted by the museum's twenty-foot-tall Tyrannosaurus Rex model, a spritely greenish fellow who has been known to sport a long red and white scarf in cold weather. They also like the hourly live-animal demonstrations, during which they become acquainted with museum regulars like Spooky the Owl.

In the Wright Medical Theater, the Transparent Woman explains how her body functions. Nearby, the Van de Graaf generator is put through its paces several times a day. There is also a planetarium to visit (small admission charge; children under five not admitted). When you arrive at the museum, ask when the next

STEVEN P. JOHNSON

Very young children are enchanted by the Museum of Science's twenty-foot-tall Tyrannosaurus Rex.

planetarium show is and purchase your tickets right away. Be certain you are on time to the show; late-comers are absolutely not admitted because opening the doors lets in light and ruins the show.

Throughout the museum, there are buttons to push, knobs to turn, tests to take, and even things to climb. A major hands-on attraction for all ages is the huge TV synthesizer in a display called How TV Works. Your child might station herself in front of the console, facing a wall of TV screens. There she can experiment with different methods of producing special effects. She might decide to turn her brother green by "colorizing" his image. Or perhaps she turns herself into a ghost by combining two images and dissolving between them. Then her brother takes a turn. He decides to "warp" himself. Really. This means he uses the sweep modulator to control the way his image is swept off the screen. Or, if he is tired of black and white, he might choose "negatizing." This technique reverses color, giving him white and black TV.

Other popular exhibits include the hot-air balloon, which rises to the ceiling as the heated air inside expands and its density decreases; the Giant Egg, where baby chicks peck their way out of their shells; and the giant wave machine. There are lots of computers to experiment with, too.

There is a cafeteria and a fast-food shop in the museum. The gift shop off the main lobby has an extensive selection of scientific-experiment kits and science artifacts, seashells, and books. If you are counting your pennies, steer your children instead in the direction of the small souvenir counter located to the left of the main entrance, where you can find lots of items priced below a dollar.

PUBLIC GARDEN. For a change of pace, visit the park area across Charles Street from Boston Common, and make the acquaintance of the great, great, great grandchildren of Jack, Kack, Lack, Mack, Nack, Ouack, Pack, and Quack, themselves born to their famous parents, Mr. and Mrs. Mallard, back in 1941. That was the year that Robert McCloskey first published his now-classic *Make Way for Ducklings*, the heart-warming saga of a young duck couple out to find a proper Boston neighborhood in which to raise their family. And find it they did.

In late April each year, the Public Garden undergoes a metamorphosis. The Swan Boats come out of storage and the garden comes to life. All around, the trees are coming into bud; enjoy the goldenleaf elm, the common linden, a dogwood, a cherry. But beware the joggers, skateboarders, bicycles, and roller skaters. Beware the stray Frisbee.

The Swan Boats have cruised the waters of the Public Garden for over a hundred years, and they haven't changed much in that time. Painted bright green with touches of red, each boat consists of a plat-

The display on jogging says a typical child's feet move about a thousand tons of cumulative weight per day!

Bring along popcorn, available from a vendor, and try to make sure children sit on the outside so they can feed the ducks, rock doves, and grackles that crowd about.

form built on two pontoon-like structures with pointed tips that tilt upward at both ends. There are varnished benches on top. Perched at the rear of each vessel is its eponym, a great white swan made of metal. Sitting between her wings, the captain propels the boat by means of pedals. You glide across the pond, past the weeping willows and under the Public Garden footbridge (constructed in 1867, it is the smallest suspension bridge in the world), and then around the island where the Mallard couple nested.

Each boat holds thirty-five people and the ride lasts ten to fifteen minutes. Bring along popcorn, available from a vendor, and try to make sure children sit on the outside so they can feed the ducks, rock doves, and grackles that crowd about.

At one end of the pond, you see a small gazebo-like structure; your children will probably wonder why it is there. We thought it was a nesting station, but a little research proved us wrong. The gazebo houses the plug. "The plug?" you ask. Yes, the plug — and the drain, the place where the water runs out. The truth is that the pond is a manmade structure, with little natural water motion. In order then to keep it clean and attractive, the city drains the whole area twice a year and scrapes the litter from the bottom. If you have a child who is still uncomfortably close to the age where he worries about being sucked down the bathtub drain, don't tell him about the plug. (You might, however, like to store the knowledge away as a truly original threat for one of those sweaty summer days when everyone is in a bad mood.)

Like Faneuil Hall Marketplace, the Public Garden is popular with street entertainers, so be sure to plan a leisurely visit.

ACCESS

TO GET TO BOSTON. From the north, head south on I-93. From the south, head north on Route 3 (which becomes I-93). From the west, head east on I-90 (Massachusetts Turnpike) to I-93, then head north on I-93.

TO GET TO MUSEUM WHARF. From the north, take I-93 south to High Street/Congress Street exit. Take the third left, onto Congress Street, and follow signs. From the west, take I-90 east to Expressway (I-93) and follow Expressway north to Atlantic Avenue/Northern Avenue exit. From the exit, turn right and cross Northern Avenue bridge, then turn right onto Sleeper Street and follow signs with milk-bottle logo. By Boston MBTA: Take the red line to South Station. **Note:** A large parking garage is nearby; watch for signs.

CHILDREN'S MUSEUM AND MUSEUM OF TRANSPORTATION. Directions: The two museums are located next to each other, at 300 Congress Street.

Seasons: Year round. **Admission** charged. Children's Museum: (617) 426-8855. Museum of Transportation: (617) 426-6633, or 426-7999.

BOSTON TEA PARTY MUSEUM. Directions: Located next to Congress Street Bridge, a short distance from Museum Wharf. **Season:** Year round. **Admission** charged. (617) 338-1773.

WATERFRONT PARK AND NEW ENGLAND AQUARIUM. Directions: Follow Northern Avenue/ Atlantic Avenue to Central Wharf, on your right as you head north. The aquarium is at Central Wharf, next to Waterfront Park at the foot of State Street. By Boston MBTA: Take the blue line to Aquarium station. **Season:** Year round. **Admission** charged to aquarium. Aquarium: (617) 742-8870. **Note:** Parking is available in a garage opposite the aquarium.

FANEUIL HALL MARKETPLACE. Directions: From aquarium parking garage, walk along State Street away from the harbor, passing under the expressway. Turn right onto Commercial Street, and walk a short distance to Quincy Market (North Market, which houses Durgin-Park, is to the right). Or, take I-93 Callahan Tunnel/Dock Square exit, and park in any of the nearby garages. By Boston MBTA: Take the green line to Government Center station. Marketplace: (617) 523-2980. Durgin-Park: (617) 227-2038.

MUSEUM OF SCIENCE. Directions: Located at Science Park, off Monsignor O'Brien Highway. By Boston MBTA: Take the green line to Science Park station. **Season:** Year round. **Admission** charged. (617) 742-6088, or (617) 723-2500.

PUBLIC GARDEN. Directions: From the Museum of Transportation, head toward downtown Boston on the Longfellow Bridge, and enter the rotary. Exit right onto Charles Street, and go five blocks to the Public Garden. By Boston MBTA: Take the green line to Arlington station. **Season:** Year round. **Admission** charged to Swan Boats. **Note:** The Swan Boats operate spring through fall, but do not operate in poor weather.

Charlestown

USS *CONSTITUTION.* Travel to the Charlestown Naval Shipyard by car or MBTA for a visit to the oldest commissioned warship afloat anywhere in the world. Her proper name is the United States Ship *Constitution,* but once you get to know her you will want to call her "Old Ironsides." First launched in 1797 at the tremendous expense of $302,718, she was equipped to carry some eight thousand gallons of rum along with her crew and other provisions.

Your visit is guided by a young Navy man dressed

Children enjoy scuttling down the ladder-like steps to the lower decks, grabbing the rope handrails for balance.

The floor is painted red because sailors were very superstitious about the sight of their own blood. This way, it would just blend in with the color of the floorboards.

in sailor's garb of the early 1800s. He takes you past cannons with names like Sweet Sue and Raging Eagle as you stroll the main deck. Up in the bow, children will be fascinated by the "head," which consists of a long board with holes cut out, three in a row. Peering down through a hole, you see the sea. So much for plumbing.

Children also enjoy scuttling down the ladder-like steps, grabbing the rope handrails for balance, to the lower decks. The purser's quarters are particularly interesting. Because the purser needed a desk in his room, there was no room for a bed. Each night, therefore, he would open his desk and toss a mattress on it.

The surgeon's quarters are also intriguing. Your guide explains that the floor is painted red because sailors were very superstitious about the sight of their own blood. This way, it would just blend in with the color of the floorboards. "Back then," the trusty guide explains further, "if a surgeon was good he could cut off an arm or a leg, burn the end, and put tar on it in about thirty seconds."

Nevertheless, some of the children aboard are right ready to sign up for a tour of duty when they hear about the powder monkeys, young boys who passed buckets of gunpowder from the powder magazine to the upper decks in times of combat. In the old days, children were indeed chosen for this task because they were fast, short, and nimble — in other words, monkey-like! A tour of the ship takes less than thirty minutes.

USS CONSTITUTION MUSEUM. Round out your visit by dropping in at this nearby museum, located directly across the parking lot from the ship. Your visit here begins with a fifteen-minute sound-and-slide show focusing on life at sea in the 1800s, and includes stories about Old Ironsides' many victorious confrontations. There are also collections of equipment used by sailors; children can examine handguns, muskets, cutlasses, boarding pikes, and the like.

For most children, the best part of the museum is the rigging, which they are welcome to climb.

For most children, the best part of the museum is the rigging, which they are welcome to climb. They can't go very high but at least they can get the feel of it. There are hammocks to try out, too, and a knot-tying setup, where they can try their hands at whipping up a "bowline," "clove hitch" or "fishermen's bend."

ACCESS _____

TO GET TO CHARLESTOWN. From I-93, take the Northeast Expressway.

USS CONSTITUTION. Directions: From Charlestown City Square, follow the red Freedom Trail signs on Constitution Road to the naval yard. By Boston MBTA: Take the green line to Haymarket station, or bus 92, 93, or 111 to Charlestown City Square; follow red Freedom Trail signs to the naval yard. **Season:**

Some of the youngest visitors like this old-timer the best. It's the USS Constitution.

Year round. **Admission** free.

USS CONSTITUTION MUSEUM. Directions: The museum is located directly across the parking lot from the ship. **Season:** Year round. **Admission** charged. (617) 426-1812.

Dorchester

JOHN F. KENNEDY LIBRARY. For a more contemporary experience, do take a trip out to the elegant new facility at Columbia Point. While parents wander through the nine-room exhibit area, children from seven to eleven years of age can participate in Kids' Caucus, a special program designed to explain the American political system to them. The ninety-minute sessions are held from 11:30 AM to 1 PM on Saturdays and Sundays; a reservation is required. There is no fee except for regular admission.

Although the program changes, a recent caucus focusing on taxes is representative of the sort of experience you can expect here. Children learn why we pay taxes, who spends them, and what they are spent on. They watch an animated film on the subject and then participate in a mock town-budget meeting. A mini-tour of the museum is also included in the program. Older children might enjoy the video tapes, particularly "The President and the Press," showing both humorous and historic moments of real press-conference footage. Also, the biographical film *John F. Kennedy, 1917-1963,* is shown continually.

Children learn why we pay taxes, who spends them, and what they are spent on.

KEN WEEDEN

While visiting the John F. Kennedy Library, young ones learn how local government actually works.

ACCESS _____

JOHN F. KENNEDY LIBRARY. Directions: From Boston, take the Southeast Expressway exit 17 to Morrissey Boulevard and the University of Massachusetts in Dorchester; signs point the way to the library. **Season:** Year round. **Admission** charged. (617) 929-4523.

Framingham

MACOMBER FARM. It's now time for you and your children to visit a farm like none you have ever visited before. The Massachusetts Society for the Prevention of Cruelty to Animals has created an excellent educational center, where visitors learn about the needs of various farm animals by becoming acquainted with their physical characteristics and patterns of behavior. Because each year thousands of people mistreat their pets, mostly out of ignorance rather than malice, the exhibits at Macomber Farm are designed to help animal owners to realize what is meant by good and thoughtful animal care.

The creatures who call this farm home are indeed among the most fortunate members of the animal kingdom. The care they are given is intended to serve as an example of the very best ways in which to meet an animal's requirements. Indeed, the stalls are so clean that sometimes you even forget that you are on a farm. Here you find the typical farm animals, but instead of one type of horse or cow there are members of many different breeds. In the horse barn, for example, you meet a standardbred, an Arabian, an appaloosa, a saddlebred, and a pinto, to name just a few.

There are six different barns to visit; you also see animals out to pasture and waterfowl enjoying the ponds. If the animals are feeling sociable, they come to the fence to have their muzzles scratched. In addition, many demonstrations are held each day, during which visitors can become acquainted with pigs or poultry, learn to draw animals, see sheepshearing, or watch horses work under harness. In the cattle barn, you can watch a milking demonstration carried on by the most modern machinery.

Actually, there is a lot more than just milking going on in the cattle barn. If you unhook that earphone from the milk can over there, you can tune in on the soundtrack accompanying an overhead video tape showing the birth of a calf. Or you can join in on a round of Getting the Milk to Market, a game designed to illustrate how milk is produced and how it reaches the consumer. To play the game, you must navigate a set of yellow balls (symbolizing sunshine) and white balls (for milk) through a series of hazards ("farmer doesn't keep bedding clean," "government doesn't help small and large dairy farmers to survive") by tilting a series of panels, avoiding holes. The idea is to use sunshine to provide feed to help the cow produce milk, and then deliver the milk to the breakfast table as efficiently as possible. There are twelve work stations, so cooperation is a big part of the game.

There are other games at the farm, most of which are also designed to solve problems or illustrate concepts of animal behavior. For example, by manipulating laser markers on an electronic game board, you learn how cattle rely on certain rules of dominance as they follow a leader from barn to pasture, pasture to water. The existence of a set pecking order among chickens is illustrated by a similar game.

In the goat barn you find old-fashioned moving-picture machines called zoetropes, which you can crank up in order to watch the various ways in which goats move. But you can become even more intimately involved with the animals. Instead of just looking, it's really fun to feel what it is like to be a horse, cow, goat, pig, or chicken through role playing. There are displays called "I'm seeing like a . . ." (fill in with the animal of your choice), in which you look through the viewer to see how a particular animal perceives the world around him. You discover that cows don't have very acute sight but that they have nearly a 360° field of vision. And you find that a sheep's vision is blurrier than ours, but that he can see quite well at night; a pig, however, has difficulty seeing after dark.

There are also many ramps that encourage children to match an animal stride for stride. By stepping in a horse's footprints, you discover that the hind foot lands almost exactly in the footprint made by the front foot. Or, you may discover that while a chicken has a walking style similar to that of a person, the chicken averages an eight-inch step while the person averages an eighteen-inch step. Do you know just how much strength is required of a horse to pull a milk cart or a covered wagon? You can learn by trying to pull a facsimile cart or wagon of the same type. And in the horse barn, you can run on a conveyor belt and watch your image projected on a video screen overhead next to a film of a running horse. How does your gait compare to that of the graceful equine?

Elsewhere, there are some fascinating computer games that focus on animal body language. Children may stand at a terminal and try their luck at interpreting questions about animal gestures: What does it mean when a horse flattens his ears back or curls his upper lip? What is a chicken really saying when she turns her back on her flock? There are also other computer terminals where you can tune in for either a simple or an in-depth explanation of the habits of a particular type of animal.

In the swine barn, there are levers to pull and

It's really fun to feel what it is like to be a horse, cow, goat, pig, or chicken through role playing.

Do you know just how much strength is required of a horse to pull a milk cart or a covered wagon? You can learn by trying to pull a facsimile cart or wagon of the same type.

Children at Macomber Farm find out that pigs are some of the very cleanest of animals.

wheels to turn as you unscramble words to form an informative statement about, say, pig behavior. It turns out that pigs are probably the most intelligent and the cleanest animals on the farm. They also have a fine sense of smell; you can learn more about what it is like to rely heavily on your own sense of smell by trying to navigate the scent maze outside the swine barn. Here you choose a particular aroma, perhaps wintergreen or peppermint, and try to follow it as you sniff your way through a field of brightly colored metal tubes that look like candy sticks. You learn that other animals depend strongly upon their sense of hearing; you can put yourself in their place by trying out the sound maze, where you must follow a particular animal's "voice" through another field of colored metal tubes.

There is so much to do at Macomber Farm that you need to be careful not to become so involved with the special effects that you forget to enjoy the real live animals. One way to encourage children to pay attention to the animals as well as to the games is to give each one a copy of the "Today's Activities" folder and map that you are presented with on arrival. It contains a simple scavenger hunt that sets them thinking as they run off to enjoy the farm; they have to find items such as: "lots of combs and no brushes" and "a sweater waiting to happen."

This is an extensive facility; you should plan to spend at least half a day. Let your children roam on

What is a chicken really saying when she turns her back on her flock?

their own; encourage them to ask questions of the many staff members, but also arrange to get together with them to play some of the games. An adult's patience is required to really get involved with some of these, as there are rules to be learned and help to be given in identifying the concept that the game is meant to illustrate.

The Macomber Farm is one of those rare spots that meets the needs of toddlers to teenagers. Be sure to take along a picnic, or plan to purchase lunch at the snack bar; in any case, look forward to a lovely day at the cleanest farm you are ever likely to come across.

ACCESS

MACOMBER FARM. Directions: Take I-90 (Massachusetts Turnpike) exit 13 (Route 30), and follow signs to Framingham. From Framingham, take Route 9 west; turn left onto Temple Street, and then right onto Salem End Road. The farm entrance is on your left, at 450 Salem End Road. **Season:** May through October. **Admission** charged. (617) 879-5345.

Plymouth

Mention Plymouth and your children will probably inform you that that is where the Pilgrims lived and that the Pilgrims invented Thanksgiving. Award partial credit. Yes, indeed, the Pilgrims did establish their original settlement here, stepping ashore at famous Plymouth Rock in December of 1620 after more than two months at sea in an overcrowded vessel, the *Mayflower*. But no, the Pilgrims did not invent Thanksgiving, the uniquely American holiday we enjoy each November.

Children may be interested to find out that our contemporary Thanksgiving celebration is rooted in three early New England traditions. Of course, the Pilgrims did prepare a feast and participate in sports and other merriment after their first successful harvest in 1621. But they also held solemn religious observances combining feasting and praying at any time of the year when events merited them; such an occasion, a day set aside to praise God, was to the early New Englanders a genuine day of thanksgiving, in contrast to the harvest-home celebration. Thus, the Pilgrims did not celebrate Thanksgiving each November; when they had a good harvest they celebrated, and when they didn't, they let a year or two or more pass without ceremony. Then, just before the Revolutionary War, interest in the Pilgrims as historical figures began to blossom, resulting in the observance of Forefathers' Day in Plymouth and several other cities; it was held on December 21st in celebration of the anniversary of the Pilgrims' arrival.

From Route 3, take the exit marked "Plimoth Plantation Highway"; the plantation is about three miles south of the center of Plymouth.

Intended as a very serious, semireligious occasion reminiscent of the early days of thanksgiving, the first national Thanksgiving was proclaimed by the Continental Congress in 1777. However, as the years passed, nineteenth-century artists, musicians, and writers began to focus on the 1621 harvest-home celebration instead of the landing of the Pilgrims; finally the harvest feast was transformed into what we now commonly accept as "the First Thanksgiving," a symbol of the Pilgrim experience.

A visit to Plymouth corrects popular myths and at the same time deepens our understanding of the people who first settled here. We begin to gain insight into their trials and tribulations as well as their pleasures and accomplishments.

PLIMOTH PLANTATION. The major attraction in Plymouth, Plimoth Plantation, unlike other "living villages" where history is brought to life in the present, is a re-creation rather than a restoration. The buildings that housed the settlers three hundred fifty years ago no longer exist. Instead of rebuilding the old buildings, staff members reproduced the buildings in their original style. It didn't make sense to furnish the "brand new" old houses with fragile antiques that needed to be protected, so village administrators decided to replace their antiques with reproductions. This decision had an important result: the plantation is completely accessible. There are no "do not touch" signs and no strings across the chairs. Instead of feeling that he is in a museum, a young visitor can begin to feel as though he is strolling through a real village.

Plimoth Plantation presents an historically accurate picture of seventeenth-century life. In this fortified village, men, women, and sometimes even children go about their daily tasks, the specific chores that vary according to the time of year. Like all farming communities, Plimoth Plantation follows the seasonal cycle. If you visit in the spring, you see the settlers planting their gardens. In the late summer they are busy harvesting their crops, and in the fall they busy themselves with preparations for the long, cold winter ahead. The settlers are dressed in period costume, but you soon discover that they differ from the costumed guides you may have met at other restorations or living villages.

Instead of leading visitors on tours of the plantation, the people who work here simply go about their routines, thatching roofs, fertilizing the fields, preparing herbal remedies, building fences, tending livestock, cooking meals, or baking in the communal oven. They practice an unusual technique known as "first-person interpretation." Instead of just pretending that they lived in the seventeenth century, they have been carefully trained to "be" the residents of early Plymouth. They absorb their roles as though playing parts in a drama, but unlike actors, their lines are con-

All in a day's work at Plimoth Plantation.

The people who inhabit Plimoth Plantation are stuck in the year 1627. Ask them a question that relates to a later year and they will stare at you blankly.

stantly changing.

Each interpreter (or informant or imposter) is steeped in the mannerisms, dialect, and personal history of a specific individual who lived in early Plymouth. You will not meet just any Pilgrim man. You will instead encounter Captain Myles Standish, or the grumpy John Billington. You will not meet just any Pilgrim woman, but instead may run into Elinor Billington or Triphosa Tracey. In addition to tending to their work, these settlers argue, fall ill, play, fall in love, and marry. The interpreters take on the characteristics of the people whose roles they are assuming, leaving visitors to arrive at their own understanding of Plimoth life.

When you arrive at the plantation, you are directed to a theater to see an orientation film that further explains the Plimoth Plantation concept and the matter of first-person interpretation. You learn here that the people who inhabit Plimoth are stuck in the year 1627. Ask them a question that relates to a later year and they will stare at you blankly. (There is no use, then, asking them what they think of the Declaration of Independence or George Washington; these things do not yet exist.) They encourage your questions, but remember that they can answer only

"Doesn't he know about germs?" asks a logical young woman, and then she catches herself. "No, of course he doesn't. They haven't been invented yet."

with seventeenth-century knowledge.

Visitors are also encouraged to join in the tasks at hand; children can help feed the chickens, cart in firewood, and assist in patching the mud and straw houses if necessary. Sometimes it is difficult, however, to understand the villagers' speech, an English which is foreign to our ears. Try this on for size: "Good morrow, Goodwife. Could'st tha help me find me three bairns? I is ga'en down to shippon to look for 'em, and if they's hid theysel' in ta ald haystack I 'spect they'll be hard to see as ferntickles come winter!" This woman is just asking her neighbor to help her look for her three children, whom she imagines are hiding in the cow shed. If they are in the haystack, they'll be as difficult to find as freckles in the wintertime.

Slipping back in time is often easier for children than for adults. Still comfortable in make-believe situations, they adapt readily to life in Plimoth. Their impressions of Plimoth will depend upon the weather, the time of year, and any special activities that happen to be going on. Should they attend a wedding, they are likely to see early Plimoth as a festive place filled with music, dancing, and games. Wander around the plantation on a cold and drizzly day, however, and you will have a glimpse of what life was perhaps more truly like. It will not make you want to be a Pilgrim. The primitive homes are dark and dank, and it becomes clear that our forebears did not have an easy existence. As you enter a dirt-floored dwelling, the figure huddled by the fireplace may offer you an herb pill to ease the pain of your aching bones. "Doesn't he know about germs?" asks a logical young woman, pointing to a bowl of porridge infested with flies. And then she catches herself. "No, of course he doesn't. They haven't been invented yet." In a way, she is right.

Allow at least half a day for your visit to Plimoth Plantation. Wear sturdy walking shoes, as the rough unpaved roads are dusty in the summer and muddy in the spring and fall. There is a cafeteria where you can purchase lunch or snacks. You'll also find an attractive book shop and gift shop. If you visit the sights in downtown Plymouth, you will find yourself many souvenir shops. Why not let them do their shopping here in Plimoth Plantation, choosing from old-fashioned toys and games and different types of ship models? It's much more interesting than many other shops, and they'll have some memorable keepsakes when they go home.

MAYFLOWER II. Most of Plymouth's other major attractions, including *Mayflower II*, are located within easy walking distance of the downtown area. This means that you can park your car once and forget about it while you explore on foot. Park as near to the harbor as possible (the crowds are heavy in the summer months), or try to find a place near the Jenney

From Plimoth Plantation, follow Route 3A back into Plymouth; turn right onto North Street, then left onto Water Street. The State Pier is almost immediately on your right. *Mayflower II* is at the Pier.

Grist Mill in Town Brook Park (the entrance is off Summer Street, opposite the huge Governor Carver Motel).

On Water Street at the State Pier, the *Mayflower II* floats gently, the cross of Saint George, patron saint of England, flying proudly from her mast. Built in England in this century to duplicate the original seventeenth-century merchant vessel, she is painted with green, blue, red, and yellow stripes and stylized flowers on a black background. Such decoration served to differentiate merchant vessels from warships. Indeed, her sides present a cheerful sight, in contrast to the tight, dark quarters hidden beneath her decks.

After purchasing a ticket, go up the gangway; here, a guide explains that once you step onto the *Mayflower II*, you will be transported back in time to February of 1621, two months after the Pilgrims' arrival in Plymouth harbor.

Just as the villagers at Plimoth Plantation know nothing of the world after 1627, the passengers and crew members you meet aboard *Mayflower II* have no knowledge of events following the "present" — February, 1621. At the time you meet them, they have lived aboard the ship in the harbor for about two months, traveling ashore to work on the crude structures that will be their permanent homes as soon as their ship departs for England.

As you step aboard, a young male "passenger" asks, "Do you take to the sickness of the sea, do you? We weren't allowed on deck much during the crossing, perhaps six days out of sixty-six we could come up." He then asks, "Are you comin' to settle with me on the shore?" It feels as though you have been asked to assume the role of one of your own forebears.

As you further explore the ship, you begin to envision the plight of the 102 passengers, stuffed like sardines in the depths of the ship for two cold, tumultuous months. Captain Christopher Jones welcomes you to steerage, with its low ceilings and notable absence of light and ventilation. He shows you his own cabin, a spacious area designed to provide an important man with proper comfort. But Captain Jones is a kind man. Pitying his unfortunate passengers, he gave up his own quarters, opting instead for a smaller space, so that sixteen people could then move into his cabin. Ask why there are no beds in the cabin now and he will explain that the settlers have taken them out: "They've paid for the wood, you see, so they are using it in making their houses."

On deck you meet a woman tending her embroidery; she is willing to pause for a chat. She explains that she is not a Separatist in search of religious freedom, but that she is instead an Anglican. Indeed, she informs, only one-third of the passengers are Separatists. Why, then, did she risk the long voyage and the

Ask why there are no beds in the cabin now and he will explain that the settlers have taken them out: "They've paid for the wood, you see, so they are using it in making their homes."

Step aboard the Mayflower II, *and you're suddenly back in 1621.*

The portico of Plymouth Rock can be seen from the deck of the *Mayflower II*, and is just a short walk away. First House and the 1627 House are right near Plymouth Rock.

perils of settlement in a wild, new land? "My husband wanted to come for the chance to own land," she explains, "and for the chance of new-found wealth from natural resources. He was a tenant farmer back home."

From conversations with other passengers and crew, you may learn that the ship belongs to the group of London businessmen who financed the Pilgrims' voyage. Indebted to these Englishmen, the settlers must attend not only to their own survival but to repaying the loan in lumber, furs, and other valuables.

One young visitor is busily taking notes. As the "crewman" speaks, he leans in her direction and whispers loudly, "Did they try to beat it out of you?" She looks confused and surprised. "You write with the hand of the Devil," he continues, pointing to her left hand and shaking his head with pity.

PLYMOUTH ROCK. From the deck of the *Mayflower II*, you can see a large stone portico. This is a protector for the famous Plymouth Rock, which marks where an expedition led by Captain Myles Standish first came ashore on December 20, 1620. As you walk from the pier to the portico, you pass a floating shallop or large sailing dory, a replica of the original boat that brought the party into the shallow waters where the *Mayflower* could not venture for fear of running aground. When you peer down at the rock, it seems small and unassuming. The more you learn about the Pilgrim story, however, the clearer the symbolism of the rock becomes.

FIRST HOUSE AND 1627 HOUSE. Just a few steps away, you approach First House and the 1627 House, two waterfront replicas of homes that illustrate early styles of colonial architecture. Here Governor and Goodwife Carver tend to their household tasks. Fish are salted down, and herbs hang from the rafters. The governor may wish to talk politics, and the lady of the house is likely to be cooking dinner— perhaps a mixture of soft cheese and eggs, or a thick porridge. If there's nothing else available, she explains, they may have to resort to lobsters and clams.

Be certain to stop at these seventeenth-century dwellings if you do not plan to visit Plimoth Plantation. At least you will get a brief taste of colonial history come to life.

COLES HILL. Now take a deep breath before you begin to climb the thirty-seven steps leading up Coles Hill. (The sign stating "climb at your own risk" makes the hill an absolute must for every child who is able to read.) This is where the Pilgrims buried half their number in unmarked graves during their first devastating winter. There is a sarcophagus containing their bones, in addition to an imposing statue of Massasoit, the Wampanoag Indian chief who befriended the Pilgrims. Here you can enjoy the panoramic view of Plymouth harbor and the open ocean beyond, with both the naked eye and the aid of a viewer. Slip in a quarter for a closer look at the Myles Standish Monument, Duxbury Beach, Gurnet Light, Clark's Island, and other landmarks.

From the First House and 1627 House, walk across Water Street to Coles Hill.

PLYMOUTH NATIONAL WAX MUSEUM. Here you can visit more than two dozen scenes depicting the Pilgrim story with the assistance of special effects. Traveling through the darkened hallways, you can activate lights, voices, and sometimes even motion by pressing buttons. Some of the scenes show historically significant moments such as the signing of the Mayflower Compact, the landing at Provincetown, and the signing of the Massasoit Treaty. Others focus on the more mundane aspects of Pilgrim life — Young Francis Billington and his buddy nearly blowing up the *Mayflower* by setting off "squibs" (balls of paper filled with gunpowder) near a powder keg, or a snoring Thomas Morton resting his head on a brick after a night of partying and overindulgence.

The National Wax Museum is located at the top of Coles Hill.

Children are often fascinated by the wax figures, but be cautious with little ones, who may be frightened by the eerie quality of the lifelike faces in the dim passages.

PLYMOUTH OCEAN TOURS. When you need a change of pace, return to the State Pier (where the *Mayflower II* is berthed) and take to the sea aboard the *American Eagle* or the *Yankee Clipper*. A thirty-five-minute narrated cruise in the protected waters of Plymouth harbor is perfect for very young children or anyone else who has never experienced life aboard. Your guide will point out landmarks and offer interesting tidbits of local history as you travel past lighthouses, monuments, and the *Mayflower II*. Children who view Plymouth Rock from the water begin to develop a sense of what it felt like to be a Pilgrim, come

Return to the State Pier and Plymouth Ocean Tours, Inc.

there to settle more than 350 years ago. Older or more durable children might enjoy the 1¼-hour sunset cruise in Plymouth harbor and Cape Cod Bay. This trip departs each evening during July and August, and you are welcome to take a picnic supper along to enjoy as you watch the sun slip below the horizon — a very pleasant way to end a hot summer day.

TOWN BROOK PARK AND JENNEY GRIST MILL. As a respite from a heavy sightseeing schedule, plan a picnic lunch or dinner in one of Plymouth's attractive green spaces. Town Brook Park at Jenney Pond is a lovely spot, with a little bridge to cross and many enthusiastic ducks to feed. If you don't have any crusts to feed the ducks, you may purchase a bag of duck corn at the Jenney Grist Mill, a twentieth-century reconstruction of the Pilgrim colony's first grist mill. Corn, wheat, and rye are ground regularly here. The water falling from Jenney Pond into Town Brook turns the huge cypress wheel, which produces power for the mill. You can watch the wheel in action as you browse in the attractive gift shop housed in the mill. You might like to add a fresh loaf of bread to your picnic fixings; this is the place to get it.

Follow Court Street (Route 3A south, which becomes Main Street), take first right from Main Street onto Leyden Street, bear left onto Market Street, and immediately turn right onto Summer Street. The parking lot is on Spring Lane, your first left.

If you visit in the early part of May, your children will witness an exciting event, the annual herring run. It's fun to watch the adult fish jump as high as two feet in the air as they make their way up the fish ladder, traveling from saltwater to their freshwater spawning ground. When the herring are "running," the brook is absolutely thick with them.

BREWSTER GARDEN. If you want to go exploring a bit, follow the path by Town Brook beneath two underpasses to find yourself in another lovely park, Brewster Garden. This is a very good spot for a picnic within easy walking distance of Plymouth Rock and other waterfront sights.

Follow the path by Town Brook beneath two underpasses to Brewster Garden, a park that fronts on Water Street within a block of Plymouth Rock.

CRANBERRY WORLD. If it's time for a break from the Pilgrim story, take your children and hop aboard the red trolley that shuttles visitors between Plymouth Rock and Cranberry World, the Ocean Spray Cranberries, Inc., visitors' center, less than a mile away. The center is located in a glass-enclosed structure, a former "clam factory," overlooking the water. The exhibits are displayed on raised platforms, and you know that children are welcome here when you see the sign saying "Touch if you want, but please keep off platforms."

A red trolley (free of charge) runs back and forth between Plymouth Rock and Cranberry World, the Ocean Spray Cranberries, Inc. visitors' center.

There are many antique and modern harvesting tools on hand, including separators that divide the superior cranberries from the average, the average from the unacceptable. Cranberries are graded according to their "bounce." Those that bounce with ease over a four-inch barrier in the separator are sold as fresh fruit, while those that find the task more demanding are relegated to sauces and drinks. Those that won't bounce properly no matter how they are encouraged are discarded. The friendly hostesses will demonstrate a separator for interested children.

Three narrated slide presentations (you can activate them yourself) focus on cranberry lore, cultivation, and harvest. You learn that the cranberry is one of only three native American fruits, the other two being the blueberry and the Concord grape. Contrary to popular opinion, cranberries do not grow on low bushes but on vines. Sand, acid peat, and an abundant supply of fresh water are the vital ingredients for cranberry cultivation; even a century-old bog can produce well if properly tended.

Cooking demonstrations are held daily at 11 AM and 1:30 PM, but if you miss those you can still take home a sheet of free recipes. Most children like the free samples of Ocean Spray juices provided at the end of their visit.

The cranberry is one of only three native American fruits.

ACCESS

TO GET TO PLYMOUTH. From Boston, follow I-93 south to Route 3, and proceed on Route 3 about thirty-seven miles south to Plymouth. In Plymouth, take Route 44 (Samoset Street); turn right onto Court Street (Route 3A), and follow Court Street into the central business district.

PLIMOTH PLANTATION. Season: April through November. **Admission** charged. (617) 746-1622. **Note:** Combination tickets for the plantation and the *Mayflower II* are available at a reduced price.

MAYFLOWER II. Season: April through November. **Admission** charged. (617) 746-1622.

FIRST HOUSE AND 1627 HOUSE. Season: Both buildings open April through November. **Admission** charged. (617) 746-1622.

PLYMOUTH NATIONAL WAX MUSEUM. Season: March through November. **Admission** charged. (617) 746-6468.

PLYMOUTH OCEAN TOURS. Season: May through October; limited operation during early spring and late fall. **Admission** charged. (617) 747-2400.

TOWN BROOK PARK AND JENNEY GRIST MILL (JENNEY POND). Season: Year round. **Admission** free. (617) 746-4604.

CRANBERRY WORLD. Season: April through November. **Admission** free. (617) 747-1000.

South Carver

For a close look at real working cranberry bogs, take a twenty-minute side trip to South Carver, long recognized as the center of America's cranberry pro-

When is a train ride more than a train ride? When it begins at Edaville Railroad, where there is a fire-engine ride, an old trolley car, a petting zoo, a museum, and more.

duction with its more than three thousand acres of cranberry bogs.

EDAVILLE RAILROAD AND MUSEUM. In South Carver you can visit this delightful railroad, a favorite with kids of all ages. Edaville was established by Ellis D. Atwood, a local cranberry grower who was also a railroad buff, and his initials — E.D.A. — were used to form the name. Atwood originally imported antique steam engines, passenger cars, and wooden train tracks from Maine to assist in harvesting his extensive bogs. Through popular demand, the Edaville Railroad has evolved into a full-fledged tourist attraction requiring at least several hours of your time.

Perhaps the most exciting part of your visit is the five-and-a-half-mile ride through the cranberry bogs of the eighteen-hundred-acre plantation via an old-fashioned steam or diesel engine. What you see depends upon the season. The bright pink blossoms are usually resplendent in late June and early July, and the berries themselves are magnificent come harvest time, usually Labor Day through early November.

You and your children will find, however, that Edaville is much more than cranberries and trains. For instance, there is a petting farm with young llamas, goats, and sheep. Children can also visit the museum to see railroad memorabilia, climb aboard a horse-drawn trolley car, take a ride on an antique fire engine, or ride on the carousel. If they prefer to travel under their own direction, there are miniature Model T cars they can pilot themselves. In November, Edaville is transformed into a Christmas fantasy land, illuminated with over two hundred thousand colored lights. The train continues to operate — it's even heated — and a

Here you take a five-and-a-half-mile ride through the cranberry bogs of the eighteen-hundred-acre plantation via an old-fashioned steam or diesel engine.

nighttime ride across the snowy landscape is a memorable event.

ACCESS _____

EDAVILLE RAILROAD AND MUSEUM. Directions: Take Route 3 south exit 6 (Route 44 west); go about six miles on Route 44, then south about three miles on Route 58 to South Carver and the railroad. **Season:** First Saturday in June through Labor Day, plus weekends and holidays through October. Inquire about winter and spring hours. **Admission** charged. (617) 866-4526.

Cape Cod

Well endowed with things to do, places to see, and dozens of beaches to enjoy, Cape Cod has long been a mecca for summer visitors. A thin hook stretching out into the ocean, the cape has banks and cliffs of continental glacier sand, gravel, and clay extending up to 175 feet in height from the beaches along the outermost section. Swimming is certainly one of Cape Cod's chief attractions, and you will be satisfied whether you prefer the pounding surf of the open Atlantic, the more docile waters of Cape Cod Bay, or the warmer stretches on the southern shore (Craigville Beach comes highly recommended). On the bay side, the swimming is excellent when the tide is in. When it's out, it's way out. Then you will have to walk about a quarter of a mile from shore to find enough water to swim in, but the children will enjoy the tide pools.

If you visit Cape Cod in July or August, anticipate crowds and traffic jams. The cape is worth the hassles, however, and once you get over the bridge and on to the cape proper, the people tend to fan out. Here follows a list of enjoyable places on this peninsula, chosen with an eye to variety in both price and the type of activity offered. You will certainly make your own discoveries as well.

Buzzards Bay

GRAZING FIELDS FARM. If your children enjoy the "Billy and Blaze" stories or any of the many other horse stories illustrated by Wesley Dennis, they will be most interested in visiting the farm where the well-known illustrator spent many summers. This is one of the last general working farms in southeastern Massachusetts; it encompasses over six hundred acres, and opens its doors to visitors in more than one way.

Tours of the farm are conducted twice a day, with programs varying according to the interests of the participants. Here you can make the acquaintance of ponies, cows, chickens, sheep, and pigs, with plenty of opportunity for petting. There are lots of wagons, buggies, and other pieces of farm equipment to see, in addition to over fifty Welsh cobs (stocky, short-legged horses), which are bred here. There is a vineyard with more than a thousand grapevines and an extensive vegetable garden too. As your guide, who works the farm, takes you around, you learn about the history of farming in this area in general and at Grazing Fields in particular. If you have the time after your hour-and-a-half tour, you can take a guided walk through the nature preserve across the road or picnic in the fields.

If you want to spend even more time on the farm, consider making it your vacation base. There is a barn-side apartment to rent, as well as three cabins located in the nature preserve. While the apartment has indoor plumbing, the cabins have only outhouses and a hand pump, both of which will be a novelty for children who have never used either. These simple facilities rent by the two-week period, although you may split that time with another family of your acquaintance if you wish. Each cabin will accommodate a family of up to six persons, and the cost is less than what you would pay for one very basic hotel room.

During your stay at the farm, children can observe and lend a hand at chores such as feeding and cleaning animals, milking cows, and working in the garden. They like riding the tractor and just getting to know the people who live and work here. If you don't have a grandfather or uncle who is a farmer, this is a great alternative. Both salt water and fresh water swimming are available nearby; you are encouraged to bring along bikes, as the parking situation at the beaches is very difficult. There's also a stand where you can purchase farm-fresh vegetables.

ACCESS

GRAZING FIELDS FARM. Directions: Take Route 6 to the Buzzards Bay rotary. Look for "Grandma's Pie House" on Head of the Bay Road; take Head of the Bay Road north about one mile, and turn right on Bournedale Road. A well-marked entrance to the farm is on your right. **Season:** Mid-May through October. **Admission** charged. (617) 759-3763.

Sandwich

HERITAGE PLANTATION. This outstanding complex in Sandwich deserves a leisurely visit. Here are seventy-six acres of magnificent gardens and trails to wander through, highlighted by a folk-art collection, an antique automobile collection, and a military museum. The folk art is kept in the Arts and Crafts Museum, which boasts the largest Currier & Ives collection in this country accessible to the public. Here you also find cigar-store figures, scrimshaw, and shell art (including a magnificent Sailor's Valentine and a mosaic of seashells), old weather vanes, mechanical banks, antique toys, and paintings of children in terribly formal poses. Children who have studied American history in school enjoy seeing real artifacts that previous generations played with or produced in their spare time.

But for most children, the special attraction in the Arts and Crafts Museum is the working Carousel protected by an elegant glassed-in rotunda. Built in Riverside, Rhode Island, about 1912 by Charles I.D. Looff (who built the original Coney Island carousel in 1876), this handsome ride is fully restored. Listen to the catchy music as you hop aboard one of the gleaming steeds for a joyous ride, and stay aboard for a second go-round if you haven't had enough. For that matter, ride as often as you like! — there's no extra charge beyond general admission. Posed against the walls of the pavilion is an assortment of carousel figures for children to climb on. Here you will find more than just the traditional equine; children may choose a rabbit, stag, zebra, lion, tiger, ostrich, or even a frog.

The Automobile Collection at Heritage Plantation is housed in a fascinating round barn. More than thirty American autos from 1899 to 1937 are all shiny and painstakingly restored. Admire the Duesenberg and the Stutz, the Packard and the Pierce Arrow. There is also a 1913 Model T, which the children can crank up or climb aboard and pilot down imaginary country lanes. In the Automobile Theater, you can watch old-time films featuring these classy cars.

The Military Museum contains collections of firearms including a rifle that belonged to Buffalo Bill Cody. There are two thousand hand-painted miniature soldiers grouped in settings showing the military units important to our country's history from 1620 to 1900. They are housed in glass display cases, and as you walk into viewing range, an electric eye automatically responds to your presence and switches on the lights to illuminate that particular scene. Out behind the museum are several cannons to climb aboard for imaginary military escapades. In front, there is a sentry box to hide inside.

An open-sided shuttle bus makes regular laps around the grounds, transporting visitors from one part of the plantation to another. But do take some time out to just walk. You are permitted to walk on the grass (but not in the flower beds, please) and you can travel the extensive trails leading through the wood groves or along the shore of Upper Shawme Lake. Who knows? You just may discover a working windmill. If you want to take a picnic, there are tables near the main entrance.

How long you spend in each of the buildings depends upon the specific interests of your young companions. Model-soldier collectors might spend a half hour in the military museum but simply dash

RUSS KENDALL

This gleaming 1876 carousel is a source of childlike merriment at Heritage Plantation in Sandwich.

Admire the Duesenberg and the Stutz, the Packard and the Pierce Arrow.

through the auto collection. On the other hand, a pre-teen enamored with beautiful cars might ignore the military museum, choosing instead to set up temporary residence in the auto museum. Your own brood will make their decisions clear to you.

ACCESS

HERITAGE PLANTATION. Directions: From the Sagamore Bridge on Cape Cod, take Route 6A into Sandwich and follow signs. The plantation is at the intersection of Grove and Pine streets. **Season:** Mid-May through mid-October. **Admission** charged. (617) 888-3300.

Hyannis

The conductor cries "All aboard!" and the train whistle blows as you set off on the fifty-five-minute journey to Sandwich.

CAPE COD & HYANNIS RAILROAD. If your children have never experienced train travel, or if they are confirmed rail fans, board the C.C. & H. Railroad for a trip with a turn-of-the-century twist. Your journey begins at the Hyannis Depot, where the conductor cries "All aboard!" and the train whistle blows as you set off on the fifty-five-minute journey to Sandwich. While you watch the scenery unfold — with glimpses of Cape Cod Bay, the sand dunes at Sandy Neck, salt marshes, and cranberry bogs — the train staff relates anecdotes filled with local color and snatches of the area's history.

Several options are available on the railroad. You can travel to Sandwich, and take time to wander the streets of what many people consider the most beautiful village on Cape Cod. Perhaps you'll choose to buy a combination ticket, which entitles you to round-trip rail transportation, bus transfers, and admission to Heritage Plantation. Or you can take the last train of the day and make the round trip without getting off the train. In any case, the ride is worth your time.

COLONIAL CANDLE OF CAPE COD. While in Hyannis, stop in for a free do-it-yourself tour of this candle "factory," the largest candle maker in the world. (In 1980, over eleven million dollars' worth of candles were sold here wholesale). There are painted lines to follow as you make your way through the factory viewing both modern and traditional modes of candle production. In the novelty department you see the manufacture of items such as Christmas, birthday, and wedding candles. Racks of graceful tapers hang in the hand-dipping department, and sturdy candle pillars are produced in the machine department. Everywhere there are great vats of colored wax, and the air is thick with a mixture of scents — cranberry, bayberry, lemon, vanilla, strawberry — some thirty-five odors in all. The tour takes fifteen to twenty minutes.

Everywhere there are great vats of colored wax, and the air is thick with a mixture of scents.

Your tour ends in the company's gift shop, where

the children are enchanted by candles in all sorts of shapes. There are pickles and Pooh bears, mice and mushrooms, and clowns, corncobs, and cupcakes, to name just a few. There is also a seconds shop, where you can find deals on hundreds of not-quite-perfect candles in a wide variety of shapes, sizes, and colors.

HY-LINE DEEP SEA FISHING TRIPS. Before leaving Hyannis, consider taking to the sea for a deep sea fishing trip. The four-and-a-half-hour trips on Nantucket Sound leave early in the morning and at midday. Cruises are billed as a family experience, and crew members are happy to get novices started on the right track. Bait is supplied and you can rent rods and reels at nominal cost. Soft drinks are sold aboard, but it's wise to bring along sandwiches and other snacks since the salt air seems to stimulate young appetites.

Trips are made during the spring, summer, and fall, and the fish you catch vary with the season. Those frequently caught include fluke (a member of the flounder family), porgy, black sea bass (very tasty!), and tautog (largest of those mentioned here, averaging about six pounds, and frequently used in chowder). The dock area is extremely congested in the summer months, so be certain to allow plenty of time to park your car and buy your ticket.

Fish frequently caught include fluke, porgy, black sea bass, and tautog.

ACCESS

TO GET TO HYANNIS. From Boston, take I-93 south to Route 3, and follow Route 3 south to the Sagamore Bridge. From the bridge, follow Route 6 (Mid-Cape Highway) to exit 6 (Route 132) and take Route 132 about two miles into Hyannis.

CAPE COD & HYANNIS RAILROAD. Directions: Follow Route 132 from Route 6, proceeding through the traffic circle to Barnstable Road. Follow Barnstable Road toward the center of town, then turn left onto Center Street to the depot. **Season:** Late June through mid-October. **Admission** charged. (617) 771-1145.

COLONIAL CANDLE OF CAPE COD. Directions: In Hyannis, continue south on Barnstable Road to South Street; at intersection of Barnstable, South, and Old Colony roads, take a sharp left on Old Colony; where Old Colony intersects Main Street, you will see the factory ahead at 238 Main Street. **Season:** Year round. **Admission** free. (617) 775-2500.

HY-LINE DEEP SEA FISHING TRIPS. Directions: From Route 6 (Mid-Cape Highway) take Route 132 to the Hyannis Airport rotary, and continue on Barnstable Road (which becomes Ocean Street). The Ocean Street Dock and Hy-Line headquarters are located on Pier 1. **Season:** Late April through mid-October. **Admission** charged. (617) 775-7185.

All self-guided trails at Cape Cod National Seashore are highlighted by trail-side labels or explanatory folders.

Cape Cod National Seashore

A visitor's dream, the national seashore was established in 1961 and will ultimately include twenty-seven thousand acres of land. The area is administered by the National Park Service, whose goal is to protect the resources, charm, and outright beauty of the area for future generations. This is a place for hiking and biking, swimming and beachcombing. Whether you prefer walks along sand dunes or shady forest trails, the national seashore will make you happy. The only facility associated with national parks that does not exist here is a campground, but there are many private ones in the area where you can pitch your tent. One of these is Nickerson State Park, a large area just south of Route 6A in Brewster. Here the campsites are on a first come, first served basis. Look for signs. Some other campgrounds accept reservations, and some don't. If you plan to visit at the height of the season and want to camp, it is imperative that you either reserve ahead or plan to arrive early in the day.

Eastham

SALT POND VISITOR CENTER. Begin your sojourn along the national seashore with a stop at this helpful starting point in Eastham. Here you can watch a brief orientation film in the comfortable theater.

Shown on the hour and the half hour, the film focuses on the features of the seashore that you will enjoy as you take advantage of the recreational opportunities offered here. There are also exhibits to examine, including a "please touch" case of Cape Cod shells and other beach findings — egg cases, mussel shells, razor clams, seaweed, and much more. A push-button slide show titled "How the Cape Was Formed" is complete with little dishes of "glacial till," "outwash," and "wave-worn debris" for fingers to explore. There is also a small book shop well stocked with books focusing on the natural resources, social history, and recreational opportunities of Cape Cod. Allow about thirty minutes here.

The Salt Pond Visitor Center also has an information desk staffed by knowledgeable park rangers who can answer your questions and suggest ways of enhancing your visit. Here you can secure a trail map (and trail recommendations suited to the age spread of your family) and sign up for scheduled activities. These include a daily series of walks through the marshes and forests and along the beaches. The themes vary, but you might choose a flora walk, a tidal flat walk, or perhaps a night hike in which the focus is on sensory perception. Each program is led by a national-park ranger or "interpreter," who helps you understand the natural and human history of the area.

The walks vary in length from barely an hour to almost half a day; you should choose among them with your children's interests and endurance levels in mind. Children might be slightly bored by a tour through the Penniman House, the 1867 home of a whaling captain, but they can't help enjoying the sunset beach walks, which feature some fine campfires and sing-alongs. And it's worth knowing that any child five years old or older who attends two interpretive programs is eligible for a Junior Ranger certificate and badge.

BUTTONBUSH TRAIL. Just outside the center, you can begin your walk along the Buttonbush Trail, a two-tenth-mile loop designed for blind as well as sighted visitors. There are signs in both large print and braille explaining that this is a trail where you will be encouraged to listen (can you distinguish between a redwinged blackbird and a grackle?) to touch (red cedar, pitch pine), and to smell (the bayberry). This is a novel way for children to exercise their senses, to learn to appreciate nature from many perspectives. You can spend a profitable fifteen minutes on this trail.

On Cape Cod National Seashore there are six beaches, all of which are manned by lifeguards. Coast Guard Beach and Nauset Light Beach in Eastham boast powerful ocean surf. Herring Cove Beach in Provincetown at the tip of the cape also has a strong surf, as do nearby Race Point Beach and Head of the Meadow Beach in Truro. On the Cape Cod Bay side, you will

Children can't help enjoying the sunset beach walks, which feature some fine campfires and sing-alongs.

You might visit a white-cedar swamp, a dune community, or the spring where the Pilgrims may well have drunk their first New England water.

find quiet Marconi Beach nestled in the protection of Wellfleet harbor at South Wellfleet.

The national seashore also includes a series of paved bicycle trails where you can pedal with your children without worrying about automobiles. The Nauset Trail begins in Eastham and extends about a mile and a half. Truro has two-mile-long Head of the Meadow Trail. In Provincetown, there is the seven-and-a-half-mile-long Province Lands Trail beginning near the Province Lands Visitor Center where you will find exhibits and services similar to those offered at the Salt Pond center.

Here, too, are ten self-guiding trails; trail-side labels or explanatory folders are available at the beginning of each trail. The trails vary in length from less than a mile to more than five.

Depending upon your choice, you might visit a red-maple swamp, a white-cedar swamp, a dune community, a pitch-pine and oak community, the spring where the Pilgrims may well have drunk their first New England water, or the spot where the first wireless transatlantic message was transmitted. Ask the park rangers for help in choosing an appropriate trail.

Both of the visitors' centers also offer evening programs in their attractive outdoor amphitheaters. It's fun to sit on a bench in the soft summer night and enjoy a narrated slide show focusing on flora or fauna or some aspect of the area's local history. There is no charge for participation in either the amphitheater shows or any of the other interpretation programs.

ACCESS

CAPE COD NATIONAL SEASHORE. For information and current calendar of events, write Superintendent, Cape Cod National Seashore, National Park Service, South Wellfleet, MA 02663.

SALT POND VISITOR CENTER. Directions: Take Route 6 about forty-two miles east to Eastham; the visitors' center is on your right and the entrance is clearly marked. **Season:** Spring through fall. **Admission** free. (617) 255-3421.

New Bedford

"The town itself is perhaps the dearest place to live in, in all New England . . ." wrote Herman Melville, describing New Bedford in his epic novel *Moby Dick.* Home of the world's largest whaling fleet in the 1800s, New Bedford still continues to rely on the sea today; it landed more than seven million dollars' worth of fish and scallops in 1980. And although whales are now an endangered species and no longer hunted, the city's name is still synonymous with whaling. A visit to New Bedford is a trip back in time to the heyday of the whaling industry, liberally spiced with a look at contemporary life at sea.

NEW BEDFORD WHALING MUSEUM. Throughout the city are information panels describing historical buildings and other points of interest listed in your pamphlet. But if you prefer a guided walking tour to the do-it-yourself version, head directly to the city's major attraction, the famous Whaling Museum atop Johnny Cake Hill. Here you can join a free one-hour walking tour of the ten-acre waterfront historic district. Wearing your most comfortable walking shoes, wander the cobblestone streets, which, with their meticulously restored buildings (indeed, the restoration is still in progress), and old-time gas lamps, evoke a strong sense of the past.

The whaling museum is a handsome, airy structure housing a huge collection of whaling material; prints and paintings depict sea voyages and figureheads, while scrimshaw, logbooks, tools, and ships' models give you an idea of the sort of items collected by the whalers on their travels throughout the world.

You might wish to prepare your children for both the film and the whaling theme in general by explaining beforehand that this is a museum of history, not conservation. Many children are appalled by the whale-butchering process; they need to be reassured that whaling was an economic necessity and that whales were taken because of their valuable oil and other products. At the time of the whaling boom, there was not the shortage of the animals there is today. Although the museum documents a period in history that is now left behind, seeking to preserve a part of the past certainly does not mean condoning such activity in the present.

As they enter the museum, even children who would just as soon have a cavity filled as look at paintings will be excited by *The Panorama,* a large section of the 8½- by 1,275-foot mural painted in 1848 by Benjamin Russell and Caleb Purrington. A testament to the great whaling days, the panels "read" like a storybook. You can almost hear the whales splash and thrash as seamen are thrown from their dories, harpoons are flung, and the dead whale is cut into pieces and pulled aboard, all in vivid detail. There is also a more serene section, showing Tahiti as it appeared to the whalemen who called there for provisions and fresh water. Souvenirs picked up on the voyages are displayed around *The Panorama.* Some of them include sharp-toothed swords and daggers from the Gilbert Islands, Eskimo dance masks, war clubs from the Marquesas, and all manner of spears.

In the main gallery, children discover the largest ship model in the world, the fifty-foot-long half-scale replica of the *Lagoda,* a square-rigged whaler that measured 118 feet. It's fun to climb aboard and explore the morass of ropes, chains, rigging, and sails. But you have to look hard to find the cookstove and the com-

Begin your visit by picking up a walking map and a guide to the Moby Dick Trail at the Information Center, at 48 North Water Street (off Elm Street, directly behind the Whaling Museum). Take the first left off Elm Street to the museum, which is at 18 Johnny Cake Hill.

Seamen are thrown from their dories, harpoons are flung, and the dead whale is cut into pieces and pulled aboard, all in vivid detail.

It's fun to climb aboard and explore the morass of ropes, chains, rigging, and sails.

pass. Can you find the bread waiting on the table?

As you walk around the museum, tell your children to imagine themselves at sea in pursuit of the world's largest mammals in one of the whaleboats (looking like oversized rowboats) stationed near the *Lagoda.* On the walls nearby you find harpoons, bomb lances, and special guns. You learn about the process of "cutting in," whereby blubber and baleen (whalebone) were removed from the whale carcass, which was hung from the side of the ship and surrounded with scaffolding for easy access. Then when you climb the stairs to the second-story balcony, you can take a walk through a whaling merchant's office, "Carter's Rigging Loft," peer into the cooper shop (where barrels for collecting whale oil were made), and examine the sails in the sail loft (each stitched by hand).

Elsewhere in the museum, you can discover an antique doll collection, a board displaying 175 different knots, a furnished eighteenth-century all-purpose room, and a magnificent scrimshaw collection. You can imagine how, when they were at sea, the sailors whiled away the long hours engraving intricate designs on whale teeth and bone. Often they even carved them into delicately detailed toys, tools, and ornaments. For instance, pie-crust crimpers were a favorite project, the handles formed in elegant animal shapes. It was said that the young man who brought his sweetheart such a gift was certain to be rewarded with a fresh fruit pie in jig time. Children are fascinated by the complexity of the designs and seem to comprehend and admire the diligence involved in crafting these pieces.

Throughout the summer months you can visit the museum's comfortable 250-seat theater to watch a 20-minute segment from the 4-hour silent film classic *Down to the Sea in Ships.* Made in New Bedford in 1922, just as the whaling industry was coming to an end, the movie features local actors and actresses in vintage 1850s clothing. A museum staff member narrates for you, and is eager for questions with the presentation over. Children find this film very interesting, as many have never seen a silent film before. Parts of the film are very exciting and parts are humorous, providing a fitting climax to a satisfying one-hour visit to the museum.

When you leave the museum, step across the street for a look inside the Seamen's Bethel.

SEAMEN'S BETHEL. Immortalized as the Whaleman's Chapel in Melville's *Moby Dick,* this lovely church was founded to protect the rights of seamen and to furnish them with moral, intellectual, and religious instruction. It was opened in 1832 as a church intended to serve the people of the waterfront. The walls are covered with engraved tablets commemorating those who lost their lives at sea, a tradition of commemoration that continues today. Children are intrigued by the pulpit, shaped and painted like the prow of a fishing boat. Services are still held here every

Fun to watch: glass blowing at Pairpoint Glass Works.

Sunday and on other special days.

NEW BEDFORD GLASS MUSEUM AND PAIRPOINT GLASS WORKS. While in the historic district, parents might enjoy a visit to the glass museum, located in a handsomely restored granite Federal-style mansion. Children will probably be more interested in the action across the street, at the Pairpoint Glass Works. After an absence of twenty years, this old New Bedford company is back at work producing fine glass products and art objects, using century-old manufacturing techniques. Glass-blowing demonstrations are held frequently during regular hours of operation. You might also wish to visit the factory store on the premises. Allow fifteen minutes for your visit here.

Follow Elm Street one block beyond Johnny Cake Hill, turn left onto North Second Street, and follow it to the Glass Museum, at 50 North Second Street. The Glass Works is across the street.

WHALING CITY HARBOR TOURS. For a look at contemporary New Bedford, walk down to the waterfront and get a firsthand look at the fishing fleet. Keep an eye out along the way for signs advertising ship chandlers, marine supply outfits, and even lawyers who specialize in boat settlements. The children soon realize here how much the sea plays a part in the whaling city today. When you reach the waterfront, how about taking a one-hour harbor cruise from Leonard's Wharf aboard a Whaling City Ferry, Inc. boat? While watching catches of scallops and fish being off-loaded, you can also observe the activity aboard longliners, lobster boats, tuna boats, draggers, and stern trawlers as they get ready to put out to sea. Your captain points out places of historical interest such as whaling wharves, shipyards, lighthouses, and Revolutionary and Civil War forts. The main deck is enclosed, but the children will probably prefer the better viewing of the upper deck. Arrive early to avoid disappointment.

As you leave the Glass Works, turn right on North Second Street; go two blocks to Union Street, turn left, and go three blocks farther. Cross the JFK Highway and turn right onto Front Street. Leonard's Wharf is on your left.

BUTTONWOOD PARK. Now it may be time to leave the historic district and the sea behind for a few hours, with a visit to ninety-seven-acre Buttonwood Park, a good spot to relax after a heavy sightseeing schedule. Children enjoy the well-equipped playground here. Slide fanciers are particularly pleased, as

There is a rocky enclosure for bears, located at the edge of the playground; children can swing here and watch the big animals lumber about at the same time.

there at least five of these: two have tunnels built over them, one has a large bump in the middle, one is attached to a climbing complex, and one is just plain regular. There is also a pleasant zoo that houses aoudads (anyone know what that is? see if you find out at the zoo.), bisons, harbor seals, sea lions, emus, mountain lions, and elephants. Who could ask for more? Well, there happens to *be* more; you'll find a contact area with rabbits, sheep, goats, and a ferret to pet. There is also a rocky enclosure for bears, located on the edge of the playground; children can swing here and watch the big animals lumber about at the same time.

Elsewhere in Buttonwood Park, you find a greenhouse to explore and a pond for tossing pebbles or dangling a fishing line. There are tennis courts and basketball courts, too, plus a small train to ride in the zoo area. There is also a concession stand for refreshments, but you might prefer to take along a picnic, since there are many attractive places to set out your feast. Plan to stay about an hour here.

FOOD AND LODGING. For a quick and inexpensive lunch in New Bedford, try the hot dogs from one of the many umbrella-topped pushcarts that ply the streets of the historic district. Order your dogs with chili or sauerkraut if you like. Then find a comfortable bench to settle on and enjoy the atmosphere. When you finish, see if you can find the Ice Cream Parlour on Front and Centre streets; walk over and enjoy a scoop of "vanilla creme" or cranberry sherbet.

If you wish to explore all the suggestions for sightseeing in New Bedford, plan to stay overnight to allow a leisurely visit. For interesting accommodations at reasonable rates, contact Pineapple Hospitality, Inc., Bed & Breakfast (384 Rodney French Boulevard, New Bedford, MA 02744; 617-997-9952). Four local ladies pool their talents in running this reservation service, which places visitors in private homes. Host families offer clean, comfortable accommodations and a complimentary continental breakfast, along with the opportunity to become acquainted with people who live in the whaling city. Many host families welcome children and some even supply cribs. You might find yourselves in a home across from Buttonwood Park, where the hostess serves home-grown rhubarb and fresh muffins for breakfast and a cocktail or a cup of tea when the occasion calls for it. Or, you might stay in a whaling captain's home in a quaint nearby village, where the son of the house enjoys taking visitors on a walking tour of the area and his mother and grandmother serve tea in their lovely garden following the tour. As you can see, it seems no two accommodations are the same.

Pineapple Hospitality provides a brief questionnaire that helps to determine which home would best fit your needs. In addition to the number and ages of

You'll find a contact area with rabbits, sheep, goats, and a ferret to pet.

the people in your party, you are asked whether you'd rather stay in a smoking or nonsmoking household, the type of bed you prefer, and whether or not anyone in your group suffers from allergies. This is a service that aims to please!

ACCESS

TO GET TO NEW BEDFORD. To reach the historic district, take I-195 exit 15, and follow signs to downtown historic area, entering on Elm Street. From Boston, take I-93 south exit 21, then take Route 24 south to exit 14 (Route 140) and follow Route 140 to New Bedford.

NEW BEDFORD WHALING MUSEUM. Season: Year round. **Admission** charged; under six free. (617) 997-0046. **Note:** Parking is available at the three-level garage on Elm Street, a block beyond the entrance to Johnny Cake Hill.

SEAMEN'S BETHEL. Season: Year round. **Donation:** accepted. (617) 992-3295.

NEW BEDFORD GLASS MUSEUM AND PAIRPOINT GLASS WORKS. Season: Year round. **Admission** charged for museum; Glass Works free. (617) 994-0115.

WHALING CITY HARBOR TOURS. Season: Spring through fall. **Admission** charged. (617) 997-1653.

BUTTONWOOD PARK. Directions: From historic district, take Union Street to Route 6, and follow Route 6 approximately two miles. The park is on the left. **Season:** Year round. **Admission** free (may change). (617) 999-2931.

Worcester

On your way to western Massachusetts, plan to stop off in Worcester to visit two special places that will leave a lasting impression on your children.

WORCESTER SCIENCE CENTER. This is an indoor/outdoor facility where you will find a main museum, a zoo area, a miniature train to ride, and a woodland nature trail to walk. The exhibits, intimate and accessible, offer many opportunities for personal involvement. Children can lean over the three-foot-high barrier that contains the two South American iguanas, actually getting close enough to see their long skinny toes (or toenails?), neatly patterned with black bands.

Children can also activate the dog-powered butter churn, which is harnessed to a full-sized plywood dog. You learn that this device was invented in colonial times to free the housewife from the tedious chore. An accompanying sign reads: "Dogs were used to power the machine until the practice was outlawed in the mid-1800s." The real dog had to run on a treadmill like

You will find, in addition to the main museum, a zoo area, a miniature train to ride, and a woodland nature trail to walk.

When you have watched the polar bears pace and lumber into their pool, walk down to the viewport, where you can see them cavort underwater.

The Worcester Science Center includes a museum, a zoo, a miniature train, and a woodland nature trail.

this one attached to the handle of the butter churn, making it go up and down. After operating the machine, children quickly perceive just how cruel it was.

In the Alden Omnisphere you can watch a planetarium show (for children five years old and older). You can also catch a live-animal demonstration including Morgan the Woodchuck. Morgan's human companion explains that if Morgan lived in the wild, he would hibernate in the winter, his body temperature dropping from one hundred degrees to between thirty-eight and fifty degrees, his heart beating only a few times a minute. He would take a breath only about once every six minutes. (This revelation causes many of the children in the audience to see if they can hold their breath for six minutes. Most soon conclude that indeed they are not in hibernation, and don't really want to be.)

Outside in the zoo area you can visit larger animals, such as Ursula Minor and Ursula Major, two very impressive polar bears who share a spacious enclosure built into a hillside. When you have watched them pace and lumber into their pool, walk down to the viewport, where you can see them cavort underwater.

The science center has a snack area that contains an assortment of vending machines and a souvenir shop. But the best way to purchase a remembrance of the center is to operate one of the machines that can mold a plastic animal right before your very eyes. Your child ends up with a five-inch model elephant or dinosaur to take home, and it is still warm as it slides from the machine. All in all, you and your group can spend an interesting one to two hours at the science center.

THE JOHN WOODMAN HIGGINS ARMORY MUSEUM. Now it's time to continue to the John Woodman Higgins Armory Museum, where you can view one of the world's largest collections of authentic arms and armor. A wealthy industrialist and collector, John Higgins built this glass-and-steel structure in

Your imagination will spin with visions of heroic lords and gracious damsels as you walk the halls.

1928 to house his impressive assortment of ancient arms and armor as well as related medieval and Renaissance art and tapestries. Your imagination will spin with visions of heroic lords and gracious damsels as you walk the halls.

The Gothic Great Hall on the first floor is populated by over a hundred suits of armor; the place feels to imaginative visitors as though ghosts are staring from behind the helmets. Because the armor is in full view — not obscured by any sort of protective barrier — there is a tendency for children to want to reach out and touch. Restrain young hands, because such treatment will cause the ages-old pieces to rust and suffer permanent damage. You can help your children to overcome this temptation by locating the "touch table," where they may handle chain mail, assorted weapons, and pieces of armor to their hearts' content.

The suits are arranged chronologically, beginning with the Crusader Knight, an imposing figure mounted upon a horse wearing its own suit of armor. And guess what! There is armor for dogs as well. You find a collection of Japanese armor and one of decorative pieces used only in tournaments. In the display of gleaming helmets, children like to look for whimsical touches such as built-in moustaches or smiling teeth.

Placards helpfully explain the uses of the armor, weapons, tools, and woodcarvings, but you make many more discoveries by talking with one of the museum guides. For instance, children are interested to know that the average knight stood 5'2" and weighed 120 pounds. The armor was custom-made for each knight; since the weight was well distributed on his body, it did not seem overly cumbersome or heavy. Nor did it clank, because it was kept well oiled. Converted into modern currency, an average suit of armor cost the equivalent of twenty to thirty thousand dollars. So, quite naturally, only the noblemen wore the stuff, not the poorer peasants.

You might also learn that castle stairways were sneakily designed so that those castle owners who were defending their homes could use their right arms freely, while those who were attacking (and thus coming up the stairs) had their right arms awkwardly pinned against the curving wall. Lectures and demonstrations on such subjects as tournaments and the history of the sword are held regularly in the second-floor auditorium (telephone ahead for times). Plan to spend about forty-five minutes here with the iron-suited ones.

ACCESS

TO GET TO WORCESTER. Take I-90 (Massachusetts Turnpike) to the Worcester exit (I-290), and head north on I-290 to Route 9. Or, head south on I-495 to the junction with I-290, then head south on I-290 to Route 9. From Boston, head west on Route 9.

Castle stairways were sneakily designed so that castle owners who were defending their homes could use their right arms freely, while attackers coming up the stairs had their right arms pinned against the curving wall.

WORCESTER SCIENCE CENTER. Directions: Follow Route 9 west past the University of Massachusetts Medical Center, on the right; then turn left onto Plantation Street, and continue one-half mile. Turn left onto Franklin Street, take a sharp right onto Harrington Street, and follow Harrington Street to the Science Center. **Season:** Year round. **Admission** charged. (617) 791-9211.

THE JOHN WOODMAN HIGGINS ARMORY MUSEUM. Directions: From the science center, return to Route 9 and continue west, toward downtown Worcester. Just before the rotary (watch for Lincoln Street sign), turn onto Lincoln Street and go two miles; then, where the road forks, bear left onto Burncoat Street. Go one and a half miles on Burncoat Street to the traffic light. Turn left onto Randolph Road; the armory is on the left, about a half mile ahead. **Season:** Year round. **Admission** charged. (617) 853-6015.

North Oxford

It's exciting just to hear the sounds of the miniature Wabash Cannonball, *assorted train whistles, and the clacking of cars.*

RAILSIDE AMERICA. Here you have a spacious museum devoted entirely to model trains, which children like because it's a noisy place with lots of motion. Proprietor Joe Olney has been collecting and building model railroads for twenty-five years, and thrives on sharing his enthusiasm for railroad Americana with visitors of all ages. The fun starts right at the entrance, which is presided over by an authentic railroad-crossing switch.

The trains travel through intricate scenes that depict a circus, an airport, a switch yard, an oil refinery, a coal-fired power plant, a harbor, and some skyscrapers. Trains run constantly; it's exciting just to hear the sounds of the miniature *Wabash Cannonball,* assorted train whistles, and the clacking of cars making their way around the 150-foot by 50-foot track layout. Buttons located at child level can be pushed to initiate action within the settings. One button starts off a fire scene, while another causes the switchman to emerge from his station; still others activate the miniature lights. Mr. Olney operates the trains from a central control booth where he also controls special effects such as night scenes, in which tiny street lights come to life to illuminate the settings. Older children and adults may visit the booth under his supervision.

Joe Olney is a treasure trove of information for model-train hobbyists. He has at one point or another in his life worked as a fireman, a machinist, and a factory worker, and it is clear that he is fascinated by what makes things tick. His dioramas show a great deal of ingenuity (the oil refinery is made from Pringles cans painted silver), and he likes to share his "trade secrets" (such as where to find logos for buildings and how to make them look authentic). He has a pleasant manner with children and is happy to answer questions.

Railside America combines a taste of the past with a fanciful look at the future. It's fun to examine the extensive collections of early track, railroad cars, and memorabilia such as conductors' hats, dining-car menus, and vintage newspaper clippings. Then you can check out Joe Olney's moon display, which contains his version of the "first railroad in space." Plan to spend about thirty minutes here.

One button starts off a fire scene, while another causes the switchman to emerge from his station; still others activate the miniature lights.

ACCESS

RAILSIDE AMERICA. Directions: Take I-90 exit 10, and follow Route 20 west. Railside America is located at the junction of routes 20 and 56 in North Oxford. **Season:** Year round. **Admission** charged. (617) 987-0288, 987-5301. **Note:** The museum is open several mornings and several afternoons each week; telephone for specifics.

Sturbridge

• The population grows apace, new land is opened for settlement, and the economy expands almost daily.

• The first grumblings of the Industrial Revolution can be heard; changes are clearly in the offing for the traditional agricultural way of life.

• Spinning wheels are relegated to the attic, as water-powered machinery turns out textiles with astounding speed.

• Universal education, women's rights, and the abolition of slavery are the hot issues of the day.

Welcome to Old Sturbridge Village.

OLD STURBRIDGE VILLAGE. Devoted to the story of inland New England in the 1830s , this 250-acre restoration re-creates a slice of life in an agricultural community during the early years of our nation's history as a republic. As you wander the expanse of woods and farmland, you see costumed interpreters going about tasks typical of 150 years ago. Farmers are busy making ox bows and shingles. The cobbler stitches together a pair of sturdy boots while the blacksmith bangs out nails on his anvil or tends to an ox's hooves. The potter bakes a batch of pitchers and bowls in a brick beehive oven, while the printer sets type for a broadside. The miller explains that if you want him to grind your wheat, he will have to deduct five percent of your grain in payment for his services. He will then either use the grain to feed his own family or perhaps trade it for a sack of sugar at the general store. (Back then, cash was a rare commodity.) Housewives busy themselves seeding rows of onions,

At Old Sturbridge Village, ox power supplements manpower in many ways — from moving a heavy object to greeting young visitors.

pulling weeds, cooking applesauce at the open hearth, carding wool, and the like.

The village contains over forty buildings to explore, only two of which were originally on the property when the land for Old Sturbridge was purchased by two collectors back in 1936. By 1946, when the village was first opened to the public, a half dozen other structures had been either built at Sturbridge or moved here and re-erected. Many of the buildings are located around the lovely village green, where today you are as likely to encounter a folk singer as a group of grazing farm animals. Based on the lifestyle of a typical New England town in the 1830s, the homes, shops, and meeting houses reflect the nature and tempo of life at that time. The costumed interpreters stationed in each building explain a little about the history and functions of that particular structure and answer any questions you might have.

When you have had your fill of "downtown" life, catch a ride on the horse-drawn wagon bound for the Pliny Freeman Farmstead. You cross a covered bridge, skim the edge of the mill pond, and pass by the sawmill, gristmill, and carding mill on your journey. Children meet horses, pigs, sheep, oxen, and other farm animals here. If you are lucky, you might arrive

If you are lucky, you might arrive in time for a sampling of gingerbread, pulled straight from the farmhouse oven.

in time for a sampling of gingerbread, pulled straight from the farmhouse oven.

Elsewhere in the village, there are formal exhibits devoted to glass and pewter as well as displays of guns, lighting devices, and clocks. Don't plan to pull a child through these sections unless he has a particular interest. There is so much going on in the village that visitors should not waste precious time on exhibits that do not particularly interest them. Most children tend to favor the more active areas. For example, they like to watch the tinsmith manufacture cups and candle holders, or the broom maker craft his graceful hearth brooms. They even enjoy attending school in the old schoolhouse, where the guide assumes the role of teacher as children take their places on the hard wooden benches and think about what it would be like to do all their lessons on a slate. Brief plays are often held in the Village Meeting House; these are a lively introduction to a particular facet of village life.

The specific activities you see under way in the village will depend upon the time of year you come to visit. For example, maple sugaring takes place in the spring, closely followed by field preparation and planting, and the birth of many farm animals. Summer means celebrations of July 4th and an abundance of garden chores, while autumn is marked by the harvest and lots of election activity. Remember, these were the days when Thomas Jefferson, James Madison, and Andrew Jackson made their marks as Presidents of the United States of America. Household chores also vary with the seasons; depending upon when you visit, you may see butter, cheese, soap, or candles being made; herbs drying; dying and weaving; fruit preservation; or sausage stuffing.

There are several places to eat within the village, with choices varying from cafeteria fare to a New England buffet luncheon with baked beans, chicken pies, and other regional favorites. There are also a number of gift shops associated with the village, where you can buy most of the items produced by the village craftspeople in addition to many other articles related to that period. It is much more fun, however, to buy peppermints, cinnamon balls, and beeswax in Miner Grant's General Store (on the village green), Quakers and Joe Froggers warm from the ovens at the village bakeshop, and a replica of a 150-year-old newspaper, still strong with the smell of ink, from the print shop.

Plan to spend a whole day here. Be sure to let your children have lots of time to set out on their own and make their own discoveries. If they have read stories about boys and girls growing up in the 1800s, their imaginations are sure to take flight as they envision themselves residents of Old Sturbridge Village. If they haven't read any good books about this period, they'll certainly be able to find some intriguing titles in the Museum Shop and Bookstore. Amidst the flurry of

You can buy peppermints, cinnamon balls, and beeswax in the general store, Quakers and Joe Froggers warm from the ovens at the village bakeshop, and a replica of a 150-year-old newspaper from the print shop.

activity, make time for everyone to just sit quietly on the village green for a few moments to savor the sights, sounds, and smells of a simpler era.

ACCESS

OLD STURBRIDGE VILLAGE. Directions: Take I-90 exit 9, or take I-86 exit 3, and travel one mile west on Route 20 to the marked village entrance. **Season:** Year round. **Admission** charged. (617) 347-3362.

Brimfield

COOK'S ORCHARD. If you visit Old Sturbridge in the fall, you can treat your children to a hands-on agricultural activity nearby: take them apple-picking! Although a number of orchards in the area permit visitors to pick their own fruits, Cook's Orchard in Brimfield is a particularly good choice. Here, children who associate apples with the produce department in the local supermarket have their consciousness raised as they enter a world of gnarled trees and freshly mowed fields.

Lucius and Marge Cook have four children of their own, and are real pros at providing a pleasant, relaxed atmosphere for visiting families. They encourage you to bring along a picnic and enjoy lunch in the orchard or at one of the tables provided. When you have finished your meal, polish off the occasion with a fresh-baked treat from the stand Marge operates; it offers only items made or grown on the premises or in the neighborhood. Jelly, honey, and cider are also usually available. While you browse at the stand, your young ones may become acquainted with the cows, pigs, and chickens that make their home here.

The highlight of your visit, of course, is the actual picking. While many orchards require that you purchase a minimum number of pounds of apples (and sometimes that amount is just too much for a family on the road), the Cooks don't worry about how much you buy, as long as you pick only as much as you are willing to purchase. Containers are provided for your convenience and you pay by the pound.

On most days, you ride into the orchard aboard an open trailer pulled by a tractor. Here you are turned loose among trees rich with McIntosh, Cortland, and Red and Yellow Delicious apples. Gently you are admonished not to climb the trees (it doesn't do them much good, and fruit tends to get wasted), and instead, to please use the stepladders provided. There is always a supervisor in the fields to lend a hand or answer questions.

To be absolutely certain of the tractor ride, plan to visit on a weekend; or better yet, call ahead. On weekends, you might also catch the small cider mill in operation. Special activities are almost always planned for Labor Day, but be sure to call ahead for specifics.

On most days, you ride into the orchard aboard an open trailer pulled by a tractor. Here you are turned loose among trees rich with McIntosh, Cortland, and Delicious apples.

Cook's Orchard is a small and accessible operation, and the people here make a special effort to extend warm, personal service.

ACCESS

COOK'S ORCHARD. Directions: Take I-90 exit 9 (Route 20), follow Route 20 west ten miles to Brimfield, and turn left on Route 19 at the traffic light in town. Proceed a half mile to Cook's Orchard, following signs. **Season:** Labor Day through mid-October. **Admission** is payment for the produce you pick. (413) 245-3241.

Hampden

LAUGHING BROOK EDUCATION CENTER AND WILDLIFE SANCTUARY. Here's the place to make the acquaintance of Hooty the owl, Jimmy Skunk, Reddy Fox, and other characters from *Mother West Wind's Children,* written by Thornton Burgess, who also lived and worked here. A real live version of Mother West Wind herself floats about the sanctuary answering questions and checking on her "children."

The sanctuary occupies 260 acres of woodlands, fields, and streams. There are four miles of trails to explore, including a "touch and see" section developed for the blind but providing an excellent sensory experience for everyone. Here children are encouraged to feel the bark of the Shadbark Bush, whose berries are favored by twenty-seven species of birds and animals, including Jimmy Skunk and Bobby Coon. Children can run their hands over the actual fossilized print of a dinosaur, fit them into the hole where a chickadee once lived, or feel the little holes in the apple trees where sapsuckers have drilled in search of food. As you leave this area, following the path out of the woods and into the field near the deer pen, encourage children to be sensitive to the changes in humidity and temperature and to think about how these changes might cause different plants and animals to live in their different habitats.

In the Animal Loop, you will see some of New England's wild animals that would not be able to survive on their own, either because of a permanent injury or because they were raised by humans and have grown dependent upon people for their care. Study the cages and dens carefully if you do not immediately spot an animal; some of them are so well camouflaged that you may be staring directly at a rabbit or bobcat without even realizing it. The only animals here that are released are the residents of the turtle pen; they are sent out on their own in the fall to hibernate. You also see small creatures such as the unfortunate skunk who was descented to make a housepet; she can no longer defend herself and so must spend her life in captivity.

Children can run their hands over the actual fossilized print of a dinosaur, fit them into the hole where a chickadee once lived, or feel the little holes the sapsuckers have drilled in apple trees.

There are reptiles and amphibians here, too, as well as birds and fish. Your children will readily pick up the lesson to be learned, that wild animals do not make good pets and should be left to their own devices.

In the Nature Center is a touch-and-feel exhibit, where children can handle items such as deer antlers, a honeycomb, porcupine quills, animal skulls, birds' nests, or a snakeskin. It is here that you also meet New England's only two types of poisonous snakes, the northern copperhead and the timber rattlesnake. Learn to recognize them.

At the Environmental Center, you can visit a solar greenhouse, among other environmental displays. This building also houses a gift shop, a craft room, an auditorium and other displays dealing with alternative technologies. From here, be sure to follow the brook (which really does laugh) to the delightful Crooked Little Path, where flowers and trees are identified in their natural settings.

Because the sanctuary, owned by the Massachusetts Audubon Society, is open year round, the different seasons bring different sights, sounds, smells, and activities. If you wish to learn about special programs and events at the sanctuary in advance of your visit, one dollar will entitle you to the quarterly publication "Programs at Laughing Brook." You are welcome to take a picnic along to the sanctuary; sheltered picnic tables are provided, but fires are not permitted. Children ten and under will particularly enjoy Laughing Brook. Older children interested in alternative-energy technology should visit the Environmental Center. Allow about forty-five minutes for your visit.

ACCESS

LAUGHING BROOK EDUCATION CENTER AND WILDLIFE SANCTUARY. Directions: From I-90 exit 8, follow signs to Monson; in Monson, turn sharply right at High Street and continue about six and a half miles to Hampden, bearing left as signs indicate. **Season:** Year round. **Admission** charged. (413) 566-8034.

Springfield

If you are traveling or camping in western Massachusetts and an unwelcome stretch of poor weather sets in, Springfield can provide welcome relief. Here you will find three indoor attractions to keep your children happily occupied at modest expense.

SPRINGFIELD ARMORY NATIONAL HISTORIC SITE. Administered by the National Park Service United States Department of the Interior, the armory houses an extensive collection of firearms, military uniforms, and related documents and paraphernalia.

Even if you have no interest in guns, there is plenty to see here; the exhibits are designed to present a piece of history rather than simply to glorify firearms. For instance, there are many dioramas depicting famous military campaigns. Here you see tiny figures representing the Royal Ethiopian Troops, a Russo-Japanese Group, an encounter of the Franco-Prussian War, members of the Royal Canadian Mounted Police and the French Foreign Legion, and the Gordon Highlander Group. Small and large boys who collect toy soldiers can't help being inspired. While some scenes depict battles, others show hospital and domestic arrangements, accessorized with tiny horse-drawn carts, tents, supply trucks, and the like.

There are handsomely cased sets of dueling pistols from France, Belgium, and England, and next to one set of guns sits a most engaging indictment of this odious custom: when challenged to a duel by a British officer in the 1790s, Judge Joseph Cabell Breckinridge wrote:

> I have two objections to this duel.
> The one is lest I should hurt you;
> the other lest you should . . . . If
> you want to try your pistols, take
> some object — a tree or barn door —
> about my dimensions, & if you hit
> that, send me word. I shall then
> acknowledge that if I had been
> standing in the same place, you would
> have killed me in a duel.

Although there is an exhibit devoted to the Evolution of the Handgun, there are also displays of cavalry sabers, bolo bayonets (for jungle warfare), and bazookas. But you don't have to be intrigued with military history to find something to interest you here. Ask the children to search out the story about the gun designer who so loved to ice skate that he flooded his parlor in the winter to create an indoor rink where he could glide in privacy!

As your children spend half an hour or more exploring the collection, you might wish to help them to put weaponry in perspective by discussing this statement from Henry Wadsworth Longfellow:

> Were half the power that fills the world with terror,
>   Were half the wealth, bestow'd on camps and
>   courts
> Given to redeem the human mind from error,
>   There were no need of arsenals nor forts.

NAISMITH MEMORIAL BASKETBALL HALL OF FAME. Is there a basketball buff in your group? He should pay homage to the sport by visiting this famous sports hall devoted to basketball. Jim Naismith, it is said, founded the popular sport right here in Springfield in 1891; in those days the players used a peach basket as the target and the janitor's ladder to retrieve

Search out the story about the gun designer who so loved to ice skate that he flooded his parlor in the winter to create an indoor rink!

the ball. The museum is housed in a replica of the original armory YMCA gym.

Here are three floors chock full of uniforms, basketballs, and other equipment used by basketball greats. You can ogle Bob Lanier's size-twenty sneakers, and see the ball used in the 1976 championship game at the Montreal Olympics. There are jerseys worn by legendary figures like Nate Archibald, Walt Frazier, Bob McAdoo, and Kareem Abdul-Jabbar as well as trophies galore. Plan to pause and rest for a moment in the set of loge seats taken from Madison Square Garden. A plaque assures you that from 1926 to 1968, "countless sports personalities undoubtedly sat in these seats . . . ."

Audio-visual displays are scattered throughout the museum, and films depicting great moments in the history of basketball are shown regularly in the Converse Theatre. You can check your basketball I.Q. by answering such questions as: 1) Who scored 64 points in one game? 2) What "iron man" played in 746 consecutive games? If you are a player as well as a fan, examine the "reboundome," a device that fits over the basket and propels the ball back to you so you can practice pulling in those all-important rebounds. There are even instructions on how to order one of your own.

Considerable attention is given to high school and college basketball here; there is a growing collection of women's basketball memorabilia on display, too. If you become overwhelmed by the exhibits, stop and read a copy of the original thirteen rules and remind yourself that basketball is actually an awful lot of fun. True basketball fanatics will spend an hour or more here, while those with a lesser commitment will probably require only thirty minutes.

(Answers to quiz questions: 1) Bob Cousy 2) Red Kerr.)

INDIAN MOTORCYCLE MUSEUM. Springfield's third museum of special interest to children is devoted to motorcycles — but not just *any* motorcycles. In 1901 George Hendee, a famous bicycle high-wheel champ, and Oscar Hedstrom, a bicycle racer, pooled their money, imagination, and technical expertise to open the Indian Manufacturing Company. Although it produced a variety of products, the firm made its reputation with the fine "Indian" motorcycle, which it manufactured until the plant was bought by the Royal Enfield Company and moved to England in 1953. Today the former plant houses the Indian Motorcycle Museum, a collection of motorcycles and memorabilia that traces the development of the famous "Indian."

Museum director Charles Manthos will probably start the vintage nickelodeon so that you can tap your toes as you examine gems such as the 1927 Indian racer that ran on a mixture of alcohol and castor oil, or the 1922 motorcycle designed specifically for women (there was no transmission). You'll find one bike here made entirely of chain; there is also a fold-up portable motorcycle, the type dropped with paratroopers in the 1950s. And then you'll see the "Daimler," the world's very first motorcycle; this particular bike is one of only two known examples now in existence and is made almost entirely of wood. Young women bikers will take a shine to the gorgeous white "Indian" propelled by trick rider Louise Sherbyn in the 1930s. Sherbyn's costume and photographs of her in action are here as well.

The museum contains an extensive collection of Columbia bicycles, the world's largest collection of toy motorcycles, associated advertising items, and other products made by Indian such as airplane engines, outboard motors, and air conditioners. Altogether, this museum is an out-of-the-ordinary experience. Your visit will be enhanced by Manthos, who knows just about all there is to know about "Indians" and who is generous with his stories and expertise. Allow half an hour for your visit.

ACCESS

TO GET TO SPRINGFIELD. Head north or south on I-91 to the junction with I-291, then head northeast on I-291.

SPRINGFIELD ARMORY NATIONAL HISTORIC SITE. Directions: Take I-291 exit 3, turn left, and go about one mile on Armory Street, which becomes Federal Street. The armory is on your right, before you reach State Street. **Season:** Year round. **Admission** free. **Information:** Superintendent, Springfield Armory National Historic Site, P.O. Box 515, Springfield, MA 01101. (413) 734-8551.

NAISMITH MEMORIAL BASKETBALL HALL OF FAME. Directions: Take I-90 exit 5 or 6, and follow signs to Springfield and to Hall of Fame. Or, take Route 20 to Roosevelt Avenue, and follow signs. **Season:** Year round. **Admission** charged. (413) 781-6500.

INDIAN MOTORCYCLE MUSEUM. Directions: From the Basketball Hall of Fame, continue north on Route 20 to I-291, exit onto Saint James Avenue, and turn right onto Page Boulevard at the light. Continue about a thousand feet to Hendee Street, on the right, and follow the sign to the Indian Motorcycle Museum. **Season:** Year round, afternoons only. **Admission** charged. (413) 737-2624.

Northampton

LOOK MEMORIAL PARK. For a picnic spot that combines lots of activity with a most pleasant setting, this rambling park in Northampton is hard to beat. You can play baseball, horseshoes, and other games here, and if you have forgotten to bring along your own equipment you can rent it all, even a baseball glove. There is lots of playground equipment spread about a pleasant, shady grove, as well as things to slide on and climb, swings, and more. Picnic tables are nearby, and there is a creek spanned by a footbridge. Young children are enchanted by the small train that circles the park in a journey that takes you past cages of deer, peacock, rabbits, and other small animals and through a tunnel, with whistle blowing. Older children enjoy propelling themselves across the pond in a pedal boat. This is an altogether satisfactory spot for combining sports and relaxation, a nice break from more conventional sightseeing.

ACCESS

LOOK MEMORIAL PARK. Directions: Take I-90 exit 4 (I-91 north); then I-91 exit 19 (Route 9) west; the park is located off Route 9 about 2 miles beyond the center of town. **Season:** Memorial Day to Labor Day. **Admission** free.

Ashfield

HIGHLAND SUGARBUSH FARM. If you want to enjoy the tastes, smells, sounds, and sights of syrup making, plan a visit to one of New England's many working sugar camps. You'll find that the older handmade wooden spiles on the trees have been replaced by metal spouts at many camps, and that entire networks of plastic tubing now pipe sap into huge collecting vats. The old sugarhouse is now a centralized boiling operation, and the enormous kettles suspended over outdoor wood fires have been replaced by oil- and gas-fired heating units.

Depending upon what maple-sugaring camp you visit, you might see everything from tree tapping to maple-sugar-candy production. But if you visit the Highland Sugarbush Farm in Ashfield, you will have the opportunity to feast on waffles and fresh maple syrup along with steaming mugs of coffee and hot chocolate. As you make your way around the farm, notice the large evaporators in operation, with tremendous amounts of evaporation in the air. You see the process of syrup making from start to finish, and how the vacuum system works. Highland Sugarbush Farm also offers small exhibits focusing on the history of sugaring off. A line of maple products is for sale.

The Pioneer Valley Association (33 Prospect Street in Northampton, MA 01060; 617-586-0321) publishes annually a free brochure listing sugar camps open to the public; there are over fifty in the Pioneer Valley. Telephone the association as well as the sugar camp on the day you plan to visit. Remember, this is an on-again, off-again business. The sap may run steadily for a week or two and then take time off during a deep freeze. Plan to spend about half an hour at the sugarhouse, longer if you plan to order food.

ACCESS

HIGHLAND SUGARBUSH FARM. Directions: Take I-91 exit 25, and head west on Route 116 to Ashfield. Continue four miles west of town; a sign points the way to the farm. **Season:** March to mid-April; waffles, pancakes, and sausages on weekends only. **Admission** free. (413) 628-3268.

North Adams

NATURAL BRIDGE AND CHASM. At this astonishing site in North Adams, your children gain a new perspective on time. Here they can see the famous bridge and chasm, a fantastic geologic phenomenon formed 550 million years ago from seashells and marine life. This is the only natural-marble water-eroded bridge in North America; it is about 50 million years older than Niagara Falls.

The nearly unfathomable age of this attraction puts our own lives in perspective, as we imagine what the world must have been like in the days when the bridge before us was formed.

Park at the end of the gravel road, where you will find picnic tables and a path that follows the course of the water through the natural bridge. There are well-protected platforms from which to view the glacial striations, potholes (formed by whirlpools), and fractures in the earth's crust. Information panels along the fences provide simple explanations and pertinent geological facts. Allow about half an hour for your visit here.

ACCESS

NATURAL BRIDGE AND CHASM. Directions: Take I-91 exit 26 (Route 2) west into North Adams, watching for signs to the Natural Bridge. Turn right onto Route 8 north and proceed a half mile. Turn left at the sign onto a gravel road and follow it to site. **Season:** Memorial Day through October. **Admission** charged. **Note:** The Mohawk Trail State Forest is located along Route 2 between Greenfield and North Adams. It includes many scenic, secluded forest areas for picnicking as well as several dammed-up river pools for swimming, one of which even has a diving board and a lifeguard. A good spot for a quick swim on a hot afternoon of driving.

This is the only natural-marble water-eroded bridge in North America; it is about 50 million years older than Niagara Falls.

White Mountain Scenic Air Flights carry you sky high for a special view.

CHAPTER IV

New Hampshire

I magine yourself aloft in a small airplane, soaring over the state of New Hampshire. The most striking feature to greet you is her wealth of mountains. Gliding along, you can count eight peaks that reach more than a mile into the sky. You see also that the last glacial age (when the "Wisconsin ice sheet" steam-rollered New England) left the state not only with high spots but also with some dramatic lows. You fly over the great gashes that we now know as the famous notches — Franconia, Pinkham, Crawford, Sandwich, and Dixville. Impressive also is the legacy of ponds and lakes bequeathed by the glacier; there are over thirteen hundred of them in New Hampshire alone. Now come down to earth, climb out of the cockpit, and prepare to get in touch with the environment. The best part about visiting New Hampshire is that your pleasure depends largely upon your willingness to explore her natural attributes. And how rewarding it is to hike her trails, climb her mountains, ply her waters.

New Hampshire is full of contrasts. Eighty percent of her land is covered with forests, including the virtually uninhabited eleven-thousand-acre White Mountain National Forest. A wide variety of wildlife makes its home here, including the abundant whitetail deer, the occasional moose and black bear, and the more usual fox, beaver, mink, and other small mammals. But for all New Hampshire's pastoral qualities, the 1970 census shows that fully forty percent of the state's residents earn their living in manufacturing, making New Hampshire (surprisingly to some) the fifth most industrialized state in the country. The shoemaking, textile, apparel, and woodworking industries that thrived in New Hampshire from the time of the Industrial Revolution to the mid twentieth century have slowly given way to space-age industries, many of which relate to the production of electrical and electronic goods. Although many new factories have been constructed, the massive old brick mills still line the river banks of the major cities; some are silent, but some are still humming, a testimony to the state's long manufacturing history.

In addition to its own traditions, New Hampshire proudly adheres to that most New England of traditions, local government by town meeting. Once a year, the citizens in nearly every New Hampshire town gather together to decide how to govern themselves in the coming twelve months. After much discussion and amid many heated offerings of opinions, they do somehow manage to pass ordinances and set policy. This emphasis on the individual and his responsibility to take an active part in government is intrinsic to the New Hampshire way of life. People here favor continuity; many families have lived in the same town for generations (wouldn't think of leaving), taking pride in setting the laws and living by them. It is no accident that Thornton Wilder chose New Hampshire as the setting for his now-classic play *Our Town* (1938), honing in on the universal aspects of human existence — growing up, growing old, living, loving, losing.

Play tick-tack-toe or find the square root of 999,999,999 on a computer terminal in the Children's Museum at the Arts and Science Center in Nashua.

Nashua

Only thirty-eight miles from Boston, the friendly, middle-sized city of Nashua is a good place to begin your vacation travels in New Hampshire. A progressive center of industry and culture, the city has many facets to show you. And one of its outstanding offerings is especially for children.

CHILDREN'S MUSEUM AT THE ARTS AND SCIENCE CENTER. This interesting establishment features educational exhibits that invite hands-on participation. Housed in the century-old Central Fire Station, the museum proudly contains the original brass fire pole that sped fire fighters to their awaiting fire trucks in the late 1800s; children are welcome to try it out. Other permanent exhibits include Granny's House, a two-story playhouse with a good supply of kitchen equipment and lots of dress-up clothes to encourage imaginative play, and the Supermarket with its well-stocked shelves, shopping baskets, and good noisy cash register to operate. The five computer terminals please older children who can challenge themselves to a variety of games. Everyone enjoys Webster the Spider, an eighteen-foot-long marionette that hangs from the ceiling. A bright yellow insect with touches of purple, red, green, and blue, he is fun to operate; all you do is pull a series of ropes that hang to the floor.

The museum also features rotating exhibits designed to involve children in verbal, math, and logic exercises painlessly. A recent display, Let's Puzzle, centered on optical illusions, rebuses, cryptograms, and secret codes. Participants are encouraged to create their own anagrams and crosswords to take home.

In visiting any children's museum, keep in mind that most children want to play, not just look. They may become involved in one exhibit and simply decide to spend all their time there, particularly if the museum is reasonably empty and there is little pressure to move on and give someone else a turn. If your little girl plays house by the hour at home, imagine what it must feel like to her to be set loose in a elaborate playhouse with all the equipment she needs! Instead of prompting her to see everything, let her set her own agenda. You might even take the opportunity to read a newspaper or write a letter in peace. Or, if you plan a longer visit to the area, investigate the different programs the museum runs in summer months, many of which visitors can participate in on a one-time basis. There are drama, music, craft, and science opportunities, as well as a family film series. Allow about forty-five minutes for your visit here.

Children are welcome to try out the original brass fire pole that sped fire fighters to their awaiting fire trucks in the late 1800s.

ACCESS

CHILDREN'S MUSEUM AT THE ARTS AND SCIENCE CENTER. Directions: From Boston, take Route 3 to the Everett Turnpike; take turnpike exit 6E to Main Street in downtown Nashua. Turn left onto Temple Street, and left again onto Court Street. The museum is located at 14 Court Street. **Season:** Year round. **Admission** charged. (603) 883-1506.

Hudson

BENSON'S ANIMAL PARK. New England is studded with commercial animal parks, story lands, and the like. Sooner or later your children will talk you into taking them to one of these, so why not choose one of the best? The quality of these amusements differs

It's like an old-fashioned circus parade, with marching elephants, pony carts, and young men with snakes wrapped around their necks.

drastically, but Benson's Animal Park in Hudson is on the high end of the scale. The exhibits here are geared to conservation and education issues and in addition provide entertainment and recreation.

Benson's combines features associated with amusement parks with those of a zoo. There are over five hundred animals here from all over the globe; they range from otters to emus, giraffes to gorillas, elephants to bears. Although the species inhabit different parts of the world, the particular animals here were not captured in the wild — they were born in zoos in the United States. It seems that such animals are less traumatized and fare better in captivity than do their counterparts born in the wild.

Some exhibits here are accompanied by recordings that provide basic information on the habits and characteristics of the animals. Other animals are discussed in conjunction with animal shows. You sit in the bleachers and watch seals, elephants, or other beasts perform for their trainers, giving Benson's a circus aspect. If you tire of animal shows, you can try a magic show for a change of pace. There is always something going on here; you might even see a parade with folks dressed up as storybook characters traipsing through the grounds, along with many of the park's animals. Children become quite excited at seeing an old-fashioned circus parade with the exotic animals out of their cages, as drummers accompany the procession of marching elephants, pony carts, and young men with snakes wrapped around their necks.

Benson's is a big place, with plenty of activity for a full day's entertainment; it offers enough variety to keep children of all ages happily occupied. The petting area is a particular favorite. Here children can mingle with dozens of sheep, goats, and even a pig for as long as they like. Then they can move on to gaze at the rhinoceros, the camels, the ostrich, the zebra, and the antelope. If it's alligators they fancy, they can have those, too. For a change of pace, they might decide on an elephant ride. There is really no end in sight.

The amusement area contains a merry-go-round and several kiddie boat and airplane rides, a medium-sized roller coaster, an old ferris wheel, and a tilt-a-whirl. These are included in the all-inclusive admission price (which covers everything except animal rides), so your young ones can ride to their hearts' content without coming to ask you for endless quarters and dollars. Later on, you might choose to take them out on the pond in a pedal boat for a little exercise. In between, they can snack on everything from pizza to popcorn, subs to salads, fudge to fried dough. It's a good plan to take along a picnic lunch to devour at one of the picnic tables while you rest a bit from the happy but hectic pace. All in all, Benson's is an excellent choice for parents reluctant to take children to the

Children can mingle with dozens of sheep, goats, and even a pig. For a change of pace, they might decide on an elephant ride.

more obviously commercial ventures of this sort. Plan to spend a full day here if you have the time.

ACCESS

BENSON'S ANIMAL PARK. Directions: Take Route 3 exit 5 onto Route 111, and follow Route 111 east about four miles. **Season:** April through Christmas season (except closed one week in November). **Admission** charged. (603) 882-2481.

A youngster at Dublin's Friendly Farm tends to some new friends.

Dublin

FRIENDLY FARM. If your very young children found Benson's just a trifle bewildering and hectic, make a special sidetrip through the beautiful Monadnock Region of southern New Hampshire for a special treat they will love: a visit to a truly friendly place. Friendly Farm in Dublin is a pleasant, low-key place where small visitors are encouraged to get to know the animals at their own pace. Your toddler may know that a pig says "oink oink" but does he know what a pig feels like? He can find out as he makes the acquaintance of pigs, sheep, cows, horses, goats, donkeys, chickens, turkeys, and even peacocks while he wanders through the fields and barns.

There are always plenty of baby animals on hand here, and children enjoy watching them play and nurse. In the stable, young visitors discover baby bunnies as well as mice in various stages of development. Here they can also see baby chicks pecking their way out of their shells into the great wide world.

The farm is alive with sound and motion as animals and visitors communicate and enjoy each other. A little boy scratches a goat behind the ears while a small girl whispers a secret in a baby lamb's ear. Everywhere you find animals to feed and pet. Take along a picnic lunch, and settle down in the pleasant picnic grove to enjoy it. The ducks and geese wander about freely, so expect to be pestered for a hand-out!

In the stable, young visitors discover baby bunnies and mice, and see baby chicks pecking their way out of their shells into the great wide world.

Children seven years old and younger seem to particularly enjoy an hour at the Friendly Farm.

ACCESS _____

FRIENDLY FARM. Directions: From Nashua, take Route 101A to Route 101, and follow Route 101 West to Dublin. The farm is located a half mile west of Dublin Lake. **Season:** May through Labor Day; weekends only through mid-October. **Admission** charged. (603) 563-8444.

Portsmouth

Walking through the charming streets recalls a time when sea captains, coopers, stage drivers, and maritime tradesmen lived and worked here.

STRAWBERY BANKE. There is no better way to touch the history that pervades this old New England seaport than to visit its restored waterfront neighborhood. Strawbery Banke is an indoor/outdoor museum with about three dozen buildings to explore, most of them standing on their original sites. This extensive complex documents the changes in architecture and lifestyle that took place in an American urban neighborhood over a period of more than three hundred years.

The neighborhood sprawls about Puddle Dock, an estuary of the Piscataqua River long since filled in. Walking through the charming streets recalls a time when sea captains, coopers, stage drivers, maritime tradesmen, and other merchants lived and worked here. Strawbery Banke, named after the multitude of wild berries that thrived by the river when the first settlers arrived in 1630, has always supported a mixture of residential and commercial activity. This trend continues today.

Here visitors can learn how historians, architects, and archeologists go about determining what existed in the past. How did this old building look two hundred years ago? Who built it? Who lived in it? Wander through homes of the 1600s, the 1700s, and the 1800s and compare their contents. Stop in at the boat shop, where skilled craftsmen turn out handmade dories, skiffs, and other traditional wooden boats for public sale. (Look for the mast shed, built to house a timber more than seventy-five feet long.) Then stop in at another shop and see the blacksmith at work.

Other craftspeople ply their trades here, too. You might see a weaver at work, or a potter. The leatherworker, the silversmith, the clockmaker, and even a spinet-maker are sometimes busy here. These artisans are not employees of Strawbery Banke. Rather, they earn a living at their crafts, renting working space from the restoration. As you walk along, consider that for all our sophisticated space-age technology, perhaps the tempo of New England life has not really changed all that much for people like these, who still make a living with their talented hands.

Special events, including militia and fife-and-drum-corps exhibitions, are held several times each summer; such performances are particularly welcomed by children. Telephone ahead to find out plans.

VIKING CRUISES. Since you are visiting a seaport, it seems only right to take to the water for a brief cruise. Viking Cruises offers several possibilities. If you are early risers, sign on for the hour-and-a-half early-bird cruise. It's great to watch the sky brighten and the birds soar while the working boats set out for a day of fishing or hauling lobster pots. The *Viking Queen* is a comfortable boat that can hold 385 people. Doughnuts and coffee are available aboard.

Daylong whale-watching cruises are offered on the Viking Sun, *and children love telling schoolmates they actually saw a live whale in the ocean.*

The even larger *Viking Sun* makes several trips each day to the **Isles of Shoals,** nine small and large islands that sit ten miles off the New Hampshire coast; they were discovered in 1614 by Captain John Smith. (As one Lucy Larcom observed in her diary in 1895, "These islands are full of strange gorges and caverns, haunted with stories of pirate and ghost." And indeed, the captain of the *Viking Sun* tells you tales of terrible murders and hidden pirate treasure; he also dispenses scientific information regarding current research projects based on Appledore Island. His commentary covers historic sites, weather signs, and bird and animal sightings. You can take a two-and-a-half hour round trip journey to the islands, or you can take a trip that includes a stopover on Star Island.

Viking Cruises also offers weekend whale-watching tours. These are day-long jaunts during which passengers are taken to the fishing grounds to look for humpback and finback whales in their native habitat. Although no promises can be made, whale sightings are frequent; if your children enjoy the water and are

On day-long whale-watching jaunts, passengers are taken to the fishing grounds to look for humpback and finback whales in their native habitat.

You can listen to a bluegrass group, a folk singer, or a string ensemble, or watch ballet or modern dance. The price is right!

patient, the rewards are great. But if they have not had experience with boats, or if more than eight hours at sea sounds like too long, save this for another year.

PRESCOTT PARK. Portsmouth has done itself proud in creating this harborside park with its lovely walkways and cheerful gardens. The park is full of life from late June to mid-August, hosting a wealth of cultural events. The stage comes alive almost every evening with favorite musicals like *Brigadoon*, *Oklahoma*, and *Carousel*. Performances are free, making this an economical way of exposing children to live theater. Dance, music, and mime events also brighten the stage, with performances held in the middle of the day and in the early evening as well as at later hours on the weekends. You can listen to a bluegrass group, a folk singer, or a string ensemble, or watch ballet or modern dance. The price is right!

You do need to take your own chairs along, or simply prepare to spread yourselves out on a blanket. In either case, plan to arrive early to get a good spot. Carry your own picnic supper with you and stake out your territory, or purchase dinner fixings from the pushcarts that work the streets near the park. You might want to bring along a sleeping bag for a younger child to snuggle into when the night grows long. There is nothing quite like growing drowsy under the stars with strong voices singing jubilantly in the background.

ACCESS

TO GET TO PORTSMOUTH. Take I-95 exit 7 to downtown Portsmouth.

STRAWBERY BANKE. Directions: From the north or south, take I-95 exit 7 (Market Street). Follow the strawberry signs. **Season:** Mid-April through mid-November. **Admission** charged. (603) 436-8010.

VIKING CRUISES. Directions: Take I-95 exit 7, and follow Market Street to the Viking dock. **Season:** Mid-June through Labor Day. **Admission** charged. (603) 431-5500.

PRESCOTT PARK. Directions: The park is in downtown Portsmouth by the banks of the Piscataqua River, on Marcy Street. **Season:** Year round (performances are held from late June to mid-August). **Admission** free. **Information:** Greater Portsmouth Chamber of Commerce, 278 State Street, Portsmouth, NH 03801.

Weirs Beach

Here in one of Lake Winnipesaukee's oldest vacation resort communities, you can swim at the pleasant public beach both in the warm afternoon sunshine and in the evening under the stars, when the beach is lighted. A broad boardwalk runs along the waterfront past the headquarters of the Winnipesaukee Flagship Corporation, and past the miniature golf course to the great big yellow building built on a pier, where you can enjoy a shore dinner or snack on caramel corn, cotton candy, fried dough, or popcorn. Both sides of the street sport amusement arcades, and there are also several photo parlors where you can have old-fashioned pictures taken. Expect large crowds if you arrive on a summer weekend, and do your utmost to avoid visiting on a holiday. Children are particularly pleased with the Weirs Beach Water Slide, which has four twisting flumes to splash down. But the biggest attraction here is that it is the point of origin of most of the boat cruises on the great lake.

LAKE WINNIPESAUKEE CRUISES. Step up to the Flagship Corporation office and purchase your tickets for the cruise of your choice. You may elect to take a three-and-a-quarter-hour trip aboard the M/V *Mount Washington,* which follows a fifty-mile route past many points of interest around the lake. There are cozy seats and wide windows inside, or you can sit on the open deck above and feel the breeze whip by. Hearty eating is very much a part of your cruise whether you catch the breakfast buffet, lunch, or dinner. Or, you can stick to snacks and ice-cream sundaes from the Ship's Galley and Soda Fountain. Crew members provide a commentary focusing on local history and legend.

If the *Mount Washington* cruise sounds too long, as it is for many children, sign on for an hour-and-three-quarters-long jaunt aboard either the M/V *Sophie C.* or the M/V *Doris E.* The former is a United States mail boat that delivers mail daily along a route originally begun in 1892. The lake contains 274 habitable islands, and the route takes you to some of those at the northern end. On the *Doris E.,* sightseeing is the name of the game. Crew members deliver commentary on both cruises; snacks and soda are available.

One of the largest natural lakes within the United States that lies entirely within one state, Lake Winnipesaukee boasts 72 square miles of water and 283 miles of shoreline. As you travel her glistening surface, you see bays and coves, bustling marinas, and sleepy cottages as well as simple camps built on stilts, and elegant summer homes. Whichever cruise you choose, think about how the lake got its name. The story goes that once Wonaton, a great chief famed for his prowess and valor, dwelt on the lake's north shore. His beautiful daughter Mineola was sought by many but desired none until she set her eye on Adiwando, the youthful chief of a rival tribe to the south. Having heard Mineola's praises sung, he had traveled across the lake seeking her, risking capture in the enemy village. Wonaton was away from his people at the time and therefore powerless to hinder the young chief; Mineola's tribesmen, admiring the youth's bravado, let

The chief assailed Adiwando, intending to kill him; only his daughter and her obvious love for the young man stopped him, and Wonaton was won over by the pair.

The name "Winnipesaukee" means "Smile of the Great Spirit," proclaimed by Wonaton to commemorate the good portents of the day.

him be, and he at once fell in love with the Indian maiden. Upon his return, not only was Wonaton loath to discover the presence of an enemy, but he was accompanied by his own choice of suitor for his daughter and therefore the more enraged at seeing Wonaton. He assailed Adiwando, intending to kill him; only his daughter and her obvious love for the young man stopped him, and Wonaton was won over by the pair.

They were married at once, and were escorted by the tribe at the start of their wedding journey. As they paddled across the lake, the black waters and gray skies became sparkling blue waters and radiant sunshine. Hence the name "Winnipesaukee," which means "the smile of the Great Spirit," proclaimed by Wonaton to commemorate the good portents of the day.

Think of Wonaton, Mineola, and Adiwando as you cruise the lake, passing an island that is for sale (the asking price is in excess of a million dollars), or a water-skier whipping gracefully in and out of the wake. In the distance on a clear day, you can see Mount Washington. Some things change, but some just endure.

ACCESS

TO GET TO WEIRS BEACH. Take I-93 exit 20, and follow Route 3 north about fifteen miles.

WEIRS BEACH WATER SLIDE. Directions: Located on Route 3 in Weirs Beach. **Season:** Memorial Day through Labor Day. **Admission** charged. (603) 366-5161.

LAKE WINNIPESAUKEE CRUISES. Directions: Ticket office is located on the boardwalk at Weirs Beach. **Season:** Memorial Day through mid-October. (Daily, July 1 through Labor Day). **Admission** charged. (603) 366-5531.

Holderness

SQUAM LAKES SCIENCE CENTER. Here is a place to visit when you feel like spending time out-of-doors, be it a warm spring afternoon, a crisp autumn morning, or any time in between. From mid-April to late November, you and your children can immerse yourselves in the many aspects of our natural environment with the aid of the live animals, formal exhibits, and nature trails here at the science center. There is a great deal to see and do, activities that appeal to both the four- and fourteen-year-old, not to mention adults. The center is composed of over two hundred acres of land and many buildings; its various ongoing programs make a point of encouraging visitors to interact with staff members. Here follows a selection of activities waiting for you; sample as many as you like

In the Discovery Exhibit, you can travel through a dark tunnel on your knees, using your sense of touch to identify items like a snakeskin or a turtle shell. Even toddlers are delighted by this.

or enjoy them all if you have the time.

Daily programs in the Barn focus on different types of animals. If "Birds of Prey" is the topic for the day, you see some stuffed specimens of a bald eagle and other birds that fit into this category. A guide talks to you about some of the eagle's habits, and you learn that he feeds heavily on fish. Did you know that he is on the endangered species list because his number has decreased so much in recent years? You then find yourself involved in a discussion in which you may apply your new knowledge to practical issues. What is the bald eagle's biggest problem? a staff member might ask. After some thought, you realize that his greatest difficulty is loss of habitat. You know that he eats fish, and therefore needs to live near the water. You hear from others in the audience that industry has come to occupy increasing amounts of waterfront property and that more and more people continue to build their homes near the water. Someone else suggests that insecticides and pesticides have polluted the water and that, in turn, the fish population has decreased. Such discussion helps form links between the bird or animal under discussion and the environmental and demographic issues that affect it. You begin to get a real feel for the way one part of our world affects another.

In addition to using visual aids such as stuffed specimens and silhouettes of birds in flight, the staff passes live specimens around for close-up examination. When you meet the live red-tailed hawk Jamaica, you learn that she has eyesight so sharp that from a ten-story height she could read the date on a penny dropped to the ground. You are also told that she is much lighter than she appears to be, and when you are given some bones from a now deceased red-tailed hawk, you realize why — her bones are hollow! A foot with sharp talons and different types of hawk feathers are also handed around.

The presentations in the barn change daily, but you might see one about nocturnal animals or another focusing on either New Hampshire mammals or reptiles. The sessions last about forty-five minutes, and slides are sometimes shown. Nature craft sessions are also held here in the barn; you might find yourself dipping candles or making a sun print.

At the Loon Exhibit, you discover why the number of loons in the area has decreased in recent years and how naturalists and environmentalists are attempting to reverse that trend. A display that uses an old balance scale clarifies the concept of homeostasis, or nature's delicate balance. You learn that the condition of the skunk population can strongly affect the loon population. Why? Well, skunks eat snapping-turtle eggs. If the skunk population decreases for some reason, the snapping turtle population may well increase. Snapping turtles eat loon eggs. If, then, the

Use a magnifier to examine a blue heron's beak, an owl's wing, or a flycatcher's nest.

snapping turtle population increases, you can expect the loon population to decrease. It soon becomes clear just how interconnected all these matters are.

In the Discovery Exhibit, you can travel through a dark tunnel on your knees, using your sense of touch to identify items like a snakeskin or a turtle shell. (Even toddlers — accompanied by adults — love this.) Here you also find the Bug Board, covered with brightly colored drawings of insects and noninsects. You are shown three insect features: three body parts, antennae, six legs. You then touch a cable to a button next to those animals on the board that you think are insects. If you are correct, a light lights up. If you are wrong, a buzzer sounds.

In the Murphy Bird Exhibit, there are many more participatory displays. Here you can use a push-button board with peek holes to match the physical characteristics (fat bill, long legs and toes) of different birds with their eating habits (cracks open seeds, eats flying insects). Or, use a magnifier to examine a blue heron's beak, an owl's wing, or a flycatcher's nest. Then try your luck sorting picture cubes into groups of birds sharing particular characteristics, such as those with two different-colored eyes or those that grasp with their feet.

In the Bear Facts Exhibit, don a set of headphones to get the lowdown on the center's two resident bears, Bert and Winnie. Bert arrived as a half-pound cub in 1973 and had to be bottle fed, but just look at him now! Today these omnivorous animals feast on whole-protein dog food supplemented with berries, nuts, molasses, and honey. Here you find an oversized puzzle challenging you to separate migrators, hibernators, and semi-active and active winter animals. You can also stroke the two full-sized bearskins (from animals shot prior to present protective legislation) and test your bear knowledge at a large board that poses questions such as: do bears hug their victims to death? Lift a flap for the answer: no, striking and biting with teeth and claws is the bear's method.

Be careful! Don't become so enchanted with the participatory exhibits here that you forget to give some time to admiring the live animals in residence. In addition to the bears, you meet a snowy owl who lost part of a wing at an airport in 1977 and can no longer fend for itself. These owls, it turns out, are attracted to airports because they resemble their home in the arctic tundra. You also make the acquaintance of a raccoon, turtles and snakes, other native birds, and some white-tailed deer.

Fact boards and small displays accompany some of the animal exhibits. After reading the information, test your sense of logic by trying to unravel the animal-track mysteries posted near many of the animals. You are told a brief story, provided with a couple of clues, and given a mystery to solve. In doing so, you must

Bert arrived as a half-pound cub in 1973 and had to be bottle fed, but just look at him now!

decipher a diagram showing different sets of animal tracks. It's not as easy as it sounds.

In the Man and the Environment area, you can visit a blacksmith shop or listen to a recorded message explain the workings of the hundred-year-old steam-powered sawmill. In the saphouse there's a slide show on maple syrup making, and elsewhere is a functioning windmill, a forestry exhibit, and a Sokoki Indian wigwam replica to explore.

The center has three lovely miles of trails to follow, trails that wind about the pond and pass through forest and fields. Climb Mount Fayal along the Gephart Trail for views of Big Squam Lake. Or make a steeper ascent up the Davison Trail for a look at Little Squam Lake, below. If you feel like just taking a relaxing walk in the woods, pick up a copy of the trail guide, "Forest Meander," which encourages you to employ all your senses in interpreting the flora and fauna you meet along the way. There are eleven stops, each pointing out a different aspect of nature. At the Hole in the Tree Stop, you can examine the home and feeding place of the pileated woodpecker. At the Fungus Stop, notice how fungi send a network of rootlike structures through a dying tree, causing decay and breakdown, while at the Hemlock Listen Stop, strain your ears to catch the "teacher, teacher" of the oven bird or the flutelike song of the wood thrush.

Search for kinsman crystals, pegmatite, impure quartzite, and more.

If there is a rock hound in your number, ask for "A Guide to the Geology of the Squam Lakes Science Center," which begins with a geologic history of the area and continues with an identification and discussion of the rocks and minerals you encounter on your hike. Search for kinsman crystals, pegmatite, impure quartzite, and more. The mile-and-a-half walk takes at least an hour to complete. As you wander the trails, keep in mind the center's philosophy: "Leave only footprints, take only photographs."

Allow a minimum of two hours for your visit to the science center if you plan to include a hike. Plan to take along a picnic lunch; or, purchase sandwiches, fruit, and cold drinks across the street at the Smith Piper Company General Store, at your service since 1888. Here you find an inventory that combines old and new, shelves stuffed with canned goods, honey, maple syrup, cheese, teapots, baskets, housewares, work clothes, and candy. Next door, at the Holderness Book Shop, you can pick up inexpensive used books to round out your vacation reading or you can purchase hand-tied fish flies.

ACCESS

SQUAM LAKES SCIENCE CENTER. Directions: Take I-93 exit 24 (Route 3) and follow Route 3 six miles east to Holderness. In Holderness, turn left onto Route 113, and go one block. The entrance is on your left. **Season:**

As they explore tunnels beneath the earth's surface, small bodies ease through Plymouth's Polar Caves more adeptly than grownups can hope to.

A visit to the caves requires caution, stamina, and dexterity, but that's part of the fun.

April through November. **Admission** charged. (603) 968-7194.

Plymouth

POLAR CAVES. Back in the Paleozoic era, more than 200 million years ago, hot molten masses were squeezed from deep within the earth toward the surface, where they cooled and solidified into what is now known as granite. During the following 200 million years or so, weathering and erosion eventually revealed the huge granite masses we now know as mountains.

At the Polar Caves, you can travel beneath the surface of the earth as you explore the caves and passageways created many thousands of years ago when a great continental glacier formed in Canada and moved slowly south over the mountains of New Hampshire. The massive body of ice covered the highest peaks and filled in the deepest valleys. As the mass slid over Mount Haycock, it shoved boulders to one side of the mountain, forming Hawk's Cliff. The cliff was fractured and cracked by the time the glacier began to melt. As the ice thawed, the great chunks of granite broke and shifted and were eventually deposited at the base of the cliff in a jumbled mass. It is this mass of tumbled granite that forms the caves and passageways through which you will journey.

A visit to the caves requires caution, stamina, and dexterity, but that's all part of the fun. There are eight stations along the boardwalks outside the cliff where you can listen to recorded messages containing information about the history, geology, and lore of the caves. For instance, you find out where to look for ice deposits (even in August) and you learn about the Pemigewasset Indian women and children who once hid in these caves. In one cave, you can see a display of phosphorescent minerals discovered there.

To have the best experience here, it is essential that children take their spelunking adventure seriously. This is no place to run or show off. There are steep, rocky ways to climb down, narrow passages to traverse. The footing is sometimes unsure, and everyone must always be careful not to bang his head on an overhanging piece of rock. Each person should take plenty of time and give the person in front of him plenty of room to navigate.

Most children find the caves exciting and mysterious, and they are usually much more adept than their parents at making their way through the tunnels. In the Cave of Eternal Chill they shiver enthusiastically, and in Fat Man's Misery, they creep through the narrow crevices far more gracefully than their older companions. Some of the more challenging caves do have detours, where a child or an adult can pass by easily if he is tired of twisting and squirming. Children seven and older enjoy scuttling through the caves. Plan to spend about an hour here.

Nearby there is a pond that is home to many varieties of waterfowl. Animal food is available for purchase in vending machines if you wish to treat the ducks and geese to a handout. There is a turkey, some lively goats, and several types of rabbits as well. Small children will probably be happier here than in the caves.

In the Cave of Eternal Chill they shiver enthusiastically, and in Fat Man's Misery they creep through the narrow crevices far more gracefully than their older companions.

ACCESS

POLAR CAVES. **Directions:** Take I-93 exit 26 (Route 25) and follow Route 25 west about five miles. **Season:** Mid-May through mid-October. **Admission** charged. (603) 536-1888.

Cornish and Meriden

It really isn't cricket to visit New England and not see some covered bridges. Although each of the six states boasts about its bridges, there are eighteen covered bridges located in this section of New Hampshire, making it a veritable paradise for covered-bridge fanciers. The bridges are clearly marked by large signs and are easily accessible. They span smooth rivers, babbling brooks, and rocky gorges. Pack up a picnic, a camera, and perhaps a fishing pole (you never know who might be lurking in the shadowy pools) and enjoy a day in western New Hampshire, visiting these bridges and others that you ferret out on your own.

CORNISH-WINDSOR COVERED BRIDGE. The bridge you see today is the fourth one on this site and the longest covered bridge in the country. The original bridge, which was probably not covered, was built in 1796, destroyed by a flood in 1824, and then rebuilt. The second structure was demolished by another flood in 1848; its replacement suffered yet again the same fate in 1866. The current covered bridge was built in 1866, and was strengthened and renovated by the State of New Hampshire in 1954. In former days, a private company operated the crossing as a toll bridge. Still in use today, the bridge crosses the Connecticut River between Windsor, Vermont, and Cornish, New Hampshire.

Traveling north on I-91 in Vermont, take exit 8 (Ascutney) to Route 5, which becomes Main Street in Windsor. Continue north on Main Street just under a half mile and turn right to the covered bridge (Route 12A), following signs to Saint-Gaudens National Historic Site.

BRIDGE-OVER-THE-GORGE OR BLOW-ME-DOWN. About one-fifth the length of the Cornish-Windsor Bridge, the Blow-Me-Down, which crosses the Blow-Me-Down River, was built in the 1860s.

MILL OR MERIDEN COVERED BRIDGE. Built in the early 1800s for three hundred dollars, the bridge was repaired to the tune of twenty thousand dollars after it was damaged by a hurricane in 1963. It crosses Blood's Brook.

If you like to draw, bring along supplies and sketch the three bridges, accentuating differences in style and setting. If you enjoy preserving your

Continue past the Saint-Gaudens site on Route 12A about four miles. Turn right about a quarter mile after passing the Maxfield Parrish House (high on a hill to your left), following the covered-bridge sign, and continue a half mile to the bridge.

Return to Route 12A and follow it through Plainfield; bear right, heading east, toward Meriden, where you pass Kimball Union Academy about seven miles east of Plainfield. The bridge is located at the foot of the hill just beyond the school.

experiences with the help of a camera, this is the perfect time to experiment.

Conway/North Conway/ Jackson Area

Located in the postcard-pretty Mount Washington Valley, the Conway/North Conway/Jackson area offers lots of opportunity to become familiar with both the history and the natural resources of this spectacular part of New Hampshire. Here you can hike, swim, fly, and canoe as you broaden your perception of a terrain rich in rivers and mountains, and visit some intriguing villages well accustomed to meeting visitors' needs.

Center Conway

SACO BOUND/NORTHERN WATERS. In order to become well acquainted with some of the area's natural features, get out there and put your children in first-person contact with some of New Hampshire's majestic mountains and wondrous waterways. The people at Saco Bound/Northern Waters in Center Conway can help you do it. When you visit their headquarters, ask to see the five-minute video-cassette show, which provides an overview of the types of adventures available. Saco Bound outfits canoe, kayak, and rafting trips; our focus is on canoeing. The Saco is a gentle, clear, and shallow river, perfect for novices. Even toddlers can be taken along safely; older children will thoroughly enjoy learning to maneuver their own craft.

The most popular section of the Saco is the forty-three mile stretch extending from just below Center Conway to Hiram, Maine. The water is crystal clear, cool, and clean, and flows mainly over a sandy bottom. You are never more than a few minutes from a beach as you glide past open meadows and river banks studded with stands of white pine and silver maple, all watched over by the White Mountains beyond. You can paddle from New Hampshire to Maine in less than an hour! During the summer, the river is so peaceful that it offers little hazard even to rank beginners, making this a trip that shouldn't be missed.

For your canoeing pleasure, there are many arrangements available. If you have never canoed before, you might choose to spend a few hours exploring the river, stopping at a sandbar for a picnic and a swim. The staff help you choose an appropriate route, provide pointers for a safe and satisfying journey, determine how long you will need to complete your trip, and outfit you with life preservers, paddles, canoes, and maps. Route and schedule established, they set a meeting time and place. You "put-in" right

Even toddlers can be taken along safely; older children will thoroughly enjoy learning to maneuver their own craft.

opposite Saco-Bound headquarters and when you arrive at your destination, a staff member is there to transport you and your equipment back to headquarters and your car. If you are a more experienced canoeist and have your own equipment, Saco Bound will still help with route planning and pick-up arrangements.

A one-day trip requiring a minimum of six hours (including lunch and swimming breaks) will take you to Canal Bridge, a distance of eleven miles. The Saco, however, is also perfect for canoe camping, so you may wish to take an overnight trip. A two-day trip takes you about twenty-three miles, ending near Lovewell Pond, while on a three-day trip you will most likely paddle all the way to Hiram, forty-three miles away. Wherever you choose to go, Saco Bound will arrange to meet you for the return trip.

There are several public campgrounds located near the river, but you are also free to camp at the many beaches along the way. The rule is that you may camp wherever signs do not expressly prohibit trespassing. Do keep in mind that the land along the river banks is privately owned and that camping privileges are granted by grace of the owners. Be certain to leave the area at least as clean as you found it. If you plan to camp outside the public camping areas, you will need a fire permit; Saco Bound can tell you where to get it. If you want to fish, you will also need a New Hampshire fishing permit; inquire of your Saco Bound guides where to get one.

In the summer months, Saco Bound turns away over a hundred canoe-rental requests on some weekends, so if at all possible, plan your expedition for midweek. You are further rewarded midweek with the fact that the river is relatively uncrowded in comparison to the often-congested weekend flow. If you must choose a weekend, reserve at least two weeks in advance to avoid disappointment. And if, even after our reassurances concerning the nature of the river, you feel that you would be happier in the company of an experienced paddler, sign up for one of the full-day guided trips offered twice a week in the summer. You're given plenty of time for swimming along the way, and your guide prepares a barbecued lunch for you at one of the sandbars.

Keep in mind that a trip on this section of the Saco is by no means a trip to the wilderness. Houses and stores are located near the river and you will be able to find assistance should any problems arise. Yet the Saco does provide a way to get out into the country, to get away from that dependence on the automobile that tends to dominate our lives. Your children develop an understanding of the river that is available only to those who have literally "gotten their feet wet." This could well become one of those treasured family vacation experiences that surface again and again in

You're given plenty of time for swimming along the way, and your guide prepares a barbecued lunch for you at one of the sandbars.

"I didn't even know how to hold a paddle when I started," one enthusiastic fourth-grader testifies, "but now I could probably go twenty miles on my own without batting an eyelash!"

conversations as the years pass. "I didn't even know how to hold a paddle when I started," one enthusiastic fourth-grader testifies, "but now I could probably go twenty miles on my own without batting an eyelash!"

ACCESS _____

SACO BOUND/NORTHERN WATERS. Directions: Traveling north on Route 16, go through Conway and turn right onto Route 302; go about three miles to Center Conway. Saco Bound is on your right. **Season:** Spring through fall. **Admission** charged. (603) 447-2177.

North Conway

"This here's a 1938 Waco," he drawls. "Now, in Texas they call it a Way-ko, and they call the pilots wacko!"

WHITE MOUNTAIN SCENIC AIR FLIGHTS. For a different kind of transportation experience, drive "up the road apiece" to the White Mountain Airport in North Conway, where White Mountain Scenic Air Flights carry you sky-high for an intimate look at the mountains and an aerial view of the valley below. There are three types of rides available; most children particularly enjoy the open-cockpit ride in a tiny biplane, say, Tom Glassburner's Waco. ("This here's a 1938 Waco [pronounced wacko]," he drawls. "Now, in Texas they call it a Way-ko, and they call the pilots wacko!") This sporty red-and-white number can carry a pair of passengers as it climbs, banks, and turns, traveling at an altitude of just 250 feet and at a speed of about 100 miles per hour. Before you climb aboard, be sure to don a flying-ace helmet complete with earflaps and chinstrap. Then clamber onto the wing and into the cockpit. The pilot sits in a seat behind. You fly over the valley for about fifteen minutes before returning to the airstrip below. The fifteen minutes seem like a mere moment, and young riders are likely to clamor for more when they return to earth. The small planes look like toys and are much less intimidating than the huge aircraft used in major commercial flights.

If your group consists of more than two fliers, you might choose a small-plane air tour of the mountain area lasting from fifteen to thirty minutes (depending upon how much you are willing to pay). The longer the flight, the greater the territory you cover, moving up into the notches and along the Presidential Range on the half-hour trip. Your pilot happily points out spots of interest below. These planes are enclosed; flights require a minimum of three passengers.

If you can muster up a group of four, consider the helicopter tours. Because of the helicopter's maneuverability, these flights provide the best opportunity to become really involved in the many facets of the landscape. There is no age minimum for any of the flights and you need not reserve a place. Just show up

With an 1874 Victorian train station, old timetables, and a sixty-year-old steam engine, the Conway Scenic Railroad is as authentically old-fashioned as can be.

at the airport and wait your turn, seldom more than fifteen minutes.

CONWAY SCENIC RAILROAD. For a genuine old-fashioned train ride, hop aboard the Conway Scenic Railroad for an eleven-mile spin through the Saco River Valley. Your train is powered by a sixty-year-old puffing steam locomotive, either 0-6-0 No. 47 or 2-6-2 No. 108. When its elders are ailing or simply fatigued, a thirty-six-year-old diesel locomotive is sometimes called upon to provide relief.

Your visit begins when you enter the sprawling yellow Victorian railroad station, built in 1874. Step up to the telegraph and ticket office; here you can obtain the long brown tickets that also serve as souvenirs. Looking around a bit, you find the room is filled with railroad artifacts; there are timetables, tickets, lanterns, and conductors' and engineers' gear. In an adjoining room, you find the Brass Whistle Gift Shop, which stocks striped engineers' caps, model trains, and other appropriate items.

Outside, you can visit the roundhouse, where the locomotives live and are cared for; notice the turntable that rotates a two-hundred-ton locomotive, and more than twenty antique railroad cars, some of them under restoration. Be certain, however, to board the train early, particularly if you want to claim the choice seats (right-side window seats) in one of the open-air Cinder Collector Club Cars. There are comfortable enclosed coaches as well.

The conductor calls "All Aboard!" several times before giving a "highball" (a hand signal indicating "ready to go"); the engineer responds with two toots of the whistle. Then off you go, chugging down tracks constructed by the Portsmouth, Great Falls, and Conway Railway in 1872. Narrated commentary over a loudspeaker occasionally makes a point about the

Off you go, chugging down tracks constructed by the Portsmouth, Great Falls, and Conway Railway in 1872.

scenery or the history of the railroad. You hear that 1961 marked the last regularly scheduled passenger ride along this Boston-North Conway route, and that the last freight run was in 1972.

The train rumbles past geese, horses, and cows, past "the largest dairy farm in New England," past corn fields, past folks swimming and canoeing along the river banks. When you come to a road crossing, the people in their autos will more than likely wave a friendly greeting. There is an eight-minute layover in Conway, where you can debark to pick up a soda and some popcorn before boarding for the return trip. The entire journey takes less than an hour, and is a delightful experience for children in the ten-and-under range as well as for people of all ages who have never traveled by train.

OTHER STOPS. There is a pleasant park located next to the train station, an attractive grassy area with swings, slide, seesaws, climbing equipment, even a wading pool and a low basketball hoop. There are picnic tables, too, making this a good spot to munch al fresco while watching the pedestrian parade in this thriving New Hampshire resort town.

If you prefer to dine in a restaurant and want to treat yourself to a special meal (but in a place where even the pickiest eater can order that beloved hamburger), try Horsefeathers, on Main Street. This very popular eatery (expect waits at peak hours) features homemade soups, creative sandwiches (heavy on the vegetables, melted cheese, and unusual mixtures of meats), and "horse fries" (oversized French fries). The atmosphere is nostalgic, accented by ceiling fans, touches of brass, and blackboards announcing house specials. It is a bustling place, and it's fun to eat here when you are not in a hurry.

The North Conway 5¢-$1 Store is located next to Horsefeathers and is marked by a bright red sign lettered in yellow. Aisles are narrow and goods are packed in tight, no matter where you turn. This is a real old "dime store," just like the ones your grandparents depended upon; for less than a dollar you can choose from dozens of little gismos capable of spicing up a long car trip.

This is a real old "dime store"; for less than a dollar you can choose from dozens of little gismos, each capable of spicing up a long car trip.

ACCESS

TO GET TO NORTH CONWAY. Take I-95 (which becomes the New Hampshire Turnpike) to Portsmouth, then Route 4 (Spaulding Turnpike) north to Rochester. From Rochester take Route 16 north to Center Conway and North Conway.

WHITE MOUNTAIN SCENIC AIR FLIGHTS. Directions: As you are traveling north toward North Conway, the airport is located on Route 16, near the intersection of routes 16 and 302. **Season:** Year round, weather permitting; biplanes do not fly during cold weather. **Admission** charged. (603) 356-2930.

CONWAY SCENIC RAILROAD. Directions: From the junction of routes 302 and 16, go north about four miles to the center of North Conway. **Season:** Early May through late October. **Admission** charged; under four free. (603) 356-5251. **Note:** Trains run rain or shine.

HORSEFEATHERS AND THE NORTH CONWAY 5¢-$1 STORE. Directions: Located next to each other on Route 16 (Main Street) in downtown North Conway, across from the Carroll Reed Ski Shop. **Season:** Year round. Horsefeathers: (603) 356-6862. The North Conway 5¢-$1 Store: (603) 356-3953.

Glen

HERITAGE-NEW HAMPSHIRE. For a crash course in New Hampshire history, take your children to Heritage-New Hampshire, a lively "museum" where Walt Disney's influence can be felt as you heed the words of lifelike mannequins and marvel at the many special effects. Walk up the wooden ramp to the thatched cottage where the purser does business, and purchase passage aboard the good ship *Reliance,* ready to depart from England on her journey to Mason's Grant in the New World. Sea gulls clamor and sails billow in the background as you read the listing of victuals supplied aboard during the crossing; one pound of beef, mutton, or pork on "flesh days," one side of salt fish on "fish days" (supplemented by butter and cheese); and half the fish allowance on "fast day," these rations to be supplemented by a daily allowance of one loaf of bread and a gallon of beer. Beware the onset of scurvy.

A guide in a tricorn hat leads you aboard the deck of the *Reliance,* which begins to roll as the sky darkens. Wind whistles past, and thunder and lightning fill the sky; in front of you (on film, of course) the sea foams and rolls. The year is 1634.

After a journey of sixty days and sixty nights, you disembark as your guide warns of the "bears, wolves, dogs with sharp noses, and savages" ahead. You wander through the forest past slides depicting native American animals (note the stuffed versions often posed dramatically in the brush), past boulders and tree trunks, and across a stream filled with real trout. The "woods" are full of the sounds of woodpeckers, waterfowl, and other beasts, and soon you hear the thunder of a waterfall. You pass an Algonquin wigwam, made by the women from bent saplings covered with heavy winter birch bark. And as you round the bend, the Amoskeag Falls appear; here the Indians are drying their fish, much as they did many hundreds of years ago here in the fertile Merrimack River Valley, well before the birth of Christ.

Wind whistles past, thunder and lightning fill the sky, and the sea foams and rolls. The year is 1634.

The sense of plenty is soon diminished by a winter scene in which you become sensitive to scarcity. Enter the modest cabin, where snowshoes and animal skins hang from the wall pegs. Up in the loft, a woman cuddles her young one and croons the sad strains of "Barbara Allen." In a nearby barn, a farmer sits planing boards while enjoying the companionship and body warmth of his horse, pig, oxen, sheep, and chickens.

As you travel through the scenes, you soon become aware of the passage of time. Your trip through Heritage-New Hampshire spans some three hundred years, the scenes growing more sophisticated as you progress. Your visit to Portsmouth Naval Ship Yard, with its cacophony of hammering and sawing sounds, is interrupted by voices discussing the new flag, the "Stars and Stripes," which will soon fly in these united colonies. As you move on to a town square, revolutionary fervor is evident everywhere. A woman grouses about the call for war as she tosses waste water from her second-story window into a barrel below. Over at the Blue Bib, an overindulgent colonist sprawls on the floor as the tavern keeper watches with disgust (you know that his name will soon be added to the list, posted at the door, of those forbidden entry). Little girls in fancy frocks recite from their hornbooks in the drawing room of an elegant brick home. The printer toils at his press, laboring to turn out another issue of the *New Hampshire Gazette*.

An old wagon bearing a small cannon sits in the courtyard; young visitors often pause to heft the puny cannonballs.

An old wagon bearing a small cannon sits in the courtyard; young visitors often pause to heft the puny cannonballs and speculate on what their own roles would have been had they lived at this historic point in time. As they look up from their musings, they see a movie of soldiers projected down at the end of State Street and realize that the American Revolution is in full swing.

The passage of time is again made real as you enter a gracious courtyard surrounded by balconied house fronts and curtained windows. Local citizens watch from balconies as the new President, George Washington, addresses them to an accompaniment of cheers and the ringing of bells. Fireworks light the sky.

You continue on across a covered bridge (toll one cent), past the prosperous coach manufactory, to make the acquaintance of Daniel Webster, who notes that "The gift of gab has stood me well. One of my first clients was charged with murder and I defended him well. Fortunately, he was hanged." In a nearby hall, a session of a New Hampshire town meeting is underway. The issue under consideration is whether or not to authorize the use of the meeting hall for Saturday-night public square dancing. Some are angered at the prospect of mixing business with pleasure, but after much dissent and humor the measure is approved.

Time continues on and the year is now 1852; the

scene is the Amoskeag Mills, at that time the largest cotton mills in the world, where twenty-seven hundred miles of cloth were produced in a single week. Small figures move methodically to and fro among the looms in the dark factory below, and children begin to ask questions about the Industrial Revolution. At one point these mills employed seventeen thousand workers; despite the poor conditions they labored under, many were grateful for the opportunity for steady employment. A sign notes the weekly wage scale, based on twelve hours of work a day, six days per week. Children under ten received seventy-five cents, grown women got two dollars, and able-bodied men were paid four dollars.

Your journey through New Hampshire's history touches briefly on the Civil War years before catapulting you into the comforts of the 1880s. You relax in the lobby of the Grand Hotel, waiting for your train ride through Crawford Notch. Later, you linger at the edge of Echo Lake, experimenting with throwing your voice (yes, it does echo), and admiring the profile of the Old Man of the Mountains far above.

Heritage-New Hampshire is full of gimmicks, but they are the kind of special effects that keep children interested. As the sights, sounds, smells, and sensations of daily life pass by, youngsters may well absorb some of the state's history and heritage. The presentation is quite a palatable way of serving up the past to children who are attuned to the immediacy and flashiness of the television age. Even skeptics will be impressed by the extent and variety of the scenes included in Heritage. Allow at least forty-five minutes for your visit. And keep this spot in mind as the perfect solution to a rainy day in the mountains.

"The gift of gab has stood me well. One of my first clients was charged with murder and I defended him well. Fortunately, he was hanged."

ACCESS

HERITAGE-NEW HAMPSHIRE. Directions: From North Conway, take Route 16 north about five miles. **Season:** Memorial Day through mid-October. **Admission** charged. (603) 383-9776. **Note:** Last ticket is sold forty-five minutes prior to closing time.

Jackson

WILDCAT VALLEY COUNTRY STORE. Moving out of the Conways now, travel 10 miles north to Jackson, a lovely mountain town by the Ellis River. Here you find the genuine article — a country store that is a welcome relief from the souvenir shops accompanying most tourist attractions. This store contains barrels, baskets, and shelves chock full of toys, books, household items, soaps, pieces of clothing, bits of hardware, foodstuffs, and the like. Here you can buy a calico-wrapped pine pillow (put it under your own pillow and dream about the New Hampshire woods

For just a nickel, you can work the Regina music box and shop to its melodic tunes.

Eager eyes will pore over wooden toys, old-fashioned candy, sunbonnets, and more at the Wildcat Valley Country Store.

If you'd like to step back into a more gracious time, check into the Eagle Mountain House, a rambling white structure reminiscent of the old-style grand resort hotel.

when you return home), a reproduction of an old-fashioned wooden toy, a sunbonnet, some soap balls, or a striped bag full of old-fashioned candy. You don't have to slog through heaps of bumper stickers and T-shirts, ashtrays, and plastic backscratchers. For just a nickel, you can work the Regina music box and shop to its melodic tunes. The aisles are narrow, the floor slanted, and the lighting minimal, so allow lots of time to browse and discover everything; it's fun to look at the braided rugs and baskets of all sizes and shapes, and perhaps make purchases from the pickle barrel, the glass-front candy counter, or one of the containers of maple cream, sugar, and syrup. A fine half-hour can be spent here, looking at the dozens and dozens of useful and fanciful things.

EAGLE MOUNTAIN HOUSE. No matter what your preference in accommodations, be it cabin, motel, hotel, country inn, or campground, the North Conway-Jackson area can meet your requirements. If you like to step back into a more gracious time, check into the Eagle Mountain House, a rambling white structure reminiscent of the old-style grand resort hotel. A casual atmosphere pervades the formerly elegant complex, and the staff is very receptive to young visitors. The 125 rooms are booked on a modified American plan only, which means that the daily per-person rate includes room, breakfast, and dinner as well as the use of all facilities. Choose from single or double rooms with or without private bathrooms, or select adjoining rooms connected by a shared bathroom, the perfect family arrangement.

Meals are served in the spacious dining room, where there is always a choice of entrees. One evening a week is set aside for an outdoor barbecue; another is delegated for the weekly buffet. Breakfast is a hearty affair featuring fresh fruit cup, homemade muffins, and omelet in addition to the standard pancakes, eggs, French toast, bacon, ham, and sausage. If you want to eat lunch at the inn, you can order sandwiches in the bar or depend on hot dogs and hamburgers grilled pool-side.

For recreation, there is shuffleboard and croquet, a tennis court and a nine-hole golf course (where many older children have gotten their first taste of the game), and a beautiful swimming pool. There is even a swing set for the very young. Indoors is a library with board games, puzzles, and a television set (that's right, there aren't any in the rooms). After dinner, guests gather at the card tables in the huge lobby or rock on the mammoth porch in one of the comfortable rocking chairs. Younger guests head for the basement game room, where they play pool and pinball. They tend to meet other children here, with whom they often explore the cavernous hallways.

Half a mile down the road you can treat the young ones to an icy plunge in the Ellis River, or you can take them on a mountain hike; ask the staff for trail suggestions. If you choose a winter vacation, you will find cross-country skiing, tobogganing, and ice skating among the activities offered. (Write to the Eagle Mountain House, Jackson, NH 03846 for further information, or call 603-383-4347.)

ACCESS

TO GET TO JACKSON. From North Conway, continue north on Route 16 about ten miles, passing Heritage-New Hampshire on your right; then take Route 16A into Jackson.

WILDCAT VALLEY COUNTRY STORE. Directions: Located on Route 16A in Jackson, about a quarter mile past the covered bridge, on your right. **Season:** Year round. **Admission** free. (603) 383-9612.

EAGLE MOUNTAIN HOUSE. Directions: From Jackson center, drive across the covered bridge on Route 16A, turn right on Route 16B, and follow signs. **Season:** Summer, fall, and winter; call for specific dates. (603) 383-4347.

White Mountain National Forest

WILDCAT MOUNTAIN GONDOLA. If you want to walk *down* a mountain instead of up (since the latter often limits you to a modest peak with limited visibility), continue on your way north along Route 16 to Pinkham Notch and Wildcat Mountain. The gondola carries you on a sky ride to the summit of Wildcat Mountain, located entirely within the White Mountain

You travel the mile and a quarter up the mountain in a tiny red, blue, or yellow cable car with windows to the front and sides providing fine visibility.

National Forest, where commercial development is severely restricted. Here you find the base lodge with a cafeteria as well as a lovely picnic area. Pick up a leaflet explaining features along the Thompson Falls Trail, an easy half-hour walk. If you want to wander a trail at higher elevation, ask for an explanatory folder for the self-guiding High Country Nature Trail, located at the summit. Request a trail map, also the same one given to skiers. This will come in handy should you decide to hike back down instead of taking the gondola.

You travel the mile-and-a-quarter distance up the mountain in a tiny red, blue, or yellow cable car with windows to the front and sides providing fine visibility. Once at the top, you enjoy fine views of Mount Washington, the highest mountain in the Northeast. Take as much time as you like exploring the summit; climb the rocky path to the observation deck or otherwise explore the trails. Stick close to the summit lodge unless you have a hiking map and know just where you are headed.

Should your time at the top still not satisfy your craving for the mountains, plan to hike down. The easiest walk is the two-and-a-quarter-mile trek down the Polecat ski trail. Designed for novice skiers, the pitch of the trail is not as steep as that of the more advanced trails and in the summer you find the trail bright with wildflowers. There are great masses of spongy moss too, perfect for taking a rest in. The woods are to either side, but the trail is broad and open, affording constant vistas of the mountain above and the peaks in the distance.

The walk takes about an hour and a half, longer if you plan a picnic. Sneakers or sturdy hiking boots are advised. Warn your children not to run, as the incline is steep enough and the footing rough enough to easily cause a sprained ankle or worse. Take your time as you hike. Walking down a mountain, contrary to popular belief, is as hard on the legs as walking up, and you may all discover muscles you never knew you had.

ACCESS

WILDCAT MOUNTAIN GONDOLA. Directions: Located on Route 16 in Pinkham Notch, twelve miles north of Jackson. **Season:** Memorial Day through mid-October. **Admission** charged. (603) 466-3326.

The Kancamagus Highway

In the early 1900s, prior to the days of strict environmental-protection measures, uncontrolled logging operations and frequent forest fires devastated many parts of the land now set aside as the White Mountain National Forest. At that time the land was privately owned. Concerned citizens lobbied untiringly over a period of years for Federal dollars to

Adults love the natural scenery along the Kancamagus Highway, while children can't gaze long enough at the covered bridge visible from the roadway.

acquire private lands; their efforts were finally rewarded with the creation of the national forest. The Kancamagus Highway, widely considered one of the loveliest roads in the east, covers a thirty-four mile stretch through the forest, linking Conway and Lincoln. The highway follows the path of the Swift River to Passaconaway Valley, where it climbs the flank of Mount Kancamagus, travels across a three-thousand-foot-high pass, and then winds down the Pemigewasset River to Lincoln.

The Forest Service abides by the principle of "The greatest good for the greatest number in the long run." To this end, it attempts to provide recreational opportunities while protecting natural resources such as water, timber, and wildlife. Taking a trip along the highway is the perfect way to help your children develop an understanding and affection for the forest as they enjoy the pleasures it provides.

The highway is punctuated by frequent scenic overlooks where you can pull off from the road and enjoy the views. Most children, however, require more than a view to pique their interest in their natural surroundings. They want to participate in nature rather than just admire it, and the Kancamagus is well suited to this purpose. There are campgrounds, swimming and wading areas, and interpretive trails located within almost immediate access of the road, making this trip far more than just a scenic drive.

THE PASSACONAWAY HISTORIC SITE. The site serves as an information center for visitors, with exhibits here focusing on the history of the people who settled in the Passaconaway Valley. There is a brief nature trail, but two self-guiding trails merit particular attention.

THE RAIL 'N' RIVER TRAIL. This is the first; be sure to get the available brochure, which contains information about natural features along the half-mile trail (though the route is also spotted with interpretive signs). You can allow as little as ten minutes (a nice break to stretch young legs) or as much as half an hour.

THE BOULDER LOOP TRAIL. This one is more demanding. At just under three miles long, it is a gradual climb with several steep pitches. Allow two to four hours, and take along a picnic. Your effort will be rewarded with magnificent views as you reach the mountains' ledges; you see Mount Chocorua (which derives its name from the courageous Indian who died on its summit) and the Swift River Valley. An informative brochure is provided for this trail, too, which tells the story of soil formation and describes the origin and growth of the forest.

SABBADAY FALLS. If you want to show your children a waterfall, you can hike to Sabbaday Falls, where a series of cascades travels down a narrow flume. This is an easy half-mile walk and there are descriptive signs along the way pointing out interesting rock formations. Allow twenty to forty minutes for the round trip from the parking lot to the falls.

CHAMPNEY FALLS. A much longer trek, although also an easy walk, is the mile-and-a-half trail to Champney Falls. This is a good route for spring or fall or after a good rainfall in midsummer. During the dry season the falls are meager or even nonexistent. At the bottom of the falls is a path to the left; follow it about two hundred feet to the base of Pitcher Falls, which has water passing over it for most of the year. Allow one to three hours for your walk.

Fishing is available at many streams and ponds located near the highway. Brook trout are stocked in the Swift River, and native brookies can be found in many of the smaller streams and ponds. A state fishing license is required.

The only formal swimming area is located at Lower Falls, where a lifeguard is on duty during the summer months. There are lovely mountain pools to swim in, and rocks to swim to and to sun upon.

Over two hundred camping sites are located at the five campgrounds along the Kancamagus: Covered Bridge, Blackberry Crossing, Passaconaway, Jigger Johnson, and Big Rock. Passaconaway and Jigger Johnson are also designated wading areas; there are no lifeguards.

Because of the splendid scenery and the proliferation of hiking trails, camping along the Kancamagus is very rewarding. Since the sites are easily accessible and well maintained, this area makes a pleasant destination for even the neophyte camping family. Jigger Johnson is an excellent choice because young ones can cool off wading in the rocky pools or go fishing without the need to load up in the car and drive somewhere.

Camping sites are allocated on a first come, first served basis, with no reservations accepted. Since this

At Lower Falls, a lifeguard is on duty during the summer months. There are lovely mountain pools to swim in, and rocks to swim to and sun upon.

is an extremely popular area, try to arrive early in the day. Also do your utmost to avoid a weekend arrival, since then you are very likely to end up without a site in the summer months. Rain gear and warm clothing are recommended for campers as temperatures in the lower 50s are not unheard of in the lower valleys, even in July. The *maximum* temperature in July in the Presidential Range normally does not exceed the upper 50s.

For additional information, contact the Saco Ranger District, Kancamagus Highway, Conway, NH 03818, or the Forest Supervisor, White Mountain National Forest, Laconia, NH 03246.

ACCESS

TO GET TO THE KANCAMAGUS HIGHWAY. From Route 16, enter the highway (Route 112) at Conway.

PASSACONAWAY HISTORIC SITE. Directions: Located on the Kancamagus Highway twelve miles west of Conway, near the junction of the Bear Notch Road and Kancamagus Highway.

RAIL 'N' RIVER TRAIL. Directions: Originates at the parking lot near the Passaconaway Information Center.

BOULDER LOOP TRAIL. Directions: Drive six miles east of the Passaconaway Information Center to the trail, which is opposite Blackberry Crossing Campground; take the road to your left, cross the covered bridge, and turn right. The trail begins on your left a short distance from the bridge.

SABBADAY FALLS. Directions: Drive three miles west of the Passaconaway Information Center to the entrance to the trail to the falls.

CHAMPNEY FALLS. Directions: Drive two miles east of the Passaconaway Information Center to the entrance to the trail to the falls.

Franconia Notch State Park

THE FLUME. Here is one natural attraction that your children *must* see in New Hampshire. A visit to The Flume is far more than a hike — it is an adventure, an awakening. Who would believe that after just a few minutes walk from the busy highway, you come to a natural gorge extending eight hundred feet along the flank of Mount Liberty, where walls of granite rise to heights of ninety feet on either side?

You can visit The Flume in a number of ways, but the more energy you are willing to invest, the more you will see. A bus runs from the entrance gate to Boulder Store. If you take the bus and then walk along the Flume Path, later returning to the store for the bus trip back, your visit will last thirty to forty minutes. This path takes you through The Flume itself; but if you want

At Jigger Johnson, young ones can cool off wading in the rocky pools or even go fishing.

You hear little except the thunder of cascading water as you approach Avalanche Falls, where the Flume Brook plummets forty-five feet into the gorge below.

"Aunt" Jess Guernsey discovered The Flume accidentally at age ninety-three while on a fishing jaunt; she had her troubles convincing her family of her discovery!

The Flume is a must-see for children. Getting there is an adventure, gazing at it an awakening.

to see more, plan to spend about an hour and a half.

The paths are easy to walk, but be prepared for many steep flights of steps as you travel up the boardwalk alongside The Flume. As you begin your ascent (and The Flume path is mostly an uphill climb), you see water flowing gracefully over a bed of large, smooth stones. Soon the chasm narrows and the water deepens. As you travel the boardwalk, you get an intimate look at the flowers, mosses, and ferns that prosper in the damp environment. You hear little except the thunder of cascading water as you approach Avalanche Falls, where the Flume Brook plummets forty-five feet into the gorge below.

If you continue on along the Ridge Path instead of returning to Boulder Store, you will come to an overlook where a rushing torrent of fast mountain water called "cascades" tumbles into narrow Liberty Gorge. Continuing ahead, you come to the pool, a deep basin in the Pemigewasset River that was formed during the Ice Age. It is 40 feet deep and 150 feet in diameter, surrounded by cliffs 130 feet high. A good view of the pool is available from the covered Sentinel Pine Bridge, the base of which is formed from the trunk of one of the largest pine trees in the state, with a girth of 16 feet and a height of nearly 175 feet. The tree was uprooted from the high cliff towering above the pool, where it had stood for centuries, in a 1938 hurricane.

As you walk the paths, think about "Aunt" Jess Guernsey, who discovered The Flume accidentally at age ninety-three while on a fishing jaunt. She had her troubles convincing her family of her marvelous discovery, but from the start she knew she was onto something special. If you wish to learn more about the social and natural history of The Flume area, take one of the guided walks offered several times each week; inquire at the ticket booth for particulars.

OLD MAN OF THE MOUNTAINS. Also known as "The Profile" and "The Great Stone Face," this natural rock formation resembling a man's face hovers on the sheer cliffs twelve hundred feet above Profile Lake. Massive granite blocks form the forehead, nose, upper lip, and chin. From chin to forehead, the Old Man measures about forty feet.

The best access to the Old Man is the parking area off Route 3, beside Profile Lake. There are benches and viewers here, too, and park naturalists hold talks here several times a week (inquire at the Flume ticket office for specifics). A verse attributed to Daniel Webster provides food for thought as you marvel at the profile:

> Men hang out their signs indicative of their
>   respective trades:
> shoemakers hang out a gigantic shoe;
> jewelers a monstrous watch;
> and a dentist hangs out a gold tooth;
> But in the mountains of New Hampshire,
> God Almighty has hung out a sign to
> show that there he makes men.

CANNON MOUNTAIN AERIAL TRAMWAY. The first aerial tramway in America began operation at this site, less than a mile up Route 3 from the Old Man, in 1938. Nearly seven million passengers traveled to the forty-two-hundred-foot summit of Cannon Mountain aboard that tram before its replacement by a new cable car in 1980. The present shiny red or yellow cars each hold up to eighty people. There are a couple of benches, but most passengers choose to stand for the five-minute ride, which affords panoramic views of the mountains and valleys. You feel your ears pop as the tram makes a 2,022-foot vertical ascent over a horizontal distance of more than a mile.

At the top, take the short path to the wooden observation platform to view neighboring Mount Lafayette, Mount Lincoln, Mount Haystack, Mount Liberty, and Eagle Cliff. From the 4040-foot summit of Cannon Mountain, you can hike along the Kinsman Ridge Trail (the entrance is marked by a sign), a brief

From the summit of Cannon Mountain, you can hike along the Kinsman Ridge Trail for a taste of mountain environment almost at the timberline.

There's been a tramway at Cannon Mountain since 1938 — and the view hasn't changed either. It still overwhelms young, first-time passengers.

distance to go for a taste of mountain environment almost at the timberline. As you walk, notice the scrubby growth, and the mushrooms and mosses that cling to the shallow layer of soil. In the summer months, naturalists are stationed at the summit to answer your questions about the wildlife and to advise on hiking routes. There is a summit station where you can consult weather instruments or have a bite to eat in the cafeteria before making your cable-car descent, watching the lakes and highways reappear as you travel down the mountain.

ACCESS

TO GET TO FRANCONIA NOTCH STATE PARK. Follow I-93 north to Lincoln, where it merges into Route 3. The park begins about three miles farther north on Route 3.

THE FLUME. Directions: Located on Route 3, just north of Lincoln. Follow signs. **Season:** Late May through fall foliage. **Admission** charged. (603) 823-5563.

OLD MAN OF THE MOUNTAINS. Directions: Located on Route 3, about five miles north of The Flume. **Season:** Year round. **Admission** free.

CANNON MOUNTAIN AERIAL TRAMWAY. Directions: Located on Route 3, less than one mile north of the Old Man. **Season:** Late May through fall foliage. **Admission** charged. (603) 823-5563.

Newport's Cliff Walk: mansions on one side and the vast Atlantic on the other.

CHAPTER V

Rhode Island

U ncompromisingly independent, Rhode Island was the renegade among the New England states. She was the first colony to declare independence from Great Britain, and the last to join the Union following the American Revolution. Traditionally a haven for dissenters, Rhode Island was first settled in 1636 by Roger Williams, a minister banished from the Massachusetts Bay Colony because of his commitment to religious freedom of conscience. The way in which Rhode Island got her start has affected the appearance and the arrangement of many of the buildings in her towns. For this is the only New England state where you will not repeatedly come upon the typical village green with its church and its surrounding cluster of homes. Since people worshipped in different ways, the church was not always the focal point of social life here as it was in the other colonies.

The smallest state, measuring only thirty-seven miles in width and forty-seven miles in length at its maximum points, Rhode Island is nonetheless the second most densely populated state in the country. Her most important natural resource is her waters. Narragansett Bay, an arm of the Atlantic, cuts deeply into her southern sections. Access to the ocean led to early commerce with the West Indies, a seagoing exchange that involved the export of horses, barrel staves, and salt fish in exchange for molasses and other exotic stuffs.

Inland waterways, most notably the Blackstone River and its tributaries, also generated power for textile mills in the Pawtucket and Woonsocket areas during the years following the American Revolution, when textile manufacturers replaced subsistence farming and the sea trade as the major economic force. The Pawcatuck, Wood, and Pawtuxet rivers also powered many smaller mills.

Today Rhode Island's water-related industries continue to dominate its economic structure. A valuable deep-water port, Providence is one of the principal oil-distributing centers in the Northeast. Newport still continues to house a Navy installation, just as it has for many years. Here elegant yachts share harbor space with formidable working Navy craft in the city that became a symbol of international wealth in the nineteenth century, when millionaires from around the country flocked here for the seaside social season. Wherever you travel in the state, you will find that water is omnipresent in Rhode Island. Whether exploring a reconstructed textile mill, a millionaire's mansion, or a 150-year-old amusement park, you are always very much aware of how important the ocean and the rivers are in Rhode Island's past and present.

LAURA J REPOSA

Take a picnic and lunch with a llama — or just observe as he indulges — at the zoo in Roger Williams Park in Providence.

Providence

ROGER WILLIAMS PARK. Every so often there is a city with one specific attraction that is so appealing that it's worth going out of your way to visit. Such is the case with the Roger Williams Park in Providence, a city that may not otherwise seem to offer much to travelers with children. Recently revitalized, this lovely 450-acre expanse of green contains a splendid variety of terrains and activities. Plan to spend the better part of a day here. Take along a picnic to eat by the side of a pond with a full view of a formal garden or on a bench overlooking exotic animals, as your tastes dictate.

As you enter the park's circular driveway, you see that a well-marked network of roads circles and crosses the park, making it easy to move from one area to another without re-entering city traffic. Children are immediately drawn to the nineteenth-century zoo, one of the oldest in the country, so follow the signs as you go. Once arrived, begin with a visit to the Children's Nature Center, an interpretive learning area featuring exhibits that illustrate how animals adapt to their environments. Small children are particularly comfortable here because the exhibits were designed with their minimal height in mind. Even a two-year-old can get eyeball-to-eyeball with a boa constrictor, a parrot, or an exotic fish. The aquariums extend low to the ground and the higher enclosures

Even a two-year-old can get eyeball-to-eyeball with a boa constrictor, a parrot, or an exotic fish.

are fronted by broad tiers of steps so that children can climb up for a better view. Be certain to stop at the nursery window, where you can see freshly hatched ducks or some other brand new animal. Right outside of the nature center are a large sand pile and sturdy climbing apparatus where children may work off excess energy before moving on.

Another popular area of the zoo is The Farmyard, across the play area from the nature center. As the name implies, this attractive setting contains domestic animals such as cows, pigs, draft horses, goats, donkeys, and chickens (including the Rhode Island Red and a placard testifying to its superiority). Many of the animals are more than willing to have their noses scratched.

The major two hundred exhibits are spread out in roomy grassy enclosures. Because of the spaciousness, you do a lot of walking here, so bring along a stroller or backpack if you have a baby in tow. The zebras, bison, elk, and camels are separated from their human admirers by a barrier of telephone poles and a layer of wire fencing. The effect is very airy and open and you feel "near" to the animals. Wild turkeys, ostriches, and other unusual birds wander among the large mammals, which makes it seem a little bit as though you are watching them in their natural habitat. Indeed, this is one of the few zoos where you don't feel sorry for the animals.

Across from the animals is an area devoted entirely to the ecology of wetlands. Here you walk through a network of paths and wooden bridges, keeping an eye out for Rhode Island waterfowl as you cross the marsh. Children may be more impressed, however, with the opportunity to almost fall into the muddy water half a dozen times than by the information placards placed along the route.

Don't miss the polar bear display. These hefty animals are housed in a rocky environment, separated from their human admirers by a deep moat. Look for a sign noting that polar bears bite, illustrated by a picture of a man being totally devoured! There is a deep pool where the bears can cool off: follow the path to your right to arrive at a viewing window where you can watch the animals swim and cavort under the water. One little girl screamed in fright and delight as a huge polar bear appeared out of the murky depths, pressing its giant paws against the glass only an inch from her nose!

Across from the polar bears is a community of monkeys that deserves attention. Housed in a tall tentlike net structure, these humorous guys swing, jump, and chatter continuously, generally knocking themselves out to keep the folks in stitches. (Are they laughing at us as hard as we're laughing at them?) In this area you also find lions, a house full of exotic birds, and a sea-lion pool, too. If the children are tired

Be certain to stop at the nursery window, where you can see freshly hatched ducks or some other brand new animal.

of walking, treat them to a ten-minute ride on a small horse-drawn cart (near the main entrance), before you take on the rest of the park. Because the zoo is only the beginning.

Wandering the grounds, about fifty yards from the zoo entrance, you can peek inside the Betsy Williams Cottage (1773) for a look at some colonial furnishings and accessories. It is so small that even young children should be able to sustain an interest for the few minutes it takes to look. Then climb into your car and drive deeper into the park, following signs to the Museum of Natural History, which specializes in American Indian, Eskimo, and Pacific area artifacts as well as local items. There is a planetarium here, too.

In the museum area, there are also several gardens and greenhouses to explore. For instance, if you venture into the greenhouse adjacent to the Japanese garden, you will find yourself in a world of exotic plants. Look for such interesting plants as the pony tail palm, the burro's tail, and the staghorn fern, all of which look exactly like what their names imply. There are also fruit trees here, bearing tiny grapefruit, nearly ripe mangos, and bunches of bananas.

One little girl screamed in fright and delight as a huge polar bear appeared out of the murky depths, pressing its giant paws against the glass only an inch from her nose!

For a change of pace, you might wish to rent a paddle boat and cruise luxuriously (albeit under your own foot power) around the pretty pond, imagining yourself part of a more gentle era as you glide beneath bridges and watch the ripples on the water's surface. There is also a merry-go-round to ride and some large Model-T-type cars that children can drive around a track. But the atmosphere here is that of a gracious park, not an amusement area.

Here's the real clincher. Except for the rides and the planetarium show, absolutely everything in the Roger Williams Park is free. The zoo, gardens, and museum are yours for the using, and on a warm summer evening you might be treated to an outdoor concert as well.

ACCESS

ROGER WILLIAMS PARK. Directions: Take I-95 exit 17, and follow Elmwood Avenue a half mile. The entrance to the park, on Elmwood Avenue, is well marked. **Season:** Year round. **Admission** free (except for planetarium and rides). (401) 421-3300.

Pawtucket

CHILDREN'S MUSEUM OF RHODE ISLAND. For indoor sightseeing, drive to nearby Pawtucket and visit this popular museum, which is designed to teach children about their surroundings through active participation. Housed in the Pitcher-Goff Mansion, a mid-nineteenth-century house with a lovely old wrap-around sun porch, brightly colored leaded windows, and a gracious stairwell (with illuminated newel post), the museum offers a houseful of fun and discovery.

Most children spend their first ten minutes hurrying through all the rooms, getting a quick look at the lay of the land before settling down to some serious play. There is a room, for instance, devoted to a climbing structure that resembles a greenhouse. There children can clamber up a ladder to the second story, which boasts a cushioned deck surrounded by protective netting to keep an overactive child from falling out. Underneath are tunnels to crawl through and curtains to draw for privacy. There is also a built-in bed and a whole box full of foam cushions to arrange as the imagination sees fit. When they tire of this, they can enter the adjoining room by way of A-Maze, a winding labyrinth that leads from one play area to the next.

In Grandma's Kitchen, little ones delve into the cabinets for pots and pans and then set to work baking imaginary bread and turning out homemade ice cream (also imaginary, alas) in the hand-cranked ice-cream maker. In the Shape Room, older children can fashion complicated geometric forms out of oversized pieces of masonite with Velcro tabs to join them together. Some of the children stick to simple forms like triangles while others tangle with six pieces to make a hexahedron. One ambitious child is determined to form a dodecahedron (twelve sides, in case you've forgotten).

In another room, a small boy rests in the lap of a huge soft sculpture, a gentle, giant-sized rag doll that could be most anybody's mom. (Adults like to sit in her lap, too.) Nearby, a little girl plays the foot-powered organ to the accompaniment of a toddler on tambourine. Three youngsters are absorbed in a world of their own in the firehouse. One is trying to climb the ladder to the burning rooftop, heavy fire hose in hand. Another screams for assistance from inside the burning building, while still another makes siren noises from his vantage point at the helm of the fire engine.

One room is full of objects made of wood: large chunks of wood to build with and display cases full of items such as a violin, some dolls, a few rolling pins, some tree bark, and even some sawdust. Kids learn how wood smells, how it feels (rough or smooth), and how it can be put to many different uses.

In Let's Pretend, there are lots of capes and hats for playing dress-up and a big curved carnival fun house mirror to admire them in. There are puppets to play with here, too. On the sun porch, you'll find Nature Walk, where little ones can pet real stuffed animals, use binoculars, check out a variety of delicate skulls, and examine specimens with a magnifying glass. In the Quiet Room, there is an oversized checker set to play with (the "board" is a rug), pretty floor pillows to nest in, and lots of baskets of bright and intriguing construction toys to play with.

The exhibits here are rotated frequently, so you

A small boy rests in the lap of a huge soft sculpture, a gentle, giant-sized rag doll that could be just about anybody's mom.

Little ones delve into the cabinets for pots and pans and then bake imaginary bread and turn out homemade ice cream (also imaginary, alas) in the hand-cranked ice-cream maker.

may not see exactly the ones described. The hands-on approach, however, is consistent in all the museum's exhibits, so whenever you visit there will be plenty of opportunity for this kind of exciting involvement. Children three to ten years old can pass a happy hour or two here.

SLATER MILL HISTORIC SITE. Your next stop in this area is the historic site that features a three-building mill complex constructed from 1758 to 1810. Billed as the birthplace of American industry, this is the spot where English immigrant Samuel Slater and two Providence merchants built a mill in 1793 for the production of machine-spun cotton yarn. The building, still standing today, was the first factory in America to successfully produce yarn with water-powered carding and spinning frames. A visit to the Old Slater Mill and the two neighboring buildings the site comprises takes the form of an hour-and-a-half guided tour focusing on both the technical aspects of the new textile technology and the social changes that accompanied it as American manufacturers made the transition from handcraft to machine production. *Note:* This tour is most appropriate for children ten years old and older. Two adults traveling with a seven-year-old and an eleven-year-old, for example, might decide to split up; one might take the younger child to the Children's Museum while the other tours this unusual site with the older child.

In Old Slater Mill itself, you see two dozen cotton machines dating from between 1775 and 1922. The machines are arranged to illustrate the factory processes that convert raw cotton fibers into cloth. Your guide will operate many of them for you, which children generally enjoy; it's difficult to understand how a machine works just by looking at it or reading about it. By observing it in action, you not only gain an understanding of how it works but also a sense of the demands made upon the person who kept it going day in, day out. The sound and strength of the machinery in action also gives you a sense of pace and of rhythm that allows you to re-create an image of early factory life in your own mind.

In the Sylvanus Brown House (1758), the only structure not original to the site, you see a home furnished with possessions listed in the inventory of a factory worker who died in 1824. Here, then, is a look at the home life of an early nineteenth-century Pawtucket mechanic.

In the Oziel Wilkinson Stone Mill (1810), visit the reconstruction of a nineteenth-century machine-building shop, designed to interpret everyday shop practices 150 years ago. You see early woodworking machinery, such as a wood-bed turning lathe, as well as machines used in sanding and sawing wood and making bobbins. More than half the space is given over to metalworking machinery, including drilling, plan-

You not only gain an understanding of how the machine works, but also a sense of the demands made upon the person who kept it going day in, day out.

Slater Mill Historic Site is called "the museum where the machines work," and thanks to on-duty guides, the machines can be demonstrated especially for children.

ing, turning, and milling machines and lathes.

The Slater Mill Historic Site bills itself as "The museum where the machines work," and this pattern of motion is enhanced by contemporary activity on the site. Here you can *see* history being reconstructed. A great water wheel has been installed in the old wheel pit under the Wilkinson Mill. Future plans call for the operation of the very large wood-and-iron wheel by water power, which means that the course of the Blackstone River, which flows by the property, must be diverted. When the extensive reconstruction work required by this project is completed, the machines in the Wilkinson Mill will be driven by the same source of energy that powered many of them in the 1800s.

By the way, there are picnic tables on the grassy banks of the river where you can spread your lunch and enjoy the sunshine while you eat.

ACCESS

TO GET TO PAWTUCKET. Head north on I-95 to exit 28, or south on I-95 to exit 29. Heading west from New Bedford, take I-195 to the junction with I-95.

CHILDREN'S MUSEUM OF RHODE ISLAND. Directions: Take I-95 north exit 28 (School Street). Cross School Street, going straight up Vernon Street, then go left on Summit Street, and left again on Walcott Street. The museum is the first building on the right. Traveling south on I-95, take exit 29 (Downtown Pawtucket).

Stay to the right on Broadway for a quarter mile, pass the Exchange Street traffic light, and turn left into Pawtucket Congregational Church/Children's Museum Parking Lot. **Season:** Year round. **Admission** charged. (401) 726-2590.

SLATER MILL HISTORIC SITE. Directions: Take I-95 north exit 28 (School Street), turn left from the exit ramp, continue straight, then cross Main Street Bridge. Turn right on Roosevelt Avenue and follow to mill site. Traveling south on I-95, take exit 29 (Downtown Pawtucket), turn right on Fountain Street, then right on Exchange Street, and left on Roosevelt Avenue. Follow Roosevelt Avenue to the mill. **Season:** March through December. **Admission** charged. (401) 725-8638.

Warwick Neck

Try out the sixteen-hundred-foot flume imported from Japan, but prepare to get splashed!

ROCKY POINT PARK. Many amusement parks are neglected places, sadly run down at the heels. Not so Rocky Point. Each winter the rides here are taken apart, readjusted and reassembled, and treated to fresh paint and upholstery. When the park opens each May, it is as fresh and shiny as the shimmering waters of neighboring Narragansett Bay. The grounds are conscientiously maintained throughout the season, and the atmosphere is lively and family oriented.

A full-scale seaside playground, Rocky Point perches at the edge of the famous bay. Cool sea breezes make this a comfortable amusement park, whether you favor the arcade or the rides. It's especially fine to look out over the water from the top of the Ferris wheel or the sky diver. And try out the sixteen-hundred-foot flume imported from Japan, but prepare to get splashed! The preschool set enjoys the miniature helicopter, motorcycle, and truck rides as well as the merry-go-round. Everyone can take a spin on the colorful Rocky Point Express Train. There are bumper cars and cable cars, too.

But rides are only the beginning. Why not try your luck in the shooting gallery or win prizes playing skee ball? You can also play a round or two of miniature golf. Or saunter over to listen to the music of rock-and-roll groups performing on the outdoor stage. Then go for a swim in the Olympic-sized saltwater swimming pool overlooking the bay. Be certain younger children visit the petting zoo where they can become acquainted with docile members of the animal kingdom.

Rocky Point is also the place to treat yourself to an old-time shore dinner, Rhode Island style. Walk right up and take a seat in "the world's largest shore dinner hall," a cavernous modern dining room overlooking Narragansett Bay. It can seat four thousand people at a time, so feel free to bring along a few friends. The complete shore dinner includes olives, relishes, cucumbers and Bermuda onions, white and brown bread, Narragansett baked clams, Rocky Point clam chowder, drawn butter, Rocky Point clam fritters, baked sausage, baked fish, creole sauce, watermelon, and a boiled lobster or half a broiled chicken. Oh yes, French fried potatoes and corn on the cob are also part of the package, in case you are still hungry.

You can order the entire shore dinner minus the lobster or chicken, at a lower price. Or if your budget is very modest, take advantage of another option, the all-you-can-eat chowder, clam cakes, and watermelon special. All meals are available in children's portions.

Plan to spend the whole day at Rocky Point. The setting is attractive, and there is lots to do and plenty to eat. Bring the toddlers, but bring the teenagers, too; and bring bathing suits for each and every one.

The complete shore dinner includes Narragansett baked clams, Rocky Point clam chowder, Rocky Point clam fritters, baked sausage, baked fish, watermelon, and a boiled lobster.

ACCESS

ROCKY POINT PARK. Directions: Traveling north or south on I-95, take exit 10 (Route 117) at Apponaug. Follow Route 117 east about four miles, then turn right onto Warwick Neck Avenue and left onto Rocky Point Avenue. Follow signs to the park. **Season:** Memorial Day through Labor Day. **Admission** charged. (401) 737-8000.

Newport

Bustling with feverish activity, Newport offers visitors a broad variety of experiences. Here you can visit the homes of millionaires or wander restored wharves, ogle the glamorous contemporary yachts, or explore the tunnels and ditches of historic Fort Adams. No matter how you choose to spend your time, you will be impressed by the omnipresent ocean. For wherever you may wander, the sea is always at hand. (There is so much to do here that we have had to be most selective. The sites that follow are our favorite child-pleasers, but we're sure you'll also make some wonderful discoveries of your own.)

VIKING TOURS OF NEWPORT. Begin your visit with a one-hour narrated harbor cruise aboard the comfortable *Viking Queen.* If you want to be certain of places on the open upper deck of the *Viking Queen* — by far the best choice from a child's point of view — plan to arrive at least fifteen minutes before departure time.

As you cruise along, you begin to get an overview and find your bearings in the harbor. Besides, since Newport's social and economic history is so closely allied with the water, it makes sense to get acquainted with her charms from this vantage point. As the boat glides out into Narragansett Bay, your guide talks about contemporary Newport, pointing out con-

One moment a seaplane deposits a well-heeled gentleman on his yacht. And then, before you know it, you are peering onto the deck of an offshore lobster boat, where a fisherman is welding his equipment.

dominiums and other new construction. As you move along past historic points, he elaborates on the history of the house built on a rock in the harbor, Fort Adams, and some of the mansions readily visible along the shore, including Hammersmith Farm, where President John F. Kennedy and Jacqueline Bouvier were married and where they vacationed frequently.

When your boat passes the wharves, the skipper points out both yachts and fishing vessels, offering on-the-spot contrast. One moment a tiny seaplane swoops down from the sky to deposit a well-heeled gentleman on his handsomely outfitted yacht. And then, before you know it, you are peering down onto the deck of an offshore lobster boat where a commercial fisherman is welding a piece of equipment. Your spokesman explains that these boats usually set eight hundred to a thousand lobster traps several hundred miles offshore, and that they are plagued by unfriendly boats who pilfer their traps and their catch.

In a historical vein, you learn about Newport's lucrative seventeenth-century slave, rum, and molasses trade with the West Indies. You hear too about the Gilded Age, when high-society figures from New York and Philadelphia (they seldom mixed), turned Newport into a fashionable resort for prominent families. Although the skipper has standard information to dispense, he is also prone to add to his presentation as the situation requires. Should you encounter a sailing race in progress, he will tell you a little about the "rules of the road" at sea as well as about the boats that are flying by. He may also add spice to his presentations by commenting on local real-estate deals he has read about lately, along with other associated gossip.

Back ashore, wander through the restored Brick Marketplace area, and Bannister's and Bowen's Wharves. Here you find a fascinating array of restaurants and shops, and good lively street life. There is a pedestrian mall in the Brick Marketplace where children can ramble without fear of cars. Here they discover all types of restaurants, several with outdoor cafés where you can all eat lunch under a bright sun umbrella. The Seaside Restaurant and Bar has a good-sized patio area, and serves the old faithful hearty hamburgers with French fries, and plates of fried chicken as well as seafood bisques and other fishy specialties. Or, pick up a picnic-to-go at The Wharf Delicatessen, which offers old-time smoked meats, fish, and cheeses along with more standard sandwich fare. Pick a dock-side spot to enjoy your lunch.

FORT ADAMS STATE PARK. To explore an aspect of Newport's history, take a very short drive out to Fort Adams, where you can tour one of the largest seacoast fortifications in the United States. Originally established after the War of 1812, Fort Adams was built to protect the entrance to Narragansett Bay. It was

This is a popular launching spot for sailboard enthusiasts, and children enjoy watching them pilot their strange craft, as they often tumble into the brink.

designed to accommodate a peacetime garrison of 200 men and a wartime complement of 2400 men with 468 cannon, to withstand both land and sea attack. The fort was never armed or garrisoned at full strength, but the weaponry was constantly updated as the years passed, and indeed, the fort served as an important command post protecting Narragansett Bay and Long Island Sound until the end of World War II.

The fort tour lasts about thirty minutes. Visitors are taken through the parade ground, the ditches and listening tunnels, the powder magazines, and more, as the guide recounts the history and technology associated with the almost two-hundred-year-old fort. Elsewhere in the park, there is a beach where you can take a dip, and some picnic areas overlooking the harbor and the fishing piers. This is a popular launching spot for sailboard enthusiasts, and children enjoy watching them pilot their strange craft (a combination surfboard/sail), often tumbling into the brink.

BEECHWOOD. Now for some equally serious but especially fun sightseeing. You cannot possibly visit Newport without treating your children to a taste of that opulent time when servants, gala balls, self-indulgence, and money-is-no-object were the rules of the game. Although all of the mansions open to the public offer a look at this lost style of life, Beechwood is the perfect choice for young visitors. The other mansions are chock-full of original art and fabulous furniture, and the emphasis on their guided tours is placed on these furnishings and on the building's architectural features. Beechwood is furnished with reproductions (find me a child who can tell a reproduction Gainsborough from an original), but its novel approach to guided tours more than compensates.

In 1881, John Jacob Astor was known as the richest man in America. (At one time, Astor owned twenty percent of Manhattan. You get the idea.)

Known as "Mrs. Astor's Beechwood," this "cottage" (as those high-society figures called their summer homes) was purchased in 1881 by her husband, John Jacob Astor, the richest man in America. (At one time, Astor owned twenty percent of Manhattan. You get the idea.) As you enter the driveway to Beechwood, a costumed lady (clothing circa 1900) asks politely if you have come to call upon Mrs. Astor. She takes your admission fee and hands you a small white ticket, instructing you to present your calling card at the main entrance. You join a small group beneath the portico and chat briefly with a man wearing a powdered wig and the livery of the House of Windsor; he introduces himself as the Astors' footman. Suddenly a Model T chugs up and the footman greets a lady and gentleman and their maid as they step from the wide running board. Dressed in turn-of-the-century garb, the lady sporting a parasol, they disappear into the cottage as the chauffeur drives off. The footman then turns his attention in your direction, welcoming you to Beechwood and escorting you into the elegant entry hall

Entering the turn-of-the-century high-society world of the Astors at Beechwood might mean watching the servants mix a bit of fun with their work.

where you deposit your calling card in a silver salaver for Mrs. Astor's consideration. He explains that twenty-four house servants are employed here, and that there are thirty-seven servants in all. The house is fashioned after an Italian palazzo but furnished in Louis XV and Louis XVI styles. He further explains that the house has something very new, something called electricity, which he describes as "something strange in the walls."

As he talks, a well-dressed fellow in spats, a tail coat, and ascot enters, and identifies himself as Mrs. Astor's private secretary. He explains that normally the butler would show us around, but that today he is detained in the cellar seeing to the proper storage of a new shipment of wine. Suddenly lovely strains of Strauss's "Tales from the Vienna Wood" fill the air, and you are escorted into an adjoining room where you take seats and watch a narrated slide show.

The show tells the story of how the first John Jacob Astor made his fortune (fur trading and, later, real estate). When asked about the difficulty of amassing such wealth, he is said to have mused, "The first hundred thousand dollars, that was hard to get, but afterwards it was easy." His manners, you are told, were crude, that indeed he was reported to have wiped his hands on the dress of his dinner partner.

The narrator then discusses "The Four Hundred," the network of 231 families and individuals whose lineage and fortune could be traced back at least three generations, which was contrived and presided over for more than 30 years by Mrs. Astor. (Coincidentally,

When asked about the difficulty of amassing such wealth, he is said to have mused, "The first hundred thousand dollars, that was hard to get, but afterwards it was easy."

400 was the number that Mrs. Astor's New York ballroom could hold.) You are then told about some of the lavish affairs held during the Gilded Age; there was, for instance, the dinner party where a mound of sand was arranged down the center of the table. Each guest was supplied with a small sterling pail and shovel so that he could dig in the sand for party favors — diamond, ruby, sapphire, and emerald chips.

The presentation concluded, the private secretary asks how long your group will be staying at Beechwood. A week? up for the season? He waits for an answer. Perhaps someone speaks up: "As long as we can!" The secretary appears pleased and by now you have come to understand that not only will you have the opportunity to view life at Beechwood, but to become involved in it as well.

You are then taken to the reception room where you meet young Charlotte Astor in her white gloves, middy dress, and shiny black patent-leather shoes. Charlotte, who appears to be about ten, is searching for her agate but stops to welcome you and tell you a little about her brother and sisters. Next you visit the morning room, where you encounter several fine ladies who have come to spend the "season" with Mrs. Astor. They are gossiping about the ball held the previous evening. It seems the orchestra was stationed in this room, which adjoins the ballroom. "You see, that's so we didn't have to gaze upon them," explains one of the ladies, referring to the members of the orchestra, in praise of this arrangement; "it's a little tedious to watch someone working so hard when you are trying to enjoy yourself!"

You meet more guests and servants as you visit the ballroom, the dining room, the pantry, and the kitchen. They discuss features of the house, social customs (the food must never cover the family emblem on the dinner plates), and any other subject you might care to raise. You learn that dinners lasted four to five hours and included twelve to twenty courses, that servants were treated well here (ten dollars a month, one day off a month, a half day of work on Sundays), and more. Children may be asked if they eat in the kitchen with their servants and if they are permitted to spend one hour per day with their mother, as is the case with Miss Charlotte. When first addressed by the Beechwood cast, children giggle and blush, but by the end of the tour they are right into the spirit of the occasion, asking such questions as: "Does Miss Charlotte have her own yacht?" or "Did Miss Charlotte ever get spanked?"

The fun at Beechwood is derived from the fact that the actors and actresses combine standard information with a lively ability and willingness to improvise as the situation suggests. Your visit lasts about forty-five minutes, and no tours are ever exactly the same. (By the way, if you take a fancy to Beechwood, you can

The orchestra was stationed in an adjoining room so the guests didn't have to see them. "It's a little tedious to watch someone working so hard when you are trying to enjoy yourself!"

always rent the ballroom and stage an extravaganza of your own.)

When you conclude your visit, stroll through Beechwood's rose garden and across the spacious back lawn toward the ocean. Here you can walk along Cliff Walk, the famous footpath that cleaves to the Atlantic shoreline and provides views of the mansion not otherwise available. The path is lined with beach roses (and a little poison ivy, too). Although it is of ample width, the footing is sometimes unsure and the drop-off on the ocean side is treacherous. Keep a tight rein on the children; toddlers are safest in backpacks. If you turn left as you face the ocean and take about a fifteen-minute walk, you will pass Rosecliff (modeled after the Grand Trianon at Versailles), and then The Breakers (built for Cornelius Vanderbilt and modeled after an Italian Renaissance palace). Or, turn right from Beech-wood and walk about five minutes to Marble House (this was also a Vanderbilt home, in the style of the Petit Trianon at Versailles). Your walk takes you up and down steps and through tunnels — always with the ocean on one side, the millionaires' legacy on the other. Children can't help being impressed by the grandeur of it all.

ACCESS

TO GET TO NEWPORT. From Boston, take Route 3 south to Route 24, follow Route 24 south to Route 114, and head south on Route 114 to Newport. From New York, take I-95 north to Route 138, and cross the Jamestown and Newport bridges (you'll traverse the island of Jamestown) into Newport.

VIKING TOURS OF NEWPORT. Directions: Heading south on Route 114, turn right on Coddington Highway and follow to the bridge. After crossing the bridge into Newport, turn right at the traffic circle, then take the first left onto Third Street and follow signs to Goat Island Causeway. Heading east on Route 138 after crossing the Newport bridge, turn right on Farewell Street, right on America's Cup Avenue, then right onto Goat Island Causeway. Boats depart from the Goat Island Marina. **Season:** May through late October. **Admission** charged. (401) 847-6921.

FORT ADAMS STATE PARK. Directions: From downtown Newport (Thames Street), travel south to Wellington Street, which becomes Halidon Avenue and then Harrison Avenue. Go right from Harrison Avenue onto Fort Adams Road. (If you reach Hammersmith Farm, you have gone too far.) **Season:** Tours from mid-June through Labor Day. **Admission** charged. (401) 847-8680 or (401) 849-5649.

BEECHWOOD. Directions: From downtown Newport, follow "mansions" signs to Bellevue Avenue. Beechwood is between Rosecliff and Marble

House. **Season:** Year round. **Admission** charged. (401) 846-3774.

Portsmouth

GREEN ANIMALS TOPIARY GARDEN. While in Newport, try to schedule a sidetrip to nearby Portsmouth, home of the "Green Animals." You can drive from Newport to Portsmouth in about twenty minutes, but for a real treat, consider a roundtrip ride aboard the 1930s vintage equipment of the Old Colony and Newport Railway. The terminal is located on America's Cup Avenue across from the Newport Fire Department Headquarters. You can also travel to the Green Animals by sea; contact the Chamber of Commerce on America's Cup Avenue across from Long Wharf for details.

Topiary gardening is the art of fashioning live plants into geometric figures and animal shapes, and it has been practiced for hundreds of years. Here you find eighty-five pieces of topiary, including sixteen animals and birds: bear, camel, boar, donkey, elephant, giraffe, horse and rider, lion, ostrich, mountain goat, dogs, peacocks, rooster, and swan. In addition to finding the birds and animals, children enjoy losing themselves along the maze of pathways as they look for the very proper pet cemetery or pause to determine the hour at the sundial. There are fruit trees, an herb garden, a dahlia garden, and annual, perennial, and biennial beds as well, with rose arbors and resting benches carefully stationed here and there.

In addition to finding the birds and animals, children enjoy losing themselves along the maze of pathways as they look for the very proper pet cemetery.

There is also a small museum (with a big name) to explore: The Rhode Island Children's Museum. Housed in two downstairs rooms in the white clapboarded residence that presides over the small estate, the museum has a collection of antique toys, including toddler-sized furnishings such as a small Victorian sofa, an overstuffed armchair, and a folding chair done in needlepoint. There are dolls, cast-iron toys, and toy soldiers to look at. Plan to spend about half an hour at Green Animals.

ACCESS

GREEN ANIMALS TOPIARY GARDEN. Directions: From downtown Newport, take Route 114 about ten miles north to Cory's Lane. Garden is on your left. **Season:** May through October. **Admission** charged. (401) 847-1000, or (401) 683-1267.

You can view Quechee Gorge from the road above; but better yet, take the twenty-minute walk to the bottom.

CHAPTER VI

Vermont

Her name derives from two French words: "vert" (green) and "mont" (mountain), a legacy from the French explorers who settled here in the 1600s. As her name implies, Vermont is composed of a profusion of mountains so formidable that only fifteen percent of her land is considered level enough for productive farming. And as the name also indicates, the mountains are covered with evergreen, thick coniferous stands of trees that keep the hills looking "vert" the year round.

The aptly named Green Mountains, extending over most of the state, are a link in the Appalachian Mountain system that stretches from Canada to Alabama. Ranged like huge soldiers in a line down the middle of the state, they form a north-to-south backbone that varies from twenty to thirty-six miles in width. Traveling east to west in Vermont is a lot like riding a roller coaster.

Dairy farming is the major form of agricultural activity in the state; this is not difficult to believe as you drive along the mountainous roads edged by steep, rocky pastures where cows graze happily on the slant. Indeed, it is said that there are more cows per capita in Vermont than in any other state. Rambling barns and towering silos punctuate the pastoral landscape, and young travelers have no difficulty spotting horses, sheep, and goats munching their greens peacefully near the roadside.

Vermont has the third lowest population in the country, largely because its inadequate supply of natural resources has allowed only minimal industrial development. Following the Civil War, many people left Vermont in search of job opportunities in other states where manufacturing was enjoying enormous growth. The Green Mountain state is, however, a major producer of timber, pulp, granite, and marble.

The state has many summer residents who own second homes here. This affluent portion of the population supports the network of elegant boutiques and treasure-stuffed antiques shops that are found in among the lovely old houses and churches edging the village greens. Thus you will find that traveling through Vermont is a study in economic contrasts. Just as there are prosperous fashionable shops designed to serve those with lots of discretionary cash, so there are dozens of modest but reliable country stores that carry stock similar to what they carried a hundred years ago: maple syrup, fly swatters, work shirts, hammers, pots and pans, a book or two. Enjoy them both as you explore this state where rural life persists, accented by frequent touches of urban chic.

Just outside the Maple Grove Honey Museum, youngsters can see what is perhaps the world's largest honey bee. Then they can enter and see the real things at work.

Route 9

One way to begin your visit to the Green Mountain State is to investigate its southernmost sector, dominated by the two small cities of Brattleboro and Bennington. Traveling west from Brattleboro on the Molly Stark Trail (Route 9), you find many interesting Vermont vistas ranging from gentle rolling hills and valleys, streams and meadows, to the ever-present mountains, which come closer and closer to the roadside as you approach the Green Mountain National Forest near Bennington.

Before you dive into some of the famous historic sites in and around Bennington, a couple of short stops on the way will whet your appetite for things to come and perhaps offer you a creative idea about overnight accommodations in the area should you wish to use them. They are located in the towns of Wilmington and Woodford, both on Route 9.

Wilmington

MAPLE GROVE HONEY MUSEUM. Bees work hard. Just how hard becomes evident when you stop in at this gift shop/museum for a look at these industrious insects going about their tasks in six glass observation hives. The tour guide tells you about the functions of various types of honeybees — the queen, the drone, and the worker. The worker, for example, feeds the queen and the drones and even the larvae who are kept warm in "the nursery," a special section of honeycomb cells constructed just for that purpose. You soon realize that these "advanced social bees" live in elaborately organized colonies characterized by a specific division of labor and responsibility.

You soon realize that these "advanced social bees" live in elaborately organized colonies with a specific division of labor and responsibility.

Here you also see a display of beekeeping equipment, old and new. Then move into the next room where you can see honey (and maple syrup) heated, filtered, bottled, and capped. Maple Grove purchases the raw materials from apiaries and sugar farmers all over Vermont. Here you see workers packaging individual candies and passing them through the labeling machine. Maple-sugar candy samples are provided at the end of the tour. You can watch a twelve-minute film, "The Honeybee — A Profile," on request.

ACCESS

MAPLE GROVE HONEY MUSEUM. Directions: Take I-91 exit 2, and follow Route 9 west to Wilmington, about half way between Brattleboro and Bennington. The museum is located on Route 100, two miles north of the junction with Route 9. **Season:** Late spring through autumn. **Admission** free. (802) 464-2193.

Woodford

Just a short way from Wilmington, Woodford offers two inexpensive forms of accommodations, a hostel and an attractive state park.

Hostels are designed for people who want to travel economically and also take the time to meet other folks along the way, sharing meals and stories with them. Hostels vary considerably, but generally speaking, they offer single-sex dormitories, private rooms, and family quarters. To stay at any hostel, you must be a member of the American Youth Hostels Association. Inexpensive trial memberships are available. Most hostels are open from late afternoon to nine or ten in the morning, with members expected to vacate the facilities during the daytime. Maximum stays are also established at most hostels. (For further information, write American Youth Hostels, Inc., National Administrative Offices, 1332 I Street N.W., Washington, DC 20005.)

Visitors are expected to sweep their own sleeping quarters, provide their own sleeping sacks, wash their own dishes, and lend a hand at cleaning up a common room.

GREENWOOD LODGE. Part of the American Youth Hostel network, Greenwood Lodge has an excellent reputation; it has been operated by the same couple since 1960, under the system common to all hostels. Visitors are expected to sweep their own sleeping quarters, provide their own sleeping sacks (or take advantage of the linen rental service), wash their own dishes, and lend a hand at a clean-up chore in one of the lodge's common rooms. In exchange, they receive low-cost sleeping accommodations, kitchen facilities, and recreational opportunities. At Greenwood Lodge, the latter means a TV set, a piano, a ping-pong table, a library, and a pond outside for swimming and boating.

WOODFORD STATE PARK. This four-hundred-acre park boasts the highest state camping area in Vermont at an elevation of twenty-four hundred feet. You can pitch your tent at a site set among the tall trees of this hardwood and spruce-fir forest, or you can rent a Green Mountain lean-to, a roofed shelter that is closed on three sides, open on the fourth. With a ten-by-thirteen-foot sleeping floor, it's big enough to accommodate five people.

The park includes a twenty-acre lake where you can swim or fish, and small boats are available for rental. Nature programs are held at the park during the summer months, with guided walks and evening programs among the offerings. The park also has its own nature trail.

ACCESS

TO GET TO WOODFORD. From the center of Wilmington, continue west on Route 9.

GREENWOOD LODGE. Directions: The lodge is off Route 9, adjacent to Prospect Ski Mountain. Enter through the ski-area parking lot, go past two posts, turn left, and continue a thousand feet to the hostel. **Season:** July and August, plus some weekends in October. **Admission** charged. (802) 442-2547. **Note:** If you wish additional information on Greenwood Lodge, or if you wish to reserve space (essential for family quarters), write Greenwood Lodge, P.O. Box 246, Bennington, VT 05201 in July and August; 197 Lyons Road, Scarsdale, NY 10583 during the rest of the year.

WOODFORD STATE PARK. Directions: From the center of Wilmington, continue west on Route 9. **Season:** Memorial Day through Columbus Day. **Admission** charged. (802) 447-7169. **Note:** The Vermont State Parks accept reservations. Write directly to the park, or request a reservation form from the Department of Forests, Parks, and Recreation, Montpelier, VT 05602.

Bennington

BENNINGTON MUSEUM. This fine museum features extensive exhibits of Bennington pottery, early-American glass, American paintings, sculpture, silver, furniture, and military memorabilia. Although children probably will not be able to appreciate the hundreds of pieces of glassware, there are sections —

exhibits within the exhibits — that will appeal to them. Look for the paperweights, for example, those exquisite glass domes containing fruits and flowers, or even a glass snake. Can you find the very tiny paperweight buttons that look like jewels? Or the blownglass paperweight delicately shaped like a pear, and the paperweight with the iridescent angelfish painted on it that looks just like a Christmas tree ornament? How about looking for the "witches' sticks" nearby? It is fun to find out about the seventeenth-century custom of keeping large sticks behind doors to ward off witches. These graceful blown-glass nineteenth-century versions of witches' sticks are decorated in yellow, blue, red, and white spirals, making them look like glass walking sticks.

Try to take this same approach as you explore the rest of the museum; find a small area of particular interest rather than encouraging children to look at everything. Another display that might interest them is the small collection of human-hair ornaments. It was a handwork fad in the mid-Victorian era to fashion rings, brooches, watchbands, necklaces, and the like from hair. Friends exchanged these trinkets as symbols of affection. (Pity the poor redhead! Victorians disapproved of red hair, favoring blonde and dark tresses at this stiff-necked point in history.)

The collection of early instruments includes a nineteenth-century mouth organ, an autoharp, and a cornet as well as a wooden flute owned by Colonel Orsamus Merrill. You think you don't have time to practice? Consider the colonel's schedule: he was a lawyer, printer, editor, soldier in the War of 1812, and member of Congress from 1817 to 1819.

If you fancy old-fashioned clothes, each member of the family can pick out garments from those displayed here. Imagine Mom decked out in a "Panama Cloth" dress with brown basque, skirt, and overskirt, the first ready-made dress to appear in Bennington. Dad might look good in a handsome nineteenth-century double-breasted velvet vest in black with small purple flowers. There is a boy's blue velvet suit, with shiny white buttons attaching the short pants to the jacket. And a young lady would look proper in the dress of plum-and-black-striped silk that was worn in 1888 by ten-year-old Jennie Carrier.

There is also a lot of clothing in the military exhibit, where you see uniforms, weapons, and military accessories; can you find the wooden canteen? Here you see everything from a pair of cannonballs found on the Bennington battlefield, to World War II anti-tank shells.

The museum also contains a hall of toys that children played with during the last half of the nineteenth century. There are Jenny Lind paper dolls, teddy bears, puzzles, a Noah's Ark, and lots of little sets of dishes; one set even has a tiny pressed-glass punch bowl with

Pity the poor redhead! Victorians disapproved of red hair, favoring blonde and dark tresses at this stiff-necked point in history.

There are Jenny Lind paper dolls, teddy bears, puzzles, a Noah's Ark, and lots of little sets of dishes.

You come upon the dress Grandma Moses wore on her ninetieth birthday, and a moment later discover the one she wore on her hundredth birthday!

thimble-sized cups hung from the rim. There is a fine collection of marbles that includes agates, Venetian swirls, and some small English clay ones called "commoneys" as well as a pair of early roller skates called "automobile cycle skates." You will see games called Attack and Grandma's Game of Useful Knowledge, as well as a two-story doll house with six fully furnished rooms to play with.

From the toy exhibit, walk outdoors to the connecting building, which houses paintings by the famous Grandma Moses. Beyond the painting gallery, step into the Schoolhouse Museum, the very building in which Grandma Moses and many of her children, grandchildren, and great-grandchildren attended school. Before becoming a painter (she didn't consider it a serious career until she was seventy-eight), Grandma worked as a hired girl, helped her husband on his milk route, and made hand-sliced potato chips to sell.

Grandma's paintings feature scenes of people working and playing — collecting the sap, bringing in the hay, making apple butter, and ice skating. The personal artifacts exhibited in the schoolhouse include her kitchen utensils, china, crafts projects, and articles of clothing. You come upon the dress she wore on her ninetieth birthday, and you're surprised a moment later to also discover the one she wore on her hundredth birthday! Her paintings and personal possessions give a strong sense of nineteeth-century rural life.

MELINDA MACAULEY

What do Jenny Lind paper dolls, Grandma Moses paintings, and World War II antitank shells have in common? They're all on display at the Bennington Museum.

BENNINGTON BATTLE MONUMENT. As you travel through southern Vermont you soon ask yourself, Who is this Molly Stark, whose name is evident everywhere, on roads, shops, and campgrounds? The lady in question was the wife of General John Stark, a New Hampshirite who fought under General George Washington at Trenton and Princeton, and who defeated British General John Burgoyne's invading army near Bennington on August 16, 1777. As history tells it, General Stark expressed his fierce determination to win the crucial battle as follows: "There stand the red-coats and they are ours, or this night Molly Stark sleeps a widow!"

The Battle of Bennington was actually fought two miles west of the site of the Bennington Battle Monument, on land that is now part of New York State. But the confrontation was named for Bennington because that is where General Stark assembled his force and because Burgoyne wished to acquire the valuable military stores that were kept at Bennington. In addition, Bennington was the only large town near the battle site.

The 306-foot-high monolith commemorating the Battle of Bennington was built in 1891. You can take an elevator ride to the top to see the Green Mountains to the north and east, New York State to the west, and Massachusetts and Mount Greylock to the south. You peer out of tall, narrow windows that somewhat hamper the view, but you gain an understanding of the countryside where the famous battle took place. A visit to the monument takes about ten minutes.

FAIRDALE FARMS. At this 785-acre dairy farm, visitors are welcome to wander the grounds and make the acquaintance of the herd of championship Ayrshire cattle. Stroll past rambling red and white barns, past cows grazing in the pastures. Then visit the Calf Nursery, where you see calves ranging from just a couple of weeks to robust six-month-olds. In the main section of the barn, you can visit their mothers. A sign requests visitors to "Please keep off the girls' table," — or, don't walk where they eat! After you leave the gentle mooing and munching sounds behind, you can wander over to the Small Animal Barn, where the speckled hens peck for food and the spotted pigs root in the dirt with their formidable snouts.

Take a break on the swings, if you like, before moving on to the modern Milking Parlor, with its carousel arrangement. Each cow has her udders sanitized in the anterooms before moving into the milking parlor, where there are eight stations on a revolving platform. Each animal is hooked up to a milking apparatus on the carousel, which milks eight cows on each revolution. As one child remarked, "They've got their own merry-go-round; now all they need is music." As each cow reaches the exit, she is released and another animal takes her place. If you

Visit the Calf Nursery, where you see calves ranging from just a couple of weeks to robust six-month-olds.

As one child remarked of the cows, "They've got their own merry-go-round; now all they need is music."

plan your visit for late afternoon, you can watch the milking process, which generally takes place daily at 3:30 PM, give or take a few minutes.

You learn in passing that the milk taken from the cows is transferred directly to a large tank, where it is cooled to thirty-five degrees Fahrenheit to maintain highest quality. After cooling, it is pumped into a truck for transport to the nearby processing plant, also at the farm. You and the children are welcome to visit the plant, where the milk is pasteurized (heated to 161 degrees Fahrenheit for 24 seconds) and homogenized (forced through a tiny metal cone under 2000 pounds of pressure to distribute fat globules). In addition to its own milk, Fairdale Farms buys and processes milk from about thirty-five other farms in the Vermont/Massachusetts/New York area. You see milk (as well as fruit juice) automatically packed, sealed, put into cases, and loaded into refrigerated delivery trucks. The processing plant is most active in the morning, when you might see men in white work clothes and hard-hats monitoring thousands of half pints of chocolate milk as they travel along conveyor belts.

When you have finished your tour, stop in at the Dairy Bar, with the twin cow weather vanes on top, for ice cream made right here at the farm. Perhaps it has been made from milk supplied by the very cows you met in the barns just a few minutes ago! Choose from such flavors as orange pineapple, raspberry twirl, and Dutch apple as well as traditional favorites. Sandwiches are available, too. You can eat at one of the red-and-white-checkered tables indoors, or under an umbrella on the veranda. There are tables for picnickers, too; you need not make a purchase at the dairy bar to visit the farm.

Your visit to the farm takes about thirty minutes to an hour, depending upon whether you stop at the dairy bar. Plan to see either the activity in the processing plant or the milking. If you choose to spend a full day in Bennington, visit the plant in the morning and return in the afternoon to see the milking.

ACCESS

TO GET TO BENNINGTON. Take I-91 exit 2, and follow Route 9 (Molly Stark Trail) west to Bennington. From Williamstown, MA, follow Route 7 north to its junction with Route 9 (Main Street) in downtown Bennington.

BENNINGTON MUSEUM. Directions: From downtown Bennington, at the junction of Routes 7 and 9, go west one mile on Route 9 to the museum. **Season:** March through November. **Admission** charged. (802) 442-2180.

BENNINGTON BATTLE MONUMENT. Directions: Follow Route 9 past the Bennington Museum; where Route 9 bears sharply left, about an eighth mile beyond

Stop in at the dairy bar for ice cream made right here at the farm. Perhaps it has been made from milk supplied by the very cows you just met!

the museum, bear right onto the access road to the monument. **Season:** April through October. **Admission** charged. Monument: (802) 442-2456. Chamber of Commerce Information: (802) 442-5900.

FAIRDALE FARMS. Directions: From the junction of routes 7 and 9 in downtown Bennington, follow Route 9 west two miles. **Season:** Mid-May to mid-October. **Admission** free. (802) 442-6391.

Shaftsbury

PETER MATTESON TAVERN. An old-time Vermonter, Peter Matteson made his living primarily as a farmer, and built his home originally as a farmhouse, although it later became known as a tavern. Indeed, Matteson was listed as a tavern keeper in 1784 records since he supplemented his family's income by serving hearty meals to travelers and neighbors. Today the tavern table stands set for dinner, ready for farmers and lumberjacks from nearby Glastenbury (now a ghost town) to drop by for a spot of rum, a plate of stew, and some good conversation by the hearth.

Because the tavern is staffed largely by volunteers, it is difficult to anticipate what you will find happening on any particular day. But craft and cooking demonstrations are often on the agenda; you might also see a display of shoemaking, basket weaving, or tinsmithing techniques, or perhaps butter being churned or pies and breads being baked in two-hundred-year-old ovens.

Children enjoy running along the paths and into the fields outside the tavern, past the eighteenth-century gardens, past sheep and chickens and ducks.

Children enjoy running along the paths and into the fields outside the tavern, past the eighteenth-century gardens, past sheep and chickens and ducks. In the outbuildings, they might find the blacksmith at work or a volunteer demonstrating shingle making. Inside the tavern, they can enjoy the second-story ballroom, equipped with a room partition that neatly swings down from the ceiling to divide the spacious area into two family bedrooms when the party is over. Your guide explains the functions of furnishings such as the mammy bench and the crank bellows.

The tavern sponsors special events: a Fourth of July Celebration, an autumn turkey shoot (firing muzzle-loaded guns at targets), and an apple festival. Because the tavern depends so heavily on volunteers who offer both their time and talents, it is wise to telephone ahead to determine what demonstrations or special events are planned for the day you'd like to visit. Plan to spend about forty-five minutes, longer on a special-events day. The tavern is best suited to the seven-and-over crowd.

ACCESS ⸻

PETER MATTESON TAVERN. Directions: From

Bennington, take Route 7A north to South Shaftsbury, then turn right on Buck Hill Road. Follow signs to the tavern, which is located on East Road, about nine miles north of the Bennington Museum. (The tavern is located on a dirt road way out in the country; don't be discouraged before you get there.) **Season:** May through October. **Admission** charged. (802) 442-5225.

East Arlington

CANDLE MILL VILLAGE. This eight-shop complex is housed in three different buildings: a two-hundred-year-old grist mill, an old hay barn, and a colonial house where the Tories held secret meetings during the Revolutionary War. A lively mountain stream with a fine waterfall rushes behind the shops; you are encouraged to wade in the cool water, to climb on the rock ledges, and even to have a picnic on the grass-covered banks.

The stores offer clothing, cookware, Scandinavian imports, music boxes, specialty goods, candles, and pottery. Two shops are of particular interest to young visitors. At the Candle Mill itself, you can browse among fifty thousand candles from around the world. There are candles that float and candles that drip a rainbow of colors; there are candles with Vermont wildflowers embedded in them and candles in Pepsi bottles! And look at those candles in the shape of cupcakes and ice-cream sundaes — they not only look edible, they smell that way too. The shop also carries dozens of different candle holders, including the delicate clip-ons for Christmas trees, should you dare.

Children are suitably impressed by the huge 248-pound red candle on display here. They also enjoy the candle-making demonstrations held twice a day from July until mid-October. But best of all, there's the opportunity to dip your own candles. You purchase an inexpensive pair of small plain candles and carry them over to the eight pots of colored wax. Dip each candle five times in the colors of your choice. (Be sure to act quickly, about a half second per dip, so that the wax doesn't burn.) You will end up with brightly striped or mottled candles uniquely yours. If you get hooked on candle making, you can choose from the full line of supplies sold here — waxes, wicks, molds, scents, and everything else you need to do it yourself back home.

You purchase an inexpensive pair of small plain candles, carry them over to the pots of colored wax, and dip each candle five times in the colors of your choice.

For those with other cravings, there are other opportunities here. At the Dutch Door (in the Candle Mill Village complex), you can still get a big fistful of candy for less than a quarter. Homemade fudge is also available to satisfy your sweet tooth: choose from chocolate, chocolate nut, peanut butter, and penuche, and make your purchases by the piece or by the pound. Another intriguing feature of this small gourmet shop is the "tasting table"; here you can sample more than half a dozen cheeses, crackers, and smoked cold cuts. As a matter of fact, why not select an instant picnic and eat it outside by the stream?

ACCESS

CANDLE MILL VILLAGE. Directions: From Bennington take Route 7A north about fourteen miles to Arlington (where Route 7A becomes Route 7). Shortly after passing the state liquor store on your left, turn right from Route 7 onto East Arlington Road. East Arlington Road becomes Old Mill Road, and Candle Mill Village is on your right. **Season:** Year round. **Admission** free. (802) 375-6068.

MELINDA MACAULEY

What's a Bevel Bear Grinder? Mechanically minded youngsters will know, and they can see one — plus many other antique tools — at the American Precision Museum.

Windsor

THE AMERICAN PRECISION MUSEUM. If you travel north in Vermont along I-91 and just happen to have a mechanically minded teenager in your entourage, make a stop at this small but unusual institution. Here you find an extensive collection of hand and machine tools (along with the products they were used to make) housed in a three-story structure of handmade bricks capped with a slate roof. When it opened in the mid-nineteenth century, the building contained the most modern armory then in existence. Production later turned to sewing machines and in 1872 it changed again, this time becoming a cotton mill. Then in 1898 the building began service as a hydroelectric power station. It has served as a museum since 1966.

The machinery is displayed in a white brick room with a shiny hardwood floor and lots of light. Everywhere you turn, you see it — gray, red, black, green, and blue arrangements of wheels, handles, belts, and

Everywhere you turn, you see machinery — gray, red, black, green, and blue arrangements of wheels, handles, belts, and levers.

levers. They are displayed so you can examine them from all sides, but this is strictly a "look-don't-touch" museum, as even fingerprints can cause rust. There is a circa 1895 Bevel Gear Grinder, a 1911 Multiple-Spindle Automatic Lathe, a 1900 Grindley Automatic Lathe, and dozens of others. Sewing machines, firearms, and a printing press are also displayed. It's a really special museum for folks with a special interest in machinery. Allow half an hour for your visit.

As you travel north on Main Street back to I-91, keep your eye out and you will see to the right the world's longest covered bridge. Built in 1866, the bridge traverses the Connecticut River between Windsor and Cornish, New Hampshire, and is still in use today.

ACCESS

THE AMERICAN PRECISION MUSEUM. Directions: Take I-91 north exit 8 (Ascutney) to Route 5 (which becomes Main Street), and follow Route 5 about five miles to Windsor. The museum is located in Windsor at 196 Main Street, on your left as you travel north. **Season:** Memorial Day through October. **Admission** charged. (802) 674-5781.

Quechee

QUECHEE GORGE. As you leave the interstates and set about exploring central Vermont, this gorge is a pleasant stopping point for lunch and leg stretching. Here the Ottauquechee River has cut a mile-long chasm where the water flows across a rocky, sunken bed. You can view the gorge from the bridge above, but better still, take the twenty-minute walk down to the bottom where there are some lovely rock pools to wade in. Whether the water rushes or slides slowly along depends, of course, on the season and the rainfall situation. If you come during a drought, the pools may be still and shallow, but after a heavy rain or the spring thaw they are glistening and lively. Your walk follows a dirt path, sometimes rocky underfoot but never particularly difficult to travel. A chain-link fence separates the path from the gorge so you are out of sight of the chasm for most of the walk, but you have the consolation of not having to worry about youngsters wandering too close to the edge.

You can view the gorge from the bridge above, but better still, take the walk down to the bottom where there are some lovely rock pools to wade in.

Dana's-by-the-Gorge, located in one of the small complexes of shops at the top of the gorge, is a pleasant spot for breakfast or lunch. There is ample indoor seating, but if you have been driving for a long period, the children are sure to prefer sitting at one of the umbrella-covered tables on the open deck. The menu includes simple fare like omelets, sandwiches, and burgers, and there is a modestly priced list of children's selections for those with small appetites. Be sure to save room for a "Chocolate Whatever Sundae," a scrumptious combination of hot fudge, Vermont maple syrup, and creme de menthe tossed over your favorite ice cream.

ACCESS

QUECHEE GORGE. Directions: Take I-91 to I-89, and head northwest on I-89; then take Route 4 about three miles west to Quechee. The entrance to the gorge is a path leading behind the Route 4 bridge over the chasm, about a hundred yards from Dana's-by-the-Gorge. **Season:** Year round. **Admission** free.

Woodstock

STANLEY STEAMER TOUR. As you meander along enjoying the Vermont ambiance, you soon come to Woodstock, an exquisite village with a lovely green and tenderly restored homes throughout. Although the town caters primarily to visitors who opt for beauty and serenity (not qualities children are likely to put at the top of their lists), there is one activity here that young ones will find very satisfactory and very unusual, truly something to talk about back home. For at the Woodstock Inn, they can hop aboard a 1913 Stanley Steamer auto for a twenty-minute evening cruise about town, under the guidance of owner/operator/local resident Don Bourdon. As you revel in the luxury of this shiny, open, red twelve-seater, which also happens to be the oldest licensed commercial vehicle in the world, Don will point out local points of interest.

It's a 1913 Stanley Steamer, and owner Don Bourdon takes Woodstock visitors on tours around town in it. The young set loves the shrieking whistle and the steam cloud the best.

ACCESS

STANLEY STEAMER TOUR. Directions: From Quechee, continue west seven miles on Route 4 to Woodstock; the Woodstock Inn is to your left as you enter the common area. The Stanley Steamer is parked in front. **Season:** Mid-June through mid-October. **Admission** charged. (802) 457-3188.

Plymouth

CALVIN COOLIDGE HOMESTEAD. Your next stop in this area might well be in the town of Plymouth, where you can visit the birthplace of our thirtieth President in the tiny hamlet of Plymouth Notch. Although Coolidge himself may not stir much interest from the children, there is something awesome to them about seeing the very bed in which a United States President was born. There are several buildings to explore here, grouped together in a lovely setting of fields and mountains; most children enjoy just running around the spread, peeking into the houses and

You will see where Coolidge was sworn in as President by his father, a Vermont notary public, on August 3, 1923, the historic moment illuminated by a kerosene lamp.

Children like sticking their noses into the Plymouth Cheese Corporation, where cheese is still made today.

barns, and feeling a sense of the past. You see here the building where Coolidge was sworn in as President by his father, a Vermont notary public, at 2:47 AM on the muggy morning of August 3, 1923, the historic moment illuminated by a kerosene lamp. The rooms in the house have been arranged exactly as they were that night, with authentic furnishings. You will see the parlor, laundry, pantry, kitchen, woodshed, and privy (a two seater).

Pre-1900 farming tools are housed in the Wilder Barn, and these items give a clear picture of the types of tasks that occupied people back then. There are tools for splitting shingles, shelling corn, and harnessing dog power as well as butter churns, cheese presses, and a milking machine that depended on foot power. And you can also see some period vehicles here, including an elegant black summer hearse, the shiny yellow coach that delivered mail along the Woodstock-Reading run, and an R.F.D. mail sleigh for winter deliveries.

Children like sticking their noses into the Plymouth Cheese Corporation, the factory operated by the President's family, where cheese is still made today. Although there is no formal presentation or tour, you are welcome to watch the activity here. There are small chunks of old-fashioned Vermont cheese to sample, and to purchase if you wish. Maple syrup, brown bread, baked beans, pickles, relishes, and hash are also usually available.

If you are still genuinely hungry when you leave the factory, purchase sandwiches and ice cream in the Wilder House, the yellow building across from the barn, where the President's mother was born.

ACCESS

CALVIN COOLIDGE HOMESTEAD. Directions: From Woodstock, continue west on Route 4 about eight miles to Route 100A; turn left onto Route 100A and go about seven miles to Plymouth. Season: Mid-May through mid-October. Admission charged. (802) 828-3226.

Healdville

CROWLEY CHEESE FACTORY. Located in Healdville, this is Vermont's oldest cheese factory, where cheese is still made by hand as it was in the past century. Children may not realize that cheese itself is an historic product. History books show that it was made in the Indus Valley of Mesopotamia eight thousand years ago. David is said to have brought ten cheeses to the army before setting out to slay Goliath, and the Greeks offered the stuff regularly to the gods of Olympus. As legend has it, cheese was first discovered by an Arab merchant who stored some excess milk in a sheep's-stomach sack before setting out to cross the

It's hard to believe that what this man is raking through will soon be cheese. It's just one step of the process you observe at the Crowley Cheese Factory in Healdville.

desert on his lumbering camel. When he settled down to drink his milk that evening, he found that the heat of the day, the motion of the camel, and the rennet in the lining of his container had all cooperated to make — what else? Cheese!

Colby cheese, a member of the cheddar family but lighter and moister than classic cheddar, is produced at the Crowley factory. The cheese is simply fresh whole raw milk that is curdled, compressed, and then aged two to six months. Inside the three-story brown clapboarded factory, you see the milk poured into huge vats, heated, and soured. The resulting curds are then cut and raked and the whey drained off. In a process similar to kneading bread, the cheese is broken into small chunks. The curds are then rinsed with spring water and compressed into molding forms. It is the "working" and "washing" of the curd that makes the Colby cheese more moist and lighter in texture than a typical cheddar. What happens to the whey? Some of it is used for animal feed and some is sprayed on the meadows as fertilizer; no waste here.

After tasting the samples provided, head outside and relax on the grass (picnicking is welcome), while the children feed the ducks who float on the tranquil pond. Then travel a mile and a half down the road to

After tasting the samples provided, head outside and relax on the grass while the children feed the ducks who float on the tranquil pond.

the *Crowley Cheese Shop,* where you can purchase wheels of cheese along with Vermont-made crafts such as braided rugs, woolen sweaters, pottery, dolls, and homemade edibles. Allow about thirty minutes for your visit at the Crowley Cheese Factory.

ACCESS

CROWLEY CHEESE FACTORY. Directions: Take I-91 exit 6 and head north on Route 103 about thirty miles to Healdville. From Plymouth Union, take Route 100 south nine miles to Route 103, turn left, and follow signs two miles south to Healdville. **Season:** Year round. **Admission** free. (802) 259-2340.

Proctor

Proctor, Vermont, is the largest marble-production center on the American continent. Marble quarried here in the Green Mountains is processed into slabs for both interior and exterior building use. As you walk through Proctor, a town that literally grew up around the marble industry, notice the touches of marble everywhere. Check the sidewalks, schools, churches, and even the bridge that crosses Otter Creek. Marble can also be found in the foyers of public buildings as well as in elegant bathrooms in private homes.

VERMONT MARBLE EXHIBIT. In the marble exhibit, you can view a brief color movie explaining how marble is formed from prehistoric forms of marine life. You may then wander through a display showing examples of many types of marble in dozens of different shades, bearing names like Roman Traverline (Italy), Breche Orientale (France), Champion Pink (Tennessee), Agatan Buff (Illinois), and Vermont's own Jasper, Verdoso, Striped Brocadillo, Pearly Danley, and Vermarco Delf, to name just a few.

You see marble slabs weighing up to ten tons swinging through the air en route to the diamond-blade coping saws that will slice them into thin sheets while you watch!

Graceful marble statues are on display; in one corner a sculptor works in his open studio, adding fine details to the bird he is creating from this workable material. You can also walk through a section of the factory proper, arriving at the visitors' balcony. From this vantage point, you can observe the cutting, fitting, and drilling operations on the floor far below. Watch pieces of marble travel along the conveyor assembly lines. You see the marble slabs weighing up to ten tons (they are about four hundred million years old), swinging through the air en route to the diamond-blade coping saws that will slice them into thin sheets while you watch!

Other exhibits focus on marble production in the nineteenth century and in the present. Changes in the industry are documented with photos showing quarrying and exploration methods, block storage and handling procedures, gang sawing (many men handling one huge saw), and slab storage, finishing, and sculpting techniques. Today diesel-powered fork-lift trucks do the work formerly relegated to oxen, horses, steam winches, derricks, steel-cable railroad flat cars, men, and muscle.

For no obvious reason, the exhibit also includes a hologram of Saint George and the Dragon. A hologram is "cast in light, a photo of light waves interfering with one another as they meet." Seemingly made of nothing, floating in space, Saint George and his companion mysteriously appear and disappear. The hologram is hidden away in a corner, so ask for it if you can't find it.

If you want to take home a souvenir, you can probably find a suitable marble memento in the gift shop, which sells slabs as well as jewelry and decorative objects. Other Vermont-made items are featured, too, and every member of the family is likely to find something unusual or tasteful to keep as a reminder.

ACCESS

VERMONT MARBLE EXHIBIT. Directions: From Healdville, follow Route 103 north about seventeen miles to Route 7. Head north on Route 7 about five miles to Route 4 west, go two miles on Route 4, then take Route 3 north about five miles. Follow signs to Vermont Marble Company. **Season:** Late May through mid-October. **Admission** charged. (802) 459-3311.

Middlebury

UNIVERSITY OF VERMONT MORGAN HORSE FARM. Any child who has read Marguerite Henry's classic story *Justin Morgan Had a Horse* will be delighted to visit the Morgan Horse Farm. The progenitor of the oldest light-horse breed in America was a slight colt named Figure, who was born in Springfield, Massachusetts, in 1789, the very same year that George Washington become the nation's first President. His owner, schoolmaster Justin Morgan, brought him to Vermont in search of a better life in 1791. The teacher wanted to sell the colt, but because of his horse's diminutive size, Morgan was unable to find a buyer. But over the next thirty years, Figure proved himself strong, versatile, and fast. He was later renamed "Justin Morgan" in honor of the man who brought him to Vermont. It was through Figure's three colts, named Sherman, Bulrush, and Woodbury, that America's first breed of horse was founded.

The Morgan Horse Farm was established here in 1907, under the auspices of the United States Department of Agriculture, to perpetuate the Morgan breed. In 1951, the government turned the farm over to the University of Vermont, and the Morgan breeding program continues today. The Morgan horses have continued to grow in popularity through the years. They

The more than twenty foals born here each year are on their feet and nursing about twenty minutes after birth, and are able to run about later the same day.

have served as cavalry mounts in time of war; they have worked as ranch horses out west, tending cattle; some have pulled plows, while others have performed as stylish show horses. A patient animal with a gentle disposition, the Morgan has helped many a young rider learn the basics of horsemanship. The horses from this farm have been transported to China, Israel, Peru, and Sweden, as their reputation grows.

Your visit to the farm begins in a large area toward the front of the ornate Victorian barn. Your feet shuffle through the sawdust as you examine the displays of harnesses and horseshoes, ribbons, trophies, photographs, and other Morgan memorabilia. A slide show used to introduce the farm and its occupants teaches about selective breeding and about the management of the farm itself. Then it's off for a guided tour of the premises. Your guide takes you through the stables, introducing Hester, Jackson, Goldrush, and many others, pointing out their characteristics and describing their parentage. The more than twenty foals born here each year are on their feet and nursing about twenty minutes after birth, and are able to run about later the same day. It's interesting to learn that a Morgan does not reach full physical maturity until age six or seven, and that the typical young horse sold from this farm fetches between two and ten thousand dollars, depending upon attributes, abilities, sex, age, and disposition.

The heavy scents of leather, horse, and hay fill the air as you wander through the aisles, peering into stalls and stroking a warm muzzle here and there. Your guide gladly explains the use of any equipment that catches your eye. Can you guess what "bell boots" are? How about a "jowel sweat"? Ask your guide to point these out and explain their functions. You might see horses having their feet lubricated, or animals being exercised in the indoor training hall. All the horses are worked daily, no matter what the weather.

In addition to the horses in the main stable, you can see brood mares getting ready to give birth or foals nursing and frolicking with their mothers in the fields. The pen full of enthusiastic yearlings is also a special pleasure to visit. This is where young horse fanciers become especially emotional. "Please Dad, we could fit him in the garage . . . . I'd get up at six every morning to take care of him . . . . I'll give up my allowance . . . . I don't want anything for my birthday for the next ten years except . . . ."

This is where young horse fanciers become especially emotional. "Please, Dad, we could fit him in the garage . . . ."

If you take along a picnic lunch, you can feast outdoors at a table set in what must be one of the most glorious spots in all Vermont while you think about the spunky little horse that started it all nearly two hundred years ago. (By the way, the farm runs an annual fund-raising raffle, so if you want to take a Morgan home, stock up on tickets!) Plan to spend one to two hours here.

UNIVERSITY OF VERMONT MORGAN HORSE FARM. Directions: From Proctor, continue north on Route 3 to Route 7, then go north about thirty-two miles on Route 7 to Middlebury. In Middlebury, leave the town square by heading west on Route 125. Just beyond a small rotary, turn right on Route 23, which is Weybridge Street. Follow signs to the farm, about two and a half miles ahead. **Season:** May through October. **Admission** charged. (802) 388-2011.

Saint Johnsbury

FAIRBANKS MUSEUM AND PLANETARIUM. Located in the northeast corner of Vermont, there is nothing backwoods about this museum, which was built by one of the world's ten richest families in the 1890s. Thanks to the Fairbanks family, you can discover a wealth of treasures displayed in a building that illustrates the architectural principle of the spherical arc. A feeling of tremendous space is imparted by the thirty-foot-high barrel-vaulted ceilings in the main hall. Stained-glass windows, some of them designed by Louis Tiffany, and lots of rich, warm wood further enhance the atmosphere.

This is a natural-history museum; as such, it contains dozens of stuffed animal specimens. Unlike many such museums, the Fairbanks Museum is not dusty and sad, but bursting with activity. Indeed, it is a place that commemorates life, not death. As you enter, you hear the cooing and chuckling of the ringed turtledove, busy in its cage. Your eyes might then focus on the stuffed South American snakes, realistically positioned in a rocky setting. Then you turn to investigate the humming of the National Oceanic and Atmospheric Administration teletype machine, busily spewing forth weather maps and forecasts.

Your eye may be drawn to the intricate renditions of patriotic subjects such as the American flag, Abraham Lincoln, and George Washington. Look closely at these works to discover the artist's medium. The sign above reads "Nature's Artistry in Art," and the pictures were made by entomologist/engineer John Hampson (1836-1923). He didn't favor clay or paint, ink or chalk. He worked in . . . insects! And he incorporated over seven thousand of them in the nine works shown here. His fragile bugs were positioned with pins or fish-scale glue; each design took three to four years to complete. The horse's bridle, for instance, is made of ladybugs; Washington's boots and breeches are fashioned from overlapping layers of different-colored moths. Patriotic mottos are spelled out in glistening green beetles!

Elsewhere in the museum you discover intricate dioramas featuring preserved animals, many of whom

Here you can experience what it would feel like to come face to face with an 1150-pound, 8½-foot-long polar bear!

Not for scientists only: the Fairbanks Museum and Planetarium in Saint Johnsbury.

made their home in Vermont. Here you can experience what it would feel like to come face to face with an 1150-pound, 8½-foot-long polar bear! He poses on all fours, but a sign notes that when he rears up on his hind legs he stands over twelve feet tall. This stuffed beast is displayed in the middle of the floor so that although you are asked to please not touch the bears, you can eyeball it with this fellow's snarling teeth just inches away. You also meet a moose, an American buffalo, and groups of woodpeckers, sandpipers, and hummingbirds. In the opossum diorama, you see these animals at different stages: nursing, clinging to their mothers, and setting out on their own.

Travel up one of the winding staircases to the second-story balcony to see the exhibits devoted to history, archeology, and anthropology. Here you see how the environment (including geography, climate, and natural resources) influences and shapes cultural patterns. Whether you are intrigued by the early Egyptians, the Moslem world, Oceania, Eskimos, or the Pueblo Indians of the American southwest, you find clothes, tools, toys, and household artifacts to examine here. Be sure also to take a look at the very special photomicrographs of snow crystals exhibited near the stairwells. Taken by W. A. Bentley of Jericho, Vermont, in the late 1800s, these are photos of actual snowflakes, enlarged many times. Proving the saying that "no two snowflakes are ever the same," they indeed show how very different one snowflake is from another. There are dozens of patterns here, many resembling the finest lace. Children soon discover that the flakes differ according to weather conditions. A severe blizzard with subnormal temperatures is characterized by snowflakes with patterns very different from those flakes resulting from a light snowfall on a moderate winter's day.

In the basement of the building, the Hall of Science houses lots of participatory exhibits that encourage an understanding of basic principles in the physical sciences. You can activate a color wheel, increasing the speed of rotation to the point where the bands of color scramble to produce near white. Or you can split light into a rainbow of colors by passing it through layers of clear Scotch tape. There are also opportunities to explore the nature of fluorescence and to consider the answer to the question, "Are you color blind?"

Still in the Hall of Science, children like to ponder the answer to "What supports an airplane?" or "What if our sun shone blue or red instead of white, as some do?" Using a set of collision balls, you can illustrate Newton's third law of motion: "Momentum Lost = Momentum Gained." Or you can choose to play with a probability board, a wave machine, a sand pendulum, a radiometer, and still other displays, too. If that isn't enough, schedule your visit to coincide with a performance here in northern New England's only public planetarium. Telephone ahead for the current schedule.

MAPLE GROVE, INC. Making maple syrup is as much a part of New England tradition as Pilgrims and apple-picking. The best one hundred percent pure maple syrup has just as much in common with its mass-produced commercial counterpart as a home-made Anadama loaf has with a package of presliced white bread. Check the label of the "syrup" bottle on your kitchen shelf and consider yourself fortunate if it contains a hefty three percent maple syrup; some brands contain one or two percent and others contain none at all. Most commercial syrups are based on a combination of sugar syrup, corn syrup, and artificial flavorings. If you are accustomed to the supermarket brands, try some of the genuine article. It's quite another story.

The famous one hundred percent pure maple syrup of New England is the rich, sweet liquid you find in country stores and specialty food shops. It is expensive and it is delicious. It is the sugar that sustained our forefathers when they could not afford the refined sweeteners from other parts of the world. According to Indian legend, the old Earth Mother Nokomis was responsible for the first maple syrup. She bored a hole in a sugar maple and the liquid that flowed forth was pure syrup. Her grandson, Manabush, thought the procedure a trifle too simple. Lest the Indians become lazy, Manabush decided to make them work for their sweetener. He climbed to the top of a sugar maple and showered it with water, thus diluting the syrup to sap. Ever since, syrup making has been no easy task.

The fact of the matter is that sap is about ninety-seven percent water and three percent maple-sugar

Children like to ponder the answer to "What supports an airplane?" or "What if our sun shone blue or red instead of white, as some do?"

In order to produce a single gallon of maple syrup, you need to boil down at least forty-five gallons of sap.

content. In order to produce a single gallon of maple syrup, you need to boil down at least forty-five gallons of sap.

The New England Indians used to boil down their sap by pouring it into hollow logs and then throwing in heated stones. In the nineteenth century, white men took to the woods on snowshoes, leading horse-drawn sledges with enough gear and provisions to last a week or more, while they camped in the woods and set about collecting sap. Today most sap is reduced only to the syrup stage, but in colonial times it was often boiled down to blocks of maple sugar; these were stored in cool cellars and chipped at and traded as necessity demanded.

Although trucks, tractors, and snowmobiles have replaced the horse-drawn sledge, modern maple-syrup manufacturers remain at the mercy of Mother Nature. The flow of sap in the sugar maple is still nature's province, and until she provides the right combination of warm days and cold nights, the collection of sap cannot begin. Most syrup makers agree that the sap runs best when the days are mild and the nights just below freezing. In southern New England this means that the sap can begin to run any time from early February until the middle of March, while up north the process is delayed several weeks to a month.

The sugar maple itself is a work of genius. In the summertime the cells of the maple leaf synthesize a simple sugar, which is converted into starch and stored in the roots and trunk of the tree. When autumn arrives and the maple leaves turn brilliant red, yellow, and orange, the tree becomes inactive. It keeps to itself all winter, as do most old-time New Englanders. But come spring, the chemistry is back at work. By the time the sap begins to flow again, the glucose has converted to sucrose, a more complicated sugar.

Here at the world's largest maple-candy factory, you can get an intimate look at the processes used to manufacture those melt-in-your-mouth maple morsels that you see in all the shops. Begin your visit here with a twelve-minute guided tour of the candy kitchens, where you will see maple sugar, maple fudge, and maple butter made and packed. The specific procedures you see depend upon activity in the kitchens on the particular day you visit, as not every product is produced every day. The maple syrup, base of all the confections, is boiled and cooled, and beaten in large electric mixers into two-hundred-pound batches of maple fondant. It is then poured into copper kettles equipped with mixing blades, and more syrup is added.

If you are watching maple-sugar-candy production, you might see the mixture poured into rubber molds stationed in the depositors. The candy is then popped from the molds and placed in wire baskets. After that, it goes to the crystallizing tanks where it receives a protective sugar coating to keep it fresh. You might also see the production of maple cream or butter; take some home and try it on French toast or in cake frosting. Maple fudge is made here as well. And perhaps you'll see workers packing the candies in fluted bon-bon cups or wrapping the boxes in cellophane, up to twenty boxes per minute for a two-woman team. The sweet scent of steaming maple syrup thickens the air, and you can't help being grateful when offered a free sample to taste.

When you leave the factory, stop by next door to see the Old Sugar House, where a recording tells about the operation of the modern evaporator on display and other aspects of syrup making. Here you also see old and new sugaring equipment such as buckets, spiles, and ox yokes.

In the nearby Maple Cabin, you can purchase candy in many shapes including maple leaves, tiny figures, and seashells. You can stock up on syrup to take home; if you are feeling economy-minded, consider Grade B syrup — it's a little darker and thicker but every bit as delicious as the more expensive Fancy Grade or Grade A. At the cabin you can enter a small theater to see a fifteen-minute color film that follows the farmer out into the sugar bush in the early spring as he taps trees and hangs buckets, gathers the sap, and transports it back to the evaporators.

You learn that in boiling down sap to make syrup, large quantities of water are removed. The idea is to eliminate the maximum amount of moisture in the minimum amount of time. The film shows how the boiling-down and collection procedures have changed with time. The horses who pulled the carrying tanks have been replaced by a tractor; modern machinery now prevails in the sugar house. And you find that commercial buyers like Maple Grove purchase their syrup and make it into other products. The movie also covers procedures within the factory, so you can watch operations that may not have been active during your tour.

The sweet scent of steaming maple syrup thickens the air, and you can't help being grateful when offered a free sample to taste.

ACCESS

TO GET TO SAINT JOHNSBURY. Take I-91 exit 20, and follow Route 5 north to Saint Johnsbury center.

THE FAIRBANKS MUSEUM AND PLANETARIUM. Directions: Take Route 5 to South Main Street, which becomes Main Street. The museum is on the left. **Season:** Year round. **Admission** charged. (802) 748-2372.

MAPLE GROVE, INC. Directions: From the Fairbanks Museum, return to Route 2, and follow it less than one mile east of the business district to Maple Grove. **Season:** Memorial Day through late October (factory tours year round). **Admission** free to museum and movie; small charge for factory tour. (802) 748-5141.

Lyndonville

MISS LYNDONVILLE DINER. About 15 minutes north of Saint Johnsbury, you can feast on good hearty food in this unpretentious eating spot with the cheery orange counter and yellow stools. There are about a dozen tables covered with brightly flowered plastic tablecloths; cake domes and cookie jars full of goodies add to the homey but bustling atmosphere.

It is just about impossible to walk away hungry from the Miss Lyndonville Diner. The emphasis is on quality cooking at modest prices. Full breakfasts include all the regulars — eggs, ham, bacon, cereal, French toast — plus huge mounds of pancakes just bursting with strawberries. (If you can't come for breakfast, order the strawberry pancakes for lunch.) Of course, you might then be too full for one of the huge wedges of chocolate cream or blueberry pie, but maybe someone else will order a slab and give you a taste.

The emphasis on substantial meals can also be identified through the Miss Lyndonville's affection for potatoes; you can have French fries, steak fries, home fries, or baked potatoes. Lunches and dinners run to trusty favorites such as steaks, grilled pork chops, or huge hot turkey sandwiches overflowing with tasty gravy. Hamburger lovers might like to sample the North Country Special, "a quarter of a pound of lean chuck served on grilled homemade bread with Vermont Cheddar Cheese, tomato slice, a whisper of onions, and our own sauce." A really great place for enthusiastic eaters of all ages.

ACCESS

MISS LYNDONVILLE DINER. Directions: From Saint Johnsbury, take Route 5 south to I-91, and follow I-91 north about eight miles to the Lyndon exit (Route 5). Travel about two miles south on Route 5; the diner is on your left. **Season:** Year round. (802) 626-9890.

Graniteville

ROCK OF AGES GRANITE QUARRIES. Put this attraction at the top of your list, whether your children are four or fourteen. There are actually five separate quarries in operation here, producing granite for monuments, markers, sidings, floors, and other building parts. The granite mined here meets the needs of the Craftsman Center a mile up the road, the largest granite manufacturing plant in the world, as well as the supply requirements of about 250 outside firms.

There are several ways to visit the quarries; by a guided walking tour, by train, or by a self-guided visit to the observation platform. To participate in any of these, enter the Tourist Reception Center, where you

From the observation platform at the Rock of Ages Granite Quarries, your children can see quarrymen hard at work.

can buy granite objects and pick up a free postcard of the quarry or try your hand at a game of chess at the granite chess table. Here you may also join a guided walking tour of the quarries, or purchase tickets to board the open railroad car for a twenty-five-minute ride aboard the Rock of Ages Railroad. Here you sit on bright red benches while a diesel locomotive transports you to the work area; your guide explains the skills and responsibilities associated with the different jobs undertaken by the quarry men you see. The train ride is a favorite with most youngsters because they feel they are right where the action is.

There is also an observation platform behind the reception center where you can check out the Rock of Ages Quarries on your own. As you stand here, you wonder at the quarries' size: the opening at the top of the great hole spans an area of about 27 acres! This hole, over 350 feet deep, has been worked for over 100 years. You see the pools of rainwater that have collected at the bottom. And as you look around, notice the great heaps of granite scraps. These are "grout" piles, grout being the Scottish word for waste. Only about 15 percent of the granite mined here is used in finished products; the other 85 percent is relegated to the grout piles because of imperfections in the stone.

As you hover at the edge of the quarry, notice the maze of cables criss-crossing the sky above. There are eight derricks at work here; 13 miles of cable are used to support and operate this machinery! The derricks themselves are made from 115-foot lengths of Oregon fir trees, trees that need three railroad flat cars to carry them east to the quarries. A cubic foot of granite weighs over 166 pounds, as much as a grown man, but this is

A system of hand signals conveys information from one worker to another; experienced workers are so adept at using them that they can carry on silent "conversations" with other workers hundreds of feet away.

*Before your children
leave, they will want to
climb aboard* Hercules,
*an old saddle-tank
locomotive built
especially for use on
steep Barre Hill.*

no problem for the derricks, each of which can transport a 40- to 50-ton load. In fact, the average block removed from the quarry weighs in at about 20 tons. The
derricks are also used to lower the quarry workers (mere
fly-weights in comparison) down to their work stations.

Peering down into the great hole you notice
dozens of ladders, which are used by quarry men who
prefer to climb in and out by their own power. At first
glance, you may think there are not many people
working in the quarries, but if you check the different
levels carefully you will soon realize that there are
several dozen men at work. They wear safety helmets
for protection against falling objects, and safety shoes
with steel tips and rubber soles to protect against foot
injuries. They also wear goggles and ear plugs or earmuffs to protect eyes and ward off hearing loss — the
quarries are an extremely noisy place to work.

You'll notice that the electronically powered
hoists that drive the derricks are located in the hoist
houses or engine rooms and are operated by hoist
engineers. These engineers take instructions from the
signal men or derrick men, who follow the activities of
the quarry men. Since the din is tremendous, it's easy
to understand why a system of hand signals is
employed to convey information from one worker to
another. Some signals are complicated and some are
simple, but experienced workers are so adept at using
them that they can carry on silent "conversations"
with other workers hundreds of feet away. Scout the
quarries for a worker using hand signals and see if you
can figure out what he is saying.

Hand signals are complemented by a sound sig-
nalling system. In addition to the regular noises, you
hear many whistles blowing. Each derrick is associated
with a whistle that has a sound different from the
other derricks. The whistles are usually blown to let
the workmen know that an object is about to be moved
or swung overhead, so that they can stand clear. As
you watch the miners carve out the huge blocks of
granite with jet-channeling flame machines and see
the derricks swinging the massive chunks clear of the
quarries, you become aware of — and awe-stricken at
— how many skills are required in order to harvest the
granite.

Before your children leave the observation area,
they will want to climb aboard *Hercules,* an old saddle-
tank locomotive built especially for use on steep Barre
Hill. She worked for the Barre and Chelsea Railroad
until the Rock of Ages Quarries purchased her in 1953.
For the next five years, until her retirement in 1958,
she worked the eleven miles of company railroad
track. Children also enjoy digging through an accessible heap of granite scraps to find the perfect piece of
Vermont rock to take home as a remembrance.

But come along, there is still more to do at the
quarries. Once you have seen how the granite is

extracted from the ground, you can watch it being made into finished products at the Craftsman Center. The observation deck here provides a good view of the action on the floor below, a space that easily exceeds the size of two football fields. Cranes running on elevated tracks move heavy blocks from one part of the plant to another, as do fork-lift trucks and conveyor belts. Polishing, shaping, and hand-carving operations can also be observed. Allow about two hours for the complete Rock of Ages Quarries visit.

ACCESS

ROCK OF AGES GRANITE QUARRIES. Directions: Take I-89 exit 6 and continue four miles to Route 14; cross Route 14 and continue about three miles, following signs to the quarries. **Season:** May through October. **Admission** charged only for train ride; quarry tours and Craftsman Center are free. (802) 476-3115.

Montpelier

THE VERMONT MUSEUM. Pause in the elegant Victorian parlor for a moment and imagine yourself transported back in time a hundred years. Think of yourself as a guest waiting to be shown to your room in the Pavilion Hotel of Montpelier, the very establishment that graced this spot from 1870 to 1966. Now you can immerse yourself in the styles, economics, and events that made Vermont what she is today.

The Vermont Historical Society runs this establishment; unlike some other historical society operations, their museum is not at all a stuffy place. The brochure sets the tone: "While boisterous behavior is not condoned, we do not expect visitors to move through the museum on tiptoe or limit their conversations to whispers . . . The Vermont Museum is meant to be enjoyed."

The museum seeks to bring to life the people and events important in the heritage and history of the Green Mountain State. In A Town and Its Business, you can ring the vintage 1890 locomotive bell that belonged to the *Arthur Tandy,* a steam train that worked the Montpelier & Wells River Railroad. Here a do-it-yourself narrated slide show focuses on the interrelationship of Barre and the granite industry to illustrate the way town centers developed; two other slide shows deal, respectively, with the geology of Vermont and with historical events.

Many other exhibits here will catch your fancy. One display centers on the Civil War years, tracing the adventures of a Vermont farm boy who joined the Union Army as a musician and was killed two months later. His letters, diary, and daguerreotypes bring his story to life. Another exhibit, 200 Years of Making a Living in Vermont, contains items either important to

Children can connect calling and answering plugs on the last telephone switchboard used in Vermont. There are earphones to wear, too, and lots of switches to throw.

Adults might be enthralled by the Vermont Museum's pure Victoriana, but children most often find Grandma's Closet especially worthy of their time.

local industries or actually produced in the state. For example, you can ponder over a Fairbanks scale from Saint Johnsbury, an Estey Organ from Brattleboro, a Tyson Furnace, a Cooley Creamer, and a Sam Daniels Company Syrup Evaporator. You can also consider the fact that the seven thousand dairy farms now active in the state ship more milk today than did the thirty-four thousand such farms in 1880.

Nearby, The Making of a State focuses on political issues during the tumultuous 1760 to 1791 period, while Rural Life concentrates on daily living during the years of agrarian prosperity. Clothing, toys (check out the marbles), and needlework from early Vermont children are on display too. In Grandma's Closet there are some spiffy turn-of-the-century dress-up clothes that include a smoking jacket, a vested suit, some floor-length dresses and fringed shawls, a velvet bonnet, a cloche, and some straw hats. There is also a display of "Touch Me" kitchen implements; you'll find an old-time sausage stuffer, a meat pounder, and a pie lifter. Elsewhere in the museum, children can connect calling and answering plugs on the last telephone switch-board used in Vermont, which was in active service in Windsor up until 1967. There are earphones to wear, too, and lots of switches to throw.

Be sure to read the wall notices posted behind the first hand printing press in Vermont. One advertises the opportunity to view "A Great Natural Curiosity — A Mammoth Moose," while another urges you to put down your money to see the "Living Skeleton." You read that this unfortunate fellow, formerly five feet six inches tall and one hundred thirty-five pounds, has wasted away to five feet three inches tall and fifty-eight pounds. Yet, the poster advises, he can still ride horseback, lift one hundred pounds, and eat, drink, and sleep as well as any man. Indeed, "He attributes the cause of his wasting to having slept on the damp ground — the night after the battle of Plattsburgh, at which time he was serving in the American Army." Think about it.

Before you leave the museum, be sure to browse in the tiny shop area where you can purchase a "braiding apple" or a kit for making old-time dolls and puppets. There are also many Vermont books on sale here, including some about farming, children's stories, and nature and hiking guides. Plan to spend about forty-five minutes here.

ACCESS

THE VERMONT MUSEUM. Directions: Take I-89 exit 8 (Montpelier), turn left at the end of the ramp, and go a half mile to the State Capitol, following green signs to State Street. The museum is located in the Pavilion Building, 109 State Street, two buildings to the right of the Capitol. **Season:** Year round. **Donation** requested. (802) 828-2291.

Waterbury

COLD HOLLOW CIDER MILL. Although the apple harvest ends in autumn, the folks here at Cold Hollow Cider Mill are busy pressing apples and making cider until the crop runs out, usually not until the middle of the following summer. So do plan to make a visit here whenever you are in the area. When you drive up to the mill, you first see a porch full of old farm equipment to investigate — lots of interesting sleds, wagons, cider presses, and the like.

If your timing is fortunate, when you enter the mill you will be greeted by the aroma of freshly made cider doughnuts. The "mill" is actually a shop; however, instead of standard souvenirs, it features Vermont-made crafts and homemade foods such as peanut butter and bread. There is a full line of maple products, and you'll see those big chunky wheels of Vermont cheddar in their wax wrappers. Children like the furry slippers, handmade toys, and the quilts with pockets and animals worked into their designs. This is just the

If your timing is fortunate, when you enter the mill you will be greeted by the aroma of freshly made cider doughnuts.

right place to find something special as a remembrance of your Vermont trip.

Out back, you can watch the cider-pressing operation. Be certain to purchase some cider to quench your thirst on the road. There's no taste quite like the just-pressed freshness of apples.

ACCESS

COLD HOLLOW CIDER MILL. Directions: Take I-89 exit 10, and follow Route 100 north to Waterbury center, about three miles. The shop is located on Route 100 in Waterbury. **Season:** Year round. (802) 244-8560.

Stowe

Ride up the mountain on a double chair lift, then sit on a small sled and control your speed as you travel down the winding chute.

MOUNT MANSFIELD ALPINE SLIDE AND GONDOLA. If you take a short jaunt just a few miles north of Stowe village, you can spend a day exploring the mountains in a couple of different ways. First, consider an exciting flight down the twenty-seven hundred-foot-long alpine slide at Spruce Peak. To get to the top of the slide, take the twelve-minute ride aboard a double chair lift that transports skiers up the mountain in the winter. Then, sit on a small sled and control the speed of your descent as you travel down the winding chute. Push forward on the lever to increase speed, pull back to slow down. The choice is yours! The ride travels through a flashing panorama of woods and open meadow.

A different type of mountain experience awaits you just down the road. At Mount Mansfield, the highest peak in Vermont, you can board a four-person gondola for a 9½-minute ride up to Cliff House, located near the summit. The bright red cars travel along a 7000-foot-long cable at a speed of 690 feet per minute, carrying you to an elevation of 3650 feet; it takes your breath away!

Mount Mansfield is formed from a geologic mix called green schist, which is composed of mica, quartz, and albite, and is the official state rock of Vermont. Its formation began some five hundred million years ago, when an ocean covered Vermont and neighboring New Hampshire. Think about this as you travel above in the gondola and look down at a northern hardwood forest with its many sugar maple, birch, and beech trees. If you watch carefully, you might spot squirrels, rabbits, or a porcupine scampering below; deer can also be seen on occasion. As you reach higher elevations, conifers such as white pine, hemlock, and red spruce mix freely with the hardwoods. Eventually the conifers take over completely and all is green. As you approach the treeline, where the trees are small and stunted from the effects of wind, ice, and snow, the balsam fir predominates.

Youngsters speed down the Alpine slide.

Your gondola soon passes over the Alpine tundra where few trees are able to grow, and where those that do manage to survive on the ridge need about eighty years to grow to just two inches in diameter. After debarking from the gondola, take a walk near the mountain's summit, and look for mountain sandwort, blueberry bog, bilberry, and mountain cranberry. Look also for white-throated sparrows, dark-eyed juncos, and ravens, those hardy species of birds that manage to survive in this high zone. There is usually a forest ranger stationed at the summit to answer all your questions about the flora and fauna; ask for hiking suggestions if you wish to strike out on your own for a spell before traveling back down the mountain in the gondola. Children of all ages enjoy both the ride and exploring or hiking on the mountaintop.

There are viewers at Cliff House, which nestles just below Mount Mansfield's summit. On a clear day you can see for miles — into Canada, and into New Hampshire's White Mountains (including Mount Washington, eighty miles in the distance). To the west, you can see New York State's Adirondack Mountains, some forty miles away. You can purchase lunch here and browse in the gift shop before making your descent.

ACCESS

MOUNT MANSFIELD ALPINE SLIDE AND GON-DOLA. Directions: Take I-89 exit 10, and follow Route 100 north through Waterbury Center to Stowe. From the junction of routes 100 and 108 in Stowe, take Route 108 west for about eight miles. **Season:** Late June through mid-October and late November through the end of the ski season; plus weekends from late May through late June. Admission charged. (802) 253-7311.

Essex Junction

DISCOVERY MUSEUM. You'll be glad to find that nearly all the exhibits here need your help! They don't do anything unless you do something with them. A relatively new museum (1975), the Discovery Museum is expanding and changing. Here you can transform light energy into electricity, match wits with a computer, or see your own voice wave pattern appear on a sound wave machine, which shows what different types of sounds "look like." You can broadcast the news at closed circuit station WFUN-TV, or you can even try your hand at weather forecasting.

There is a lively animal room here, with many residents who have been injured or orphaned and brought to the museum for care. Most will eventually be returned to the wild. There are exotic animals, too, such as the red-tailed boa constrictor. Run your hands along his body; he's not at all wet or cold, as you might imagine. Fred and Barry, the two hamsters, can be held in your hands; you can pick up a red-eared ponder, too. Do be careful with the latter, though, as these turtles sometimes bite. A museum assistant will show you the proper way to handle the animals, and will answer any questions you might have.

Upstairs, you can enter the child-sized door to Childsworld, an elaborate combination of hideaway spaces, peepholes, platforms, and ladders where you can stage a puppet show or engage in any sort of imaginary adventure you might care to invent. Next door, in Grandma's Attic, there are lots of clothes to dress up in (try the silver high heels or a sergeant-major's jacket), and a large furnished doll house to play with. Across the hall you can grind corn with an Indian mortar and pestle or don a set of earphones to listen to tales of adventure on nearby Lake Champlain. There is altogether lots for children ages three to twelve to do and think about here for at least an hour. So, get involved!

ACCESS

DISCOVERY MUSEUM. **Directions:** Take I-89 exit 12 and travel about three and a half miles north on Route 2A (which becomes Park Street) to Essex Junction. The museum is at 51 Park Street. **Season:** Year round. **Admission** charged. (802) 878-8687.

Shelburne

SHELBURNE MUSEUM. Shelburne is the home of one of Vermont's most famous attractions, Shelburne Museum, otherwise known as The Shelburne Collection of Wonderful Things. Composed of thirty-five buildings situated on forty-five meticulously landscaped acres,

Shelburne embraces three hundred years of treasures instead of sticking to a specific time frame, as is the practice at Old Sturbridge Village and Mystic Seaport.

The museum contains many serious collections, and children are not permitted to enter the buildings without their parents. Yet Shelburne must be mentioned here because older travelers will insist on stopping when they are in the area, and because there are plenty of exhibits to intrigue children if you make an effort to ferret them out.

Begin, by all means, with a visit to the Shelburne Railroad Station, a Victorian structure with a handsome waiting room that makes young and old wish they could turn the hands of time back on travel modes. Among other things, there is a wonderful private railroad car to visit, with its own built-in sofas, beds, and bathtubs, giving you a glimpse of truly luxurious vintage travel. The only train you are likely to catch, however, is the open-sided tractor train that shuttles visitors about the grounds.

As the tractor train transports you to the center of Shelburne, children are quickly attracted to the great side-wheeler *Ticonderoga*, now moored on dry land after nearly half a century spent steaming up and down the waters of nearby Lake Champlain. Climb aboard to view the film that documents the trials and tribulations of moving the 220-foot ship two miles overland from the lake to its present resting place. Then roam her decks, peeking in every nook and cranny. You can explore both the crew and passenger areas and also gawk at your leisure at the mechanical workings of the ship.

A one-horse shay is parked outside with its own mock horse; children are welcome to clamber aboard and take the reins.

Children love general stores, even ones where you can't buy anything. In the Shelburne General Store, they are amazed at how many businesses used to be combined beneath a single roof. Not only is the store chock full of dry goods, groceries, hardware, and candy, but space is also allotted to a post office, a taproom, a barber shop, and doctor's and dentist's quarters. There's a well-stocked apothecary shop next door, complete with leeches and blood-letting equipment, and a one-horse shay is parked outside with its own mock horse; children are welcome to clamber aboard and take the reins.

If this popular conveyance is endlessly occupied, head over to the weaving display, where you are likely to see a young woman at work "teasing" the wool — removing clumps and knots and making it fluffy before combing. Out front is an old-time milk truck, white with red trim, bearing the words "Shelburne Dairy — Milk and Cream"; it is accompanied by another "horse" and is also "on limits" for children. Filled with milk cans and bottles, it's an easy place to pretend that one is a milkman making the rounds at the turn of the century. When children tire of this, get

SEAN KARDON

Though it once cruised the waters of Lake Champlain, it's now virtually a museum in dry dock. Your children can thoroughly explore the Ticonderoga *at Shelburne Museum.*

them to duck inside the live-bee exhibit for a gander at the observation hive. Can you find the queen? She's the one with the white spot on her back.

The stocks in front of the Castleton Slate Jail (1890) are lots of fun, but if someone in your troupe has been really naughty, why stop with this? Go on inside and throw the offender in a cell! After a jail break, you can observe the blacksmith at work. Or, you might move on to the toy shop, which is plumb full of mechanical toys, penny banks, and music boxes, several of which are in working order. You can even slip a dime into the horse-race box, and bet your money that the steed of your choice will be closest to the finish line when the music stops. It's fun, also, to ask the hostess to activate the large advertising figure of a cobbler who comes to life, pounding on the sole of a shoe.

The Schoolhouse, outfitted with dunce cap, a bucket and dipper for drinking water, and a row of lunch baskets, is also a good place to visit. Children are amused by the serious sentiments that adorn the walls: "People who throw dirt lose ground"; "After all is said and done, more is said than done"; "Honor is a priceless jewel." Now, class, how can we apply such wisdom to our daily lives?

If you and your children love the circus, take them to the imposing semicircular building constructed just for the purpose of housing a 525-foot-long scale model of a circus parade. This is a very superior rendition of a parade in that the performers come from all over the world. The carved and intricately decorated figures include acrobats and tumblers, seals, elephants, bears, magnificent circus wagons drawn by splendid horses, and dozens of clowns; there are also men on stilts, beautiful ladies, and all the other necessaries.

The stocks in front of the Castleton Slate Jail are lots of fun, but if someone in your troupe has been really naughty, why stop with this?

To a great extent, the exhibits you visit here will depend upon the age and inclination of your young companions. If they have never seen a covered bridge or a real lighthouse, they'll want to enjoy those experiences here, too. The choices are abundant and varied, but truly there is plenty for everyone. Many visitors spend a full day at Shelburne, but with children along three hours is usually sufficient.

ACCESS

SHELBURNE MUSEUM. Directions: Take I-89 exit 13, and follow I-189 west to Route 7, then follow Route 7 south through the town of Shelburne to the museum. **Season:** Mid-May through late October. **Admission** charged. (802) 985-3344.

INDEX

MICHAEL LAFFERTY

About the Author

A freelance writer ever since her graduation from college, Harriet Webster holds a B.A. in sociology from the University of New Hampshire, and an M.A. in urban studies from Boston University. With her husband, Jonathan, an English teacher, she has written two books: *18: The Teenage Catalog*, in 1976, and *The Underground Marketplace*, in 1981. She has also had articles published in *Mademoiselle, Seventeen, McCall's, Yankee*, and *Americana*, and from 1977 to 1979 wrote the column "Kids' Trips" for *Metroguide*, a Boston weekly. She lives in Gloucester, Massachusetts, with her husband and three sons, David, 15, Matthew, 10, and Benjamin, 2½.

Her sons and some of their friends accompanied her as she researched the New England trips in this book; she and Jonathan have also taken the boys on trips to Europe, Mexico, the Caribbean, and various parts of the United States. Her travels throughout New England with children, she says, proved conclusively that "what is ice cream to one child may be spinach to another," since children, like adults, have different tastes and temperaments. However, she does feel that children can be prepared positively (or negatively) by what their parents or other adults say or tell them about a given place or attraction.

And that is the reason for this book. Webster discovered New England to be ideal territory for family exploration because there is such a great variety of places to visit and the distances are not great — "it is a place to return to again and again." Most children who try these trips are bound to agree.